IN LOCAL HANDS

IN LOCAL HANDS

VILLAGE GOVERNMENT INCORPORATION
AND DISSOLUTION IN NEW YORK STATE

Lisa K. Parshall

SUNY
PRESS

Cover photo of the Wayne County court building in Lyons, New York taken by Dr. Martin J. Anisman.

Published by State University of New York Press, Albany

For information, contact State University of New York Press, Albany, NY
www.sunypress.edu

Library of Congress Cataloging-in-Publication Data

Name: Parshall, Lisa K., author.
Title: In local hands : village government incorporation and dissolution in
    New York State / Lisa K. Parshall, author.
Description: Albany : State University of New York Press, [2023] | Includes
    bibliographical references and index.
Identifiers: ISBN 9781438492452 (hardcover : alk. paper) | ISBN 9781438492476
    (ebook) | ISBN 9781438492469 (pbk. : alk. paper)
Further information is available at the Library of Congress.

10 9 8 7 6 5 4 3 2 1

For Marty

Abolition of one or the other of the [village or town] governments is almost out of the question politically. It could be done but it would take a great deal more drive than anyone seems to be willing to put into it.

—Peter Cox, Editor, *Adirondack Daily Enterprise*, 1964

Contents

x | Contents

Illustrations

Figures

Tables

Acknowledgments

I am grateful to many people for their inspiration and support of my research on village government in New York State. I rely heavily on the scholarship of Dr. Gerald Benjamin in understanding the development and evolution of New York State's local government structure as well as his work with Richard P. Nathan on regionalism. In 2017, I was honored to be named among the inaugural class of Richard P. Nathan Fellows at the Nelson A. Rockefeller Institute of Government in Albany, New York, where I continued as a policy fellow. I am especially grateful to the Rockefeller Institute's former and current directors, Dr. Jim Malatras, Dr. Patricia Strach, and Dr. Laura Schultz. The scholarly community that is the Rockefeller Institute has been instrumental to how the project has developed.

Daemen University continues to provide robust support for faculty research under the leadership of President Gary A. Olson and Executive Vice President of Academic Affairs and Provost Michael Brogan. I am very fortunate to teach at an institution that values and encourages faculty scholarship. A special thanks to my Daemen colleagues, Aakriti Tandon, Jay Wendland, and Dan Shanahan, for comments and insights, and to Robin Lauermann (Messiah University) for feedback and suggestions.

The archival research was made possible by a 2012 grant from the New York State Archives and Partnership Trust, Larry J. Hackman Research Residency. This grant supported research trips to the New York State Library and to the Frank C. Moore archives housed at the M.E. Grenander Department of Special Collections & Archives University Libraries at the University of Albany. A grant from the Howard J. Samuels State and City Policy Center at Baruch College's Austin W. Marxe School of Public and International Affairs, City University of New York, funded travel for

archival research, photography, site visits, and interviews with key participants involved in village dissolution efforts, as well as student-research
support. Research assistance was provided by the late Megan Racinowski
(1999–2018), a political science major at Daemen University, through the
funding from the Samuels Center. Megan will be forever remembered
and deeply missed by the Daemen community. Dr. Martin J. Anisman,
a skilled photographer and Daemen University president emeritus, captured images for many of the case studies. These site visits deepened my
understanding of the social context and places in which the debates over
municipal structures and services occur.

Numerous people provided insights for the project through conversations and informal interviews. While most have requested anonymity, I
would like to acknowledge a few of those who shared with me their direct
experience as participants in the dissolution debate. My initial interest was
sparked by the work of Kevin Gaughan, an attorney and local civic activist
who spearheaded downsizing and dissolution efforts in Erie County. From
this local example, I expanded my interest to a statewide and historical
understanding of municipal reorganization. The leadership of the One-
Lyons group, including Mr. Andrew DeWolfe and Jack Bailey, along with
Rhett King of NY Villagers for Effective Government, offered extensive
insight into their organizations' pro-dissolution efforts. I also spoke with
numerous village and town elected officials, including Mayor Greg Martin
(village of Champlain), Mayor Tim Currier (village of Massena), Trustee
Melanie Gurerrero (village of Highland Falls), Sandra Pagano (Macedon
town supervisor), Brian Manktelow (Lyons town supervisor), and Mayor
Sam Teresi (city of Jamestown and former president of New York Conference of Mayors). Kevin Malloy (town of Brookhaven) added perspective
to the post-dissolution efforts in the town of Brookhaven. Each provided
honest reflections on the dissolution debate in their community. I received
valuable technical advice from various policy actors, consultants, and
state officials, including Wade Beltramo of the New York Conference of
Mayors, Joseph Stefko and Paul Bishop of the Center for Governmental
Research, and Christopher Grant and Kyle Wilbur of the Office of Local
Government Services.

The research was conducted from an outsider-observer perspective;
the opportunity to speak with participants on all sides of the debate helped
to verify assumptions and ensure the inclusion of multiple perspectives.
I must also give credit and express appreciation to the many local news
reporters who cover the debate in real time. Their reporting provided

crucial insights, analysis, and color that informed and enriched the research. Local reporting is a critical function in a democratic society and an invaluable public service.

Introduction

In Local Hands

On November 8, 2022, the residents of the village of Highland Falls in Orange County, New York, went to the polls to decide the fate of their village. The question before them was whether to dissolve the 116-year-old village government and return the administration of village affairs to the town of Highlands.[1] This was not the first time that dissolution of Highland Falls (founded as Buttermilk Falls) was proposed. Residents had debated the question in 1908, just two years after the village was incorporated, and voted on the issue in 1916, rejecting it 228–66 in a referendum in which only property residents were (at the time) allowed to vote.

This latest dissolution effort in Highland Falls was prompted by growing residential concern over the village tax rate and the belief that that a community of its size (3,823 in population) could be more efficiently served by merging services (including policing and public works) with the embracing town (Randall 2016; Aiello 2021). Supporters of the dissolution were cautiously optimistic; they had collected sufficient signatures to put the issue onto the general election ballot. They had spent weeks campaigning and educating their fellow residents on the potential benefits of reuniting with the town. At the urging of several trustees, the village board commissioned a preliminary study that projected a post-dissolution reduction in property taxes for village residents. The neighboring communities of West Point and Fort Montgomery served as living examples that a separate village government was not necessary to preserve a satisfactory level of amenities and services. And because the town of Highlands' municipal buildings and facilities were physically located within the village, supporters believed the transfer of services was likely to be undramatic.

Yet dissolution advocates soon realized that they faced an uphill battle. Residents were wary. Skeptics argued that there were simply too many unanswered questions about the potential impact on critical services and amenities. Those who lived in the town-outside-the-village (TOV) had no vote on the matter, although their taxes too would be impacted by the decision. Some feared that dissolving the village government would result in a loss of a shared community identity. In other words, what proponents had anticipated would be a debate over service delivery options and relative costs had become increasingly contentious and highly emotional. By a vote of 779–450, the voters of Highland Falls rejected the measure, triggering a four-year moratorium on its resubmission.

In New York State, villages are the only form of general-purpose government that can be incorporated or dissolved solely by the local action of village residents.[2] Historically, the number of village government dissolutions has always been quite modest. From 1900 to 2009, only forty-six villages had officially dissolved. But, since the passage of the New N.Y. Reorganization and Citizen Empowerment Act (hereinafter the Empowerment Act), which went into effect on March 21, 2010, the number of New York villages actively considering dissolution has dramatically risen. Indeed, Highland Falls was the forty-seventh village to vote on dissolution under the Empowerment Act's provision—meaning that as many communities have voted on the question in the last twelve years as had dissolved in the prior century.

This book explores the contemporary village dissolution movement in New York State, the impetus behind these reforms, and the impact of the state policies and incentives that are driving local communities to reconsider the need for maintaining villages as governing units. Although New York is at the forefront of the village dissolution movement, it is not just a New York State curiosity. Similar debates are taking place in several states, including Ohio, Missouri, and Wisconsin, driven by a combination of state-level policies, fiscal pressures, and a grassroots interest in reducing local property tax burdens (Parshall 2022). Dissolution is an example of local democracy in action, an issue that is both timeless and timely, and one that is as important as it is messy and contentious.

Fundamentally, it is a debate over decentralized (local autonomy) versus centralized (or state) authority, shaped by the specific historical and legal framework of the state and against the backdrop of two competing legal theories of local power. In the first, local self-governance is a constitutional right, stemming from the rights of individuals aggregated into self-governing communities that, in turn, constitute the state as the recipient of their delegated powers. In this view, residents have the right to form their own municipal governments to manage their internal property and affairs while state authority is restricted to statewide policy concerns. Such a view comports with a Jeffersonian embrace of rural communities as centers of autonomous self-rule that predate our constitutional system (Syed 1966) and is reflected by Alexis de Tocqueville's belief that localism is the wellspring of democracy (1835). The legal theory of an inherent right of self-governance is perhaps most famously expressed in the writings of Thomas M. Cooley, a state jurist and local government scholar. Yet even under Judge Cooley's robust conception of local autonomy, "while the local community is entitled to local government," in terms of managing its own affairs, "it cannot claim, as against the state, any particular charter or form of local government" (Cooley 1880, 379).

The state-centric theory of local government, by contrast, holds that local government structure and powers exist solely at the discretion of the state. This view has been memorialized as Dillon's rule—the legal theory that local governments may exercise *only those powers expressly granted to them by state law*. On this theory, localities are mere creatures of the states, lacking independent standing under the US Constitution.

> Municipal corporations owe their origin to, and derive their powers and rights wholly from, the legislature. It breathes into them the breath of life, without which they cannot exist. As it creates, so it may destroy. If it may destroy, it may abridge and control. Unless there is some constitutional limitation on the right, the legislature might by a single act, if we can suppose it capable of so great a folly and so great a wrong, sweep from its existence all of the municipal corporations in the State, and the corporations could not prevent it. . . . [Local governments] are, so to phrase it, the mere tenants at will of the [state] legislature. (City of Clinton 1868, 475)

The United States Supreme Court embraced a state-centric view by holding that "in the absence of state constitutional provisions safeguarding it to them, municipalities have no inherent right of self-government which is beyond the legislative control of the state" (City of Trenton v. New Jersey 1923, 182). Because local governments exist for "a specific purpose," the state may withdraw these local powers of government at pleasure and may, through its legislature or other appointed channels . . . enlarge or contract its powers or destroy its existence" (U.S. v. Railroad 1872, 329). Moreover, the state may do so "with or without the consent of its citizens, or even against their protest. . . ." (Hunter v. Pittsburgh 1907, 186–87).

Yet states have been traditionally reluctant to mandate local government reform, and local governments, once granted home rule authority, have been stubbornly resistant to state directive and reorganization efforts. New York is no exception. Indeed, constitutional and statutory grants of home rule require local consent for municipal reorganization, defined here to include incorporation, consolidation, and dissolution of local entities. Thus, rather than *mandating* reform, New York has attempted to encourage local government restructuring through both positive and negative inducements, along with an eased pathway for citizen-initiated efforts. With respect to village government dissolution (the primary focus of this work), the decision is one that, despite state-level pressures, rests in local hands.

Methodology and Overview

This book adds to a growing literature on municipal formation and reorganization, much of which is focused on metro-area consolidations using a small number of cases. The case-based approach, incorporating dozens of cases of both rural and suburban character across time, reveals the deep connection that residents have to their local governing entities as reflective and protective of their community values and shared identity. This study blends historical, evidence-based research with interpretive lines of inquiry by accounting for the psychological and sociological attachments that motivate residents when considering whether to retain their incorporated status or merge their village with the embracing town (or towns). In so doing, I account for the legal frameworks, as well as the policy and political contexts in which village dissolution debates occur, to demonstrate that the decision is more than just an economic calculus yet is nevertheless shaped by the social and political interests of the residents in whose hands the decision rests. The empirical observations of the book and its claims, inferences, and theories are derived from:

- qualitative case studies of both successful and failed village dissolution attempts

- conversations and interviews with policy actors and citizen participants in selected case studies

- data, reports, audits, and policy briefings from New York State sources, including the New York Department of State (DOS), the Division of the Budget (DOB), the Office of the New York State Comptroller (OSC), the Office of Local Government Services (OLGS), and the Financial Restructuring Board for Local Governments (FRB)

- media and local news coverage of historical and contemporary (post-2010) dissolution efforts

- fiscal reports, minutes, and press releases by village and town governments

- village dissolution study reports and meetings that have been conducted by citizens groups, village-appointed dissolution committees, municipal organizations, including the New York Conference of Mayors (NYCOM), and various private consulting organizations that are contracted to perform dissolution studies and planning, including the Center for Governmental Research (CGR), the Development Authority of the North Country (DANC), Roundout Consulting, Fairweather Consulting, and the Laberge Group (LaBerge).

- archival records, including the official incorporation files maintained by the Department of State and housed at the New York State Archives, various legislative committee reports and hearings, state constitutional convention proceedings, and the New York State Session Laws database to track legislative changes to incorporation, annexation, and dissolution procedures (noted parenthetically throughout by the year and chapter number of the law).[3]

Historical cases of village disincorporation that took place pre-1900 are detailed in Appendix A on page 213. These dissolutions were identified through extensive primary source searches of local newspaper databases and New York State Session laws granting, amending, or repealing village charters. The list of incorporations and dissolutions maintained by the Department of State since 1920 (and listing dissolutions post-1900) was verified through archival and newspaper coverage, resulting in the identification of several errors and omissions. The details for dissolutions between 1900 and 2009 are provided in Appendix B on page 214.

Contemporary (post-2010) dissolution efforts were tracked through print and online media coverage, village board minutes, and dissolution studies and reports publicly released by consulting organizations. The inventory of villages that have voted on dissolution since 2010 are provided in Appendix C on page 216, which includes additional details on the method (whether under Article 19 or the Empowerment Act, or if board or citizen-initiated) along with the referenda dates and outcomes. The county in which villages are located are noted parenthetically in the text throughout. Information on the town (or towns) for contemporary dissolutions can be found in Appendix C.

Since 2010, I attended dozens of dissolution meetings (in person or virtually) and interacted with a wide array of participants through interviews and informal conversations. I have analyzed dozens of social media accounts and websites of village and town governments, as well as those of the citizen coalition groups that form on both the pro- and anti-dissolution sides of the debate. Accompanied by a photographer, I visited more than thirty villages and towns, mostly in Western and Central New York. The places visited included both recent and historical cases and villages where dissolution was rejected as well as approved. The visits were informative to the book project, providing an opportunity to observe a diverse array of villages and to speak to residents. Such portraiture and interaction with a range of actors helped to inform my interpretation of the factual artifacts of the dissolution debate (i.e., the legal records, dissolution studies, agency reports, and news coverage). To the greatest extent possible, I have tried to depersonalize often contentious debates over dissolution and to refrain from discussing the actions of specific individuals, referencing most by their title (or role) rather than by name. In this way, interviews provided context and color, allowing me to verify my observations while protecting the privacy of individuals willing to speak about their experiences as citizens and policy actors.

My primary focus is the phenomenon of village creation and dissolution *as a community-level choice*. I am not interested in how or why individual citizens vote as they do on dissolution but concentrate instead on the collective choice of the community. The book is not an argument in support of or in opposition to dissolution, but rather an effort to explain the phenomenon and the contours of this important debate. The explanations offered are not causal; that is, no general theory as to the precise combination of factors necessary to convince a community to dissolve its village government is presented. Instead, I seek to generally understand the many factors that are at play when residents consider the dissolution question. While antecedent contextual circumstances, such as depopulation and fiscal or environmental stress, are important, I argue that perceptions may matter more than objective indicators, that narrative framing fundamentally shapes public support or opposition to dissolution as a policy solution. From a state policy-making standpoint, such understanding is critical. Viewing the choice to dissolve as a purely economic decision driven solely by a demonstration of potential savings misses the mark in facilitating local government restructuring.

Part I of the book addresses the legal authority for local government reorganization by tracing changes in New York State laws controlling the incorporation and dissolution of village governments. As Burns and Gam (1997) note, local government studies too often neglect the effect of state legislative action on local outcomes. The laws and procedures under which dissolution takes place matter. To comprehend why villages sometimes dissolve, it is beneficial to understand how and why they incorporate in the first place and the legal requirements for forming and dissolving villages. To detail and contextualize changes in New York's incorporation and dissolution procedures, I relied on a variety of sources, including state constitutional conventions, legislative session laws and proceedings, gubernatorial messages, bill and veto jackets, state court rulings, and the hearings and reports of the various state legislative committees on the recodification of municipal law. Additional source material was obtained through the Frank C. Moore Papers at the Archives of Public Affairs and Policy of the University at Albany.[4]

Part II turns to the political and social context of the village dissolution debate to better understand what motivates citizens to pursue dissolution and why it is so often resisted. New York's recent policy support for local reorganization is based on the twin assumptions that an outmoded structure of overlapping and duplicative units of general-purpose governments is a major driver of New York's high property taxes and that increased fiscal pressure on local units will facilitate restructuring. State-level policies reflect a deliberate effort to encourage reorganization, incentivize reform, and tie local financial assistance to the quest for greater efficiency. As will be seen, pro-dissolution efforts are largely, although not exclusively, about the search for potential savings, but fiscal stress alone is not a reliable indicator of either dissolution activity or success. I argue that it is the everyday politics of village living, the iconography, symbolism, and psychological attachment residents have for their local government, that explains the often-fierce resistance to dissolution efforts. To help explain the contours of these local debates, I use the theories of Narrative Policy Framework (NPF) to elucidate how both pro- and anti-dissolution coalitions seek to structure the voters' choice ahead of the public referendum (Kear and Wells 2014, 161).[5] The within-case and cross-case comparisons of successful and unsuccessful dissolutions suggest that the narrative framing deployed in the community-level debate has more persuasive influence than does the cost-benefit assessment of potential tax savings (Parshall 2011; 2012b).

Studying the village dissolution movement in New York and the attempt to eliminate smaller municipal units produces a richer understanding of the myriad reasons that communities consider, accept, or reject municipal reorganization efforts. In terms of policy change, dissolution is on the radical side, reflecting a disruption of the status quo. There must be sufficient impetus behind the effort not only to overcome a natural tendency toward policy inertia, but also to promote dissolution against competing policy solutions, such as shared services. The Empowerment Act's mixed record of success, given the state's dedication of resources, suggests that even bolder reform may be in order.

Part I

The Legal and Policy Framework

Chapter 1

Incorporating Villages

A municipal corporation "is an imaginary, immaterial legal entity, with certain powers, rights, and duties. It is immortal, unless limited in duration, when created by a formal act" (Eaton 1902, 8). It is a construct "composed of individual members that die, but which continues on notwithstanding their death or withdrawal" (Eaton 1902, 9). Under English and Dutch colonial law, small settlements or hamlets were incorporated as cities or towns.[1] New York's first constitution, adopted in 1777, made no mention of villages. Village government was of a later (post-colonial) origin than that of cities, towns, or counties (Morey 1902; Fairlie 1920). The first village incorporation in New York State dates to the 1790s, with some disagreement as to whether it was Lansingburgh in 1790, Waterford in 1794, or the villages of Troy and Lansingburgh in 1798 (Morey 1902; Feeney Commission 1975). The incorporation of villages was undertaken "partly to circumvent the legal confusion about the nature and scope of town government," when "clusters of people in otherwise sparsely settled towns" wanted to secure dedicated police, fire, or other services not available, or not needed, on a townwide basis (New York Department of State 2018b, 82).

Between 1790 and 1847, incorporation as a village required a special act of the state legislature. Village powers therefore varied, dependent on the unique chartering act. Powers were sometimes conferred through reference to another existing village's charter, granting a new village the same powers as a village previously incorporated. This ad hoc, piecemeal approach reflected a "pervasive spirit of localism," wherein the state responded to local demands and local needs. But it also led to frequent, and sometimes highly specific, local requests to amend village charters, creating an ever-increasing lack of uniformity in the powers granted to the state's growing number of villages (Bishop and Attree 1846, 964). It was not until New York's Constitution of 1821 that villages were legally recognized as a civil division, although even then the term "village" was still sporadically and "haphazardly" referenced in state legislation and often used interchangeably with references to "town" government (Feeney Commission 1975).

To eliminate this confusion, the 1846 Constitution (Article VIII, Sect. 9) expressly directed the legislature to "provide for the organization of cities and incorporated villages" and to restrict their "power of taxation, assessment, borrowing money, contracting debts, and loaning their credit," thereby setting the stage for the adoption of a General Village Law in 1847. This new General Village Law was intended to remove the growing "incongruities" between special charters and to draw local government more firmly under the auspices of state authority.

In so doing, the legislature shifted power over community affairs from the residents and into the hands of an elected village board (Wallace 1911). The *authority* to incorporate or disincorporate villages, however, was given directly to residents via local action, shifting the model of incorporation from one of legislative *responsiveness* to one of direct *local control over the formation of new village governments*. Most existing villages voluntarily reincorporated under the new general law, although incorporation by special charter continued. The result was to create three categories of legal villages: those that were specially incorporated prior to 1847; those that were incorporated under the provisions of the General Village Law; and those that continued to operate under special act (by legislative charter) even after 1847.

The Evolution of the General Village Law

The mechanism for incorporating an otherwise unincorporated area as a village, under the first General Village Law of 1847, was by a petition to the courts. A proposed village had to have a "a population of not less than 300 per square mile within boundary of more than one square mile (L. 1847, Ch. 426). Those persons interested in incorporating were required to post a survey, map, and census, along with the application, six weeks before petitioning the court. The court could hear from all interested parties before incorporation was put to a public vote.

The 1847 law thus provided the basic elements of incorporation: legislatively prescribed territorial and population requirements; a clear delineation of boundaries; an application (and later petition) process to initiate the legal creation of a village; and final approval of a majority of residents of the proposed village at the polls. These basic requirements for the incorporation of new villages have evolved only modestly over time, even though the General Village Law has been recodified and revised several times.

The Laws of 1870 expanded village powers, keeping the grants "liberal and flexible" so as not to restrict village governments from accommodating variations in local needs (Wallace 1911). The adoption of a uniform structure and powers for villages was intended to reduce state interference in local affairs (Lincoln 1909, 120). As Governor John T. Hoffman explained, the goal was to meet varied local demands while keeping special acts and amendments to a minimum. To this end, in 1874, the New York State Constitution was amended to formally ban incorporation by special act (Article III, §18, effective January 1, 1875). Villages previously chartered by special act were not, however, required to reincorporate; thus, existing village charters continued to be amended by the state legislature for relatively mundane matters.[2]

The major revisions to the General Village Law in 1897 were two years in the making but reflected a "culmination of a half century of reform" (Benjamin 1990; *New York Times* 1897). For the first time, a system of classification of villages was introduced. Based on population, this system prescribed the size of the village board and defined its relative powers for each class: first-class villages were defined as those containing a population of 5,000 or more and were authorized to elect between two and eight trustees; second-class villages were those between 3,000 and 5,000 and allowed two to six trustees; villages between 1,000 and 3,000 in population were limited to no more than four trustees; and villages of the fourth class were those with fewer than 1,000 residents and limited to only two trustees (L. 1897, Ch. 414). The 1897 law retained the same territorial and population requirements but now required that twenty-five adults who were resident freeholders bring an incorporation petition forward to the town supervisor(s) (L. 1897 Ch 414, §3). It also required, for the first time, that a report of incorporation be filed with the secretary of state.

In 1899, the legislature lowered the population requirement for new incorporations to 200, adding provisions for the consolidation of adjoining villages (later amended by the laws of 1902) and clarifying the grounds on which any objection to the proposed incorporation might be made (Becker and Howe 1902). The purpose of these revisions was to "provide a simple method of incorporating villages, with an equally simple method of testing the legality of the proceedings and a prompt remedy for any mistake rendering those proceedings invalid" (People v. Snedeker 1899; Fitzpatrick 1924).

In 1903, provisions requiring the special consent of property owners were added (L. 1903, Ch. 139). The petitioning process further required a list of inhabitants and the signatures of the owners of property constituting one-third of the real property within the village—those on whom the taxation for village services would disproportionately fall. A year later, the legislature revised the territorial and population requirements for the incorporation of territory in towns with more than 10,000 in population in which there were existing cities and villages. In such cases, an otherwise unincorporated area within a town could only incorporate as a village if its population exceeded 1,000 (L. 1904, Ch. 35). The change reflected the increasing friction between growing cities and their adjacent residents. The higher population requirements made it more difficult for smaller communities to defend against being annexed by incorporating as a village.

In 1905, the legislature added a requirement that the petitioners pay the expense of the incorporation application and referendum if incorporation failed to pass (L. 1905, Ch. 404). The legislature also clarified the process for the expansion of village boundaries through the annexation of adjacent territory and placed limits on the frequency of attempts to dissolve a village (L. 1907, Ch. 607; Benjamin 1990). Changes made in 1907 and 1909 were minor adjustments to the General Village Law, which, by now, had firmly established the authority of the state legislature to provide for uniform government of villages and for the election and appointment of their officers. Per the courts, it was affirmed that "a municipal corporation is a creature of the state, and *the adjustments of its powers and duties of the relevant right of the citizens and the municipality is the province of the legislature*" (Scott v. Village of Saratoga Springs 1909, emphasis added).

Revisions in the incorporation process made in the 1910s and early 1920s represented more legislative tinkering in response to the frictions created by ongoing incorporation battles. For communities between 50 and 200 in population, the incorporation requirements were changed in

1910 to now require the consent of the owners of three-fourths of the assessed value of real property and passage by three-fourths of the voters at referendum (L. 1910, Ch. 258, amended by L. 1913, Ch. 358 to authorize initiation of petition by ten adult freeholders).[3] The legislature added a ban on the resubmission of defeated incorporation propositions for at least one year in 1917 (L. 1917, Ch. 541). In 1920, it eased the requirements for villages with populations between 50 and 200 to the consent of owners of one-half of the value of the assessed village properties and approval by simple majority. The next year, consent requirements for incorporations of villages greater than 2,000 in population were adjusted to require *either* a petition containing the signatures of the owners of one-third the assessed property of the proposed village *or* of a majority of the resident freeholders. A 1921 law accordingly added challenges to a petition based on the insufficiency of these new territorial, population, and consent requirements (L. 1921, Ch. 453).

In 1927, the General Village Law underwent a major recodification following a two-year study by a joint legislative committee and vigorous lobbying by village government representatives (*New York Times* 1926). The overhaul was an effort to "modernize" village law in the direction of expanded local authority and control, affecting nearly all the state's then 450-some villages by providing a model village charter, replacing village presidents with mayors, adopting the direct election of mayors and trustees, imposing budgeting systems, and limiting matters requiring mandatory public referenda to appropriations, bonds, debt, and dissolution (*New York Times* 1927). Incorporation now required a territory of not more than three square miles or fewer than 250 in population, with boundaries established in metes and bounds or by reference to the boundaries of one or more existing water, lighting, fire, or school districts, or of the boundaries of a town. The petition to incorporate had to be signed by twenty-five adults, freeholders with the consent of the owners of property amounting to at least one-third of the village's assessed value, *or* a majority or more of resident freeholders (L. 1927, Ch. 650). Objections to the population requirements had to be raised by witnesses at the incorporation hearing and were strictly limited to compliance with the statutory requirements.

The population requirement was raised to 500, and the number of freeholders necessary to bring a petition forward was raised to fifty in 1933 (L. 1933, Ch. 392). Consent requirements for incorporation where population exceeded 2,000 were restored to approval by one-third of owners of assessed property or a majority of freeholders, and the definition of inhabitants was clarified to exclude summer residents or those not residing in the village for at least one year (L. 1933, Ch. 392). These minor adjustments to the basic elements of incorporation were legislative response to competing local desires to ease or restrict incorporation requirements and to expand or restrict who could participate on the question. Property and residency requirements, in particular, demonstrated ongoing concern over who would shoulder the costs of incorporation and pay for the enhanced level of services.

A redesign of both town and village laws in the 1920–60 period reflected growing tensions between these two municipal forms over the issue of annexation (Lansing and Jones 1903; Boynton 1916). Annexation "has been the dominant method of physical municipal growth in the United States, dating back to the early 1800s" (Edwards and Xiao 2009, 147). By annexing territory, an existing municipality expands its tax base and extends zoning and taxing authority over new or growing development along its periphery. Incorporating is a way to defend against being annexed. Outside Nassau County, town governments have no authority other than verifying that the petition to annex does not include territory that is already incorporated as a city or village.[4] Much to the dismay of towns, recommendations to grant general town authority over the annexation of otherwise unincorporated areas were regularly either legislatively stalled or vetoed (Legislative Document No. 41 1956; Legislative Document No. 47 1956).

Between 1955 and 1959, the New York legislature engaged in an intensive study of municipal relations and rivalries. A Temporary Commission on Town and Village Laws (established by L. 1954, Ch. 533) and several joint legislative committees issued several reports on ongoing village-town conflict particularly as regarded new village incorporations.[5] In 1961, New York enacted legislation, sometimes referred to as the "Selkirk" law, requiring that a city's proposed annexation of otherwise unincorporated (town) territory be approved by both municipal boards followed by the approval of both city and annexed-area residents in concurrent referenda. The requirements were extended to cover annexations by villages in 1963, and the principle of local consent was integrated into New York State constitutional amendments and associated Home Rule Acts in 1964. These changes made annexation impossible without the consent of the residents of all the affected municipalities (Moore 1964).

Village law was substantially revised again in 1964, altering the previous classification of villages that "no longer serve[d] an up-to-date functional purpose" (Legislative Document No. 27 1971, 11).[6] The population and territorial requirements remained the same (no fewer than 500 and not exceeding three square miles or conforming to an existing town or district), but the consent requirements were revised to require petition signatures of at least one-fourth of the real property owners of the village *or* the signatures of the owners of at least one-half of the village's assessed property value. The petition elements were clarified, requiring a territorial description through traditional metes and bounds descriptions or by maps or by reference to an existing district(s), to be accompanied by a list of regular inhabitants (L. 1964, Ch. 755). Also refined were the duties and responsibilities of the town supervisor(s) in conducting the hearing and reviewing the petition.[7]

When the General Village Law was again recodified in 1972 (the last major overhaul), village incorporation provisions were reconstituted as Article 2 of the General Village Law (where they presently remain). Territorial requirements were raised to not more than five square miles, and the population requirement to not fewer than 500. Village boundaries still had to be described in metes and bounds or else by reference as geographically coterminous with one or more existing districts, or with a town. Under Article 2, the petition requirements were lowered to 20 percent of residents qualified to vote for town officers *or* the signatures of the owners of more than 50 percent of the assessed value of the village.[8]

The contemporary contours of village incorporation law were thus substantially set in 1964 with modest revision in 1972. Under these provisions, challenges are authorized *only with respect to the sufficiency of the petition and its required elements, including the submission of surveys, maps, and a list of regular inhabitants.* In the early 1980s, New York courts rejected the authority of towns to add to the incorporation requirements as spelled out in Article 2.[9] In *Marcus v. Baron* (1981; 1982), the court acknowledged that towns may have significant interest in the creation of new villages, but that such "questions are for the Legislature and not for the courts" (138–39). In other words, the addition of substantive review as to the merits of incorporation would require *legislative* authorization and revision of Article 2 of the village law. The Empowerment Act changed the processes for consolidation and dissolution but left the incorporation process intact so that the procedure for creating new villages remains subject to minimal review, even as the state has expended resources to encourage villages to dissolve.[10]

The Parallel Development of Municipal Home Rule Authority

Article VIII, Section 9 of the New York State Constitution of 1846 (the provision establishing the basis for the creation of the General Village Law of 1847) had recognized the "plenary power of the legislature in relation to the creation, alteration, and consolidation of municipal incorporations" (McGovern 1953, 159). Yet the General Village Law, as enacted, reflected self-government principles that can be traced to English and colonial roots (Eaton 1902). With each major revision of the General Village Law, the powers granted to villages expanded but pertained exclusively to internal, community affairs—covering everything from the administration of village elections to the prohibition of kite-flying and hoop-rolling on village streets (L. 1846, Ch. 426, §§57–58). Villages were thus self-governing communities, well regulated from within and exercising authority over a limited sphere of purely local affairs (Novak 1996, x). The subsequent expansion of such home rule authority would further restrict state encroachment into the internal concerns of local government.

The constitutional foundation of home rule originates from the New York State Constitution of 1894, which created classes of cities and specifically granted them authority over their own "property, affairs and government" through a "suspensory veto"—or a rejection by mayors that was subject to legislative override (N.Y. Const., Article XII, §§2–3). The initial push for augmented home rule power was driven by urban concerns that the rurally dominated state legislature was not attentive to the unique needs of the cities. Cities were given additional statutory grants of home rule in 1913–14 with the passage of the Home Rule Act (L. 1937, Ch. 247), and in 1923 under the Constitutional Home Rule Amendment (Article XII, §§2–7) (Lazarus 1964; L. 1924, Ch. 363).[11]

The 1923 amendment embraced the legal theory of the city as *imperium in imperio* (an empire within an empire), limiting state authority to general laws and converting the suspensory veto into a ban on special laws except when the governor declared an emergency supported by two-thirds of the legislature (Hyman 1965, 342). Cities could now adopt and amend local laws without authorization by special act from the state, "*but only with respect to the five matters enumerated in Article XII, Section 3*" (Weiner 1937, 564). A 1928 amendment lifted this restriction, and, after extensive study, the 1938 Constitutional Convention gave every city the power to enact "local laws not inconsistent with the constitution and laws of the state relating to its property, affairs or government" (Article

IX, §11). The legislature, in other words, could not act in relation to local property, affairs or government, except by general law or upon special request of the locality (Article IX, §11).

Calls for greater protection for the other municipal classes was, in part, a reaction to the growth of urban city powers as well as backlash to the incorporation of the greater New York City area. Indeed, the consolidation of dozens of towns, two cities, and more than twenty villages in five counties to re-create the city of New York was soon publicly decried as "the Great Mistake of 1898." By the mid-1920s, organized by the Conference of Mayors, the state's larger villages had begun coordinated lobbying to secure the same home rule powers that had been granted to cities (*New York Times* 1926).

Whereas previous constitutional conventions had considered home rule proposals of counties and villages together, village proposals were considered by a separate committee of the 1938 Constitutional Convention and received far less attention than did the county provisions (Moore 1938). Village home rule proponents argued that the rationale for granting cities home rule powers applied equally to larger villages. They objected to governance under the General Village Law, arguing that its provisions were not responsive to "special conditions or particular community desires" (Problems Related to Home Rule and Local Government 1938, 104). Opponents to village home rule authority maintained that its grant would blur the distinctions between municipal forms and insisted that larger villages could achieve the same ends simply by reincorporating as a city (Problems Related to Home Rule and Local Government 1938, 104–5).

The 1938 convention ultimately adopted a proposal that gave the state's approximately fifty-three first-class villages home rule on par with cities, directing the legislature to pass implementing legislation. Voters approved, and the new Village Home Rule Act was enacted in 1940 (*New York Times* 1937; Moore 1938; McGovern 1953, 166). In so doing, it was believed that the number of special laws would be reduced, resulting in greater uniformity while still allowing localities the flexibility necessary (through local law power) to meet local needs without constant appeal to the legislature. As importantly, it would free state legislators from refereeing local battles of limited state concern, keeping them from being drawn into conflicts between municipal constituencies, and shielding them from the opportunities for favor trading and corruption. In this way, village home rule was as much about offloading state legislative accountability as venerating localism.

The extension of home rule authority to larger villages that was undertaken as a somewhat insular development and without full intentionality and consideration by the 1938 convention opened the gateway for municipal pressure by other governing units. Counties too were given authority to adopt alternative forms of government in 1935 and similarly received constitutional grants of home rule powers from the 1938 convention (to be further enhanced by amendments to county home rule provisions in 1958).

Yet, despite these statutory and constitutional gains, home rule proponents were increasingly dissatisfied (Putrino 1964; Hyman 1965).[12] Restrictive and inconsistent judicial interpretations of local authority (i.e., of what constituted matters of internal property, affairs, and government), confusion over the competing state concern doctrine, and the frequency of state legislative preemption rendered home rule powers limited in practical application. While "all of the local governments of our state were dissatisfied with the inadequacy or lack of powers," the municipal units that were most desirous of change were smaller villages and town governments, which, "regardless of size," lacked the powers of local legislation now enjoyed by cities, counties, and first-class villages (Marshlow 1964, 3–4; *Buffalo Evening News* 1965).

In advance of a constitutionally mandated referendum on the question of whether to convene a convention to amend or revise the New York State Constitution, a Temporary Commission on the Revision and Simplification of the Constitution was established in 1959. That commission spent considerable time developing even more robust home rule provisions for New York's localities.[13] This push was inexorably bound up with concern over annexation of territory by adjacent, larger, or expanding municipalities. Suburbanization and demographic changes had greatly contributed to concerns of municipalities on the peripheries of urban areas. The increasing number of defensive incorporations reflected the desire of local residents to preserve their communities from encroachment—whether in the form of new development or the influx of new, more racially or economically diverse residents.

Although the Temporary Commission's various proposals failed to achieve legislative support for an overhaul of the heretofore patchwork of home rule provisions, its progress was handed off to the Office of Local Government and an advisory committee on home rule that would put forward the proposal to create a new local government article of the New

York State Constitution (Article IX).[14] This major constitutional amendment passed two successive legislative sessions (in 1962 and 1963), was ratified by the voters, and took effect on January 1, 1964 (Marshlow 1964, 4). Implementing legislation, in the form of the Home Rule Law and the Statue of Local Governments, was passed in 1963 (currently codified as Chapter 58-A of the Consolidated Laws of New York). These revisions constitutionally extended to *all counties, cities, towns, and villages* the power to enact local laws relative to their own "property, affairs, and government." The provisions further protected the localities' right to elected representation and instituted local consent as a safeguard against involuntary annexation. Annexation now uniformly required the acquiescence of voters in both the annexing jurisdiction and territory to be annexed, as well as the agreement of the boards of all affected municipalities and a review process allowing input from all affected units of government.

The Statute of Local Governments, as enacted in 1963, did not add new local powers into the constitution, but rather "froze" the specified powers of local governments, further requiring that the withdrawal of any such local powers be passed by two successive legislatures. In this way, the 1963–64 changes "unite[d] counties, cities, towns, and villages in interest by treating them alike in their basic powers" (Recent Developments in Home Rule 1964, 3). Small towns and villages now had the home rule powers enjoyed by cities and first-class villages. These changes were enacted with the full support and advocacy of municipal organizations like the New York Conference of Mayors (NYCOM) but with "little evidence of any groundswell of public demand of such powers" (Grad 1964).[15]

While seemingly enhancing local autonomy, the standardization of home rule and local powers (much like the adoption of general laws) functionally served to transfer control *out of the hands of residents and into the hands of their local elected officials* (Wallace 1911; Grad 1964). The paradox of home rule, in other words, was that it shifted the locus of local powers to local governing boards. Moreover, new provisions allowing executive intervention in local affairs via emergency powers were apparently, and surprisingly, approved "sight unseen" by NYCOM (Lazarus 1964).

Local government powers continued to receive substantial attention from the Constitutional Convention of 1967. The Committee on Local Government and Home Rule failed to adopt a final majority report, and its calls for fiscal autonomy failed to garner convention support (Dullea 1997, 274). In the end, even modest changes to the Local Government

Article were denied when the voters rejected the work of the 1967 Constitutional Convention in a single (i.e., up-down) vote. Since then, no major constitutional revisions of local governing powers have been enacted.

Despite these long and hard-fought efforts for greater local autonomy, the 1983 Commission on State-Local Relations still likened home rule to a "paper tiger," noting that, in practice, it exists more as a function of state legislative discretion than robust constitutional protection for local government (New York State Legislative Commission on State-Local Relations 1983, 9). Overarching and limiting state laws and the imposition of state mandates create regular friction between state-level policies and local choice. Tensions over the exercise of home rule authority are exacerbated by home-district influences over state lawmakers and by partisan pressures on the executive to respond to local concerns (Benjamin 2017b, 27). Moreover, state intervention into local affairs can still be achieved by "techniques . . . developed to systematically bypass home rule provisions," including the adoption of general laws that in their specificity effectively apply only to select localities, by the enactment of special law by local request, and by local reluctance to exercise the autonomous authority they have been granted (Benjamin 2017b, 27–28). As Benjamin explains, similar authority over functions, structure, personnel, and fiscal matters exercised by multiple local jurisdictions has produced a "clash of laws" and ongoing conflict between local governments and between localities and the state (2017b, 27).

The impact of this lengthy and piecemeal evolution of constitutional and statutory home rule authority nevertheless had a twofold impact on village incorporation and dissolution. First, it has essentially placed all municipalities on equal footing, blurring the functional distinctions between municipal types and making their proliferation and maintenance harder to rationalize (Benjamin 1990). Indeed, the 1983 State Legislative Committee on State-Local Relations concluded that there was now striking similarity among the powers of local government units (New York State Legislative Commission on State-Local Relations 1983, S-2). An already outmoded and ossified structure, in other words, has been increasingly burdened by growing rivalries between municipal forms of similar authority and overlapping jurisdiction (Atkins 1968).

Second, although Article IX, Section 2 grants the legislature the power to create and organize local governments, the evolution of municipal powers has made incorporation, dissolution, and annexation *contingent on local consent*.[16] Reorganization remains an "obvious" mechanism of change at the state's disposal, and the state retains its legal authority to "create or dissolve local governments" (New York State Legislative Commission on State-Local Relations 1983, 107). But, as a *practical matter*, once control over municipal structure is entrusted to local choice, the state's ability to command (or incentivize) municipal reorganization becomes *politically infeasible*.[17]

The Purpose and Patterns of Village Incorporation

New York was a poor record keeper of its early village incorporations and dissolutions. In 1881 and again in 1896, the secretary of state wrote to each of the counties to try to establish a complete and correct inventory of the number of incorporated places. The state made another attempt in 1931, sending a survey to all villages asking for 1) the date of incorporation and the law under which the village was incorporated; 2) any recorded name changes or dissolutions; and 3) verification as to whether the village was still functioning as a corporate entity. The responses to these surveys (available in the archives of the New York Library) reveal that an astonishing number of village officials lacked basic information on their communities' incorporation history, often leaving the field blank, entering conflicting information, or confessing ignorance as to when and under which law their village was legally incorporated. In many cases, local postmasters supplied the necessary information or offered their own best guess.

To ensure accuracy of early dissolutions, I compiled an inventory of incorporated villages using assorted *Civil Lists* (Hough 1858; 1860; 1867; and Werner 1888), *New York State Guides* (Disturnell 1842; 1843), *New York Field Codes* (1850–65), the *Special Report of the Statutory Revision Committee* (1897), and *Bender's Village Law* (Grattan 1903; 1914; 1918; Birdseye 1897; Parker and Danaher 1906; McKinney 1918) along with a review of New York State Session Laws (1789–2020) and historical newspaper coverage. The compilation of village incorporations allows us to see the patterns of village government formation as well as to verify past dissolutions by comparing once incorporated places with the current list of villages.

The incorporation of villages in New York can be attributed to three main reasons: entrepreneurial development, service provision, and establishing boundaries for the purposes of land-use regulation and zoning authority or the definition of community. The founding stories reflect both intentionality and happenstance: Some villages were transplants from New England, others were established for religious purposes or selected as an ideal site for a specific economic enterprise (such as mining, tanning, or lumber harvesting). Still others sprang up more organically without intentionality or planning (Bates 1912). Smith's (1966) classic study differentiates between such covenanted and cumulative communities. Covenanted communities are those "composed of individuals bound in a special compact with God and each other," driven by colonial aspirations or having foundations in religious societies (17). Its citizens are collectively bound in moral obligation as a self-governed body politic that is often utopian in aspiration (Elazar 1998). The desire for internal harmony, stability, and conformity still permeates the idea of small-town living (Lingeman 1980, 35).

In more secularized covenants, local government is constituted to promote a collective, public purpose to the mutual benefit of all inhabitants. These "civil communities," as Lutz (1988) calls them, reflect "the American pioneer tradition" and were regarded as self-organizing and self-governing communities" until they were "legally redefined as creatures of state governments" (Agranoff 2017, 21). Lingeman (1980) explains how the profit motive frequently drove the settlement of new, speculative towns, sparking competition between towns and between established towns and new development. He highlights tensions between existing residents and "newcomers" and their rival interests in development and growth (35). "A town meant trade, a seat of rudimentary government and law enforcement, a center of sociability, a hearth fire of civilization in the forest. Above all, to the speculator, the town promised a way to make money" (1980, 105). Speculators engaged in "town jobbing"—creating "paper towns" or grabbing up land in favorable locations where a town might be built (108–10). Much of this planning, from site location and proximity to commerce routes, was future oriented. Such places either "grew slowly but stubbornly, or else faded into economic decay and quiescence" (108).

By contrast, cumulative settlements sprang up without intentionality in planning, their growth organically driven by entrepreneurism, geographic convenience, or proximity to the crossroads or channels of trade. Their incorporation too was typically motivated by the economic interests of their inhabitants, who desired greater services than was available from the town or who wanted to protect their property interests through more localized land-use authority.

The stories of New York's villages well illustrate the variables of fortune that could benefit or befall a community. External forces, such as the routing (or rerouting) of commerce by rail or canal, boomed some places and doomed others. Downturns in fortune, like resource depletion, natural disasters, or fire, resulted in devastation from which some villages could never recover. By the 1870s, the populations of many villages had naturally stagnated or declined, draining the community of its former vitality. The view was that, once deterioration set in, "the tendency of things becomes strong in this direction" (Egleston 1878, 22).

ENTREPRENEURIALISM AND DEVELOPMENT

As seen in figure 1.1, the number of village incorporations increased steadily in the period of 1790 to 1840.[18] Some villages were forged out of the wilderness by founding figures looking for a location suitable to building their fortune or embarking on some entrepreneurial venture. Locations on or close to rivers, with access to stands of trees, or cheap land, were often places where mills, tanneries, foundries, or factories could be envisioned and built. The names are often telling: Prospect (Oneida County), Speculator (Hamilton County), Deposit (Broom County). Geographical attributes, like waterway access, sand deposits, creeks, hot springs, or streams for energy and mill production, frequently provide the explanation as to why a particular community was founded *there* in that place, at that time (Hall 2016).

Many of the earliest villages owe their existence to the entrepreneurial ambitions of specific individuals. An 1852 biography of Zadock Pratt, founder of Prattsville (Greene County), for example, reads like a cross between the story of the real-life Daniel Boone and the fictitious Jebediah Springfield of *The Simpsons*. In the 1820s, Pratt set off in search of a suitable location for his tannery, finding in the unsettled expanse of the town of Windham (Greene County) an abundance of resources, including hemlock forests, where he planned out a community anchored by a great tannery. The location was perfectly positioned for what he foresaw as a corridor of commerce linking the untapped resources of the state's western territory with the commercial centers of the east. In 1824, he began construction, "predict[ing] that the rich meadows all about him would be covered with a beautiful village."[67] In this enterprising spirit, he dammed Schoharie Creek, laid out streets, strategically planted trees, and courted turnpike companies. Foreseeing the "disadvantages and inconveniences of a

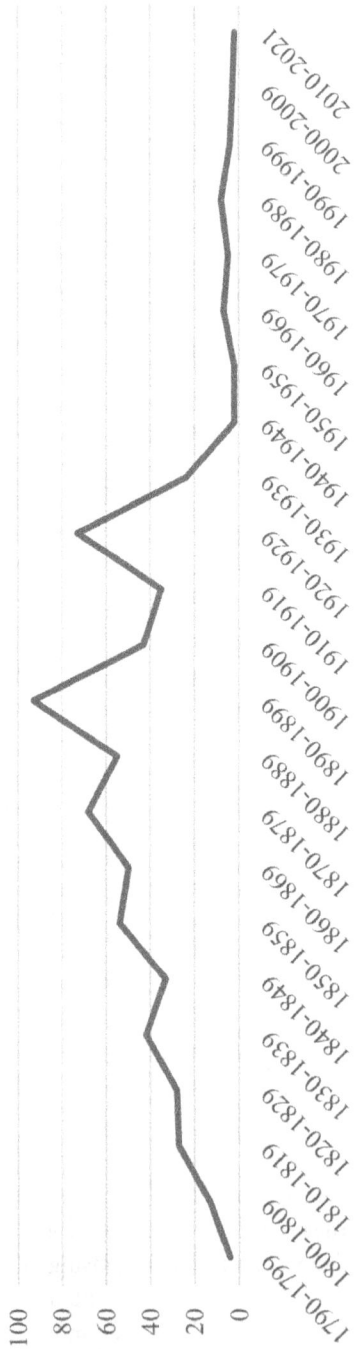

Figure 1.1. New York Village Incorporations by Decade (1790–2021). *Source:* Author created graphic.

village at a distance from the center of town influences and privileges" and recognizing the "the force of the opposition which would most probably be made by the sudden application for a separate incorporation," he laid the groundwork for a new town of Prattsville in 1832.[19] But the prosperity of the new village could not long outlive the man. Once the hemlock stands were depleted, the tannery closed and the population dwindled (Schupe, Stein, and Pandit 1987). Prattsville officially dissolved in 1899.

After the adoption of the General Village Law in 1847, the rate of incorporation increased to more than three per year. By 1860, there were 204 incorporated villages. The number of new towns peaked by the 1860, then all but ceased after the Civil War. Villages, "the town's major competitor as a local municipal form," continued to flourish (Feeney Commission 1975). Fueled by the opening of the Erie Canal in 1815, the expansion of railroads, and surges in immigration, the new industrial economy led to a boom in new villages from the 1830s to the 1920s. The peak decade for incorporation was 1880–99, when ninety-three new villages were created. The competition and growth of prosperity demanded greater local governing capacity and civic boosterism.

Between 1910 and 1933, when population requirements for incorporation were eased, there was another boom with 143 new incorporations. The Great Depression had created something of a "back-to-the-land-movement" as migrants seeking work in the cities returned to their rural roots (Lingeman 1980, 294). More than half (59 percent) of these new villages were created in downstate suburban counties, with incorporations in Nassau and Suffolk Counties accounting for 53 percent of new village formation in this twenty-three-year period. In the 1940s, the number of new villages dropped to just two.

Annexation of villages by adjacent cities,[20] the reincorporation of villages as cities, and village dissolution all subtracted from the growing total of village governments.[21] Of New York's sixty-three incorporated cities, all but five (New York, Albany, Schenectady, Hudson, and Lackawanna) were incorporated first as villages.[22] Reincorporating as a city was another way to "divorce" a village from the town (Atkins 1968; 1969b).[23] But there is no singular explanation for why villages transitioned to city status, although the evidence suggests that population growth, civic prestige, avoiding annexation, and desire for enhanced representation were the primary motivators.

The more limited scope of village powers was another (Ducker 1931; Rochester Bureau of Municipal Research 1958). The General Village Law of 1897, for example, had been likened to a "straight jacket" for village governments. When the 1927 recodification "released them from much of that straight jacket, the desire to become cities evaporated" (Village Committee of the New York State Constitutional Convention 1938, 11). Residential dissatisfaction with town-level control over zoning and planning decisions along with a desire to avoid town taxes fueled renewed interest in village creation in the 1960s (New York Conference of Mayors 1964; 1965).

The Feeney Commission (1975) suggested that there is a "normal pattern of municipal development" in which villages emerged out of the deficiencies of the towns, transitioning into cities with time and growth. As an example of that optimism, Medina's village municipal building, built in 1908, was inscribed as "City Hall" in anticipation that it was only a matter of time before the village reincorporated as a city. But municipal classification is not a function of size in New York. Not all villages made this transition from a hamlet to a village to a city; indeed, *most did not*. Nevertheless, this view that there is a "normal pattern" of municipal growth and development remains a progressive narrative against which present-day villages continue to struggle.

SERVICE PROVISION

While not every incorporated village thrived or survived, the ranks of villages nevertheless swelled, in part because incorporation was a legally convenient (and relatively easy) means by which residents in populated areas could secure services that were not needed or provided on a town-wide basis. Such services would then be funded exclusively by the taxes of those residing within the new village. Particularly in rural counties and towns, populated areas incorporated mostly to secure services, such as lighting, sanitation, or street maintenance, that were appropriate for the higher densities of residences and businesses.

Villages thus grew as a derivation of town government, driven by patterns of settlement and the demand for services. That a significant number of new villages retained or echoed the name of their embracing town further indicates that villages were created out of a desire to supplement, not separate from, the town.[24] Executive refusal to empower towns in the nineteenth century contributed to these developments. Gubernatorial veto messages expressed the view that it was unnecessary to expand town government because the needs of populated areas could be readily accommodated by their incorporation as a village (or city) (Benjamin 1990, 30–31).

In 1926, a General District Law, was enacted and the "incorporation rate of villages began its downward trend parallel to the rise of the district" (Feeney Commission 1975; L. 1926, Ch. 470).[25] The proliferation of special districts had a "profound effect" in slowing the creation of new villages by allowing the service needs of more populated areas to be accommodated through the creation of special taxing districts within the town (New York Department of State 2018b, 77). As seen in Figure 1.1, the formation of new villages drops precipitously in the 1930s and 1940s and remains flat in the period following, with just a handful per decade.

Nationally, the 1940s and 1950s witnessed a growth in new municipalities. That trend was muted in New York by the expansion of town powers in the 1930s and the granting of general-service powers to counties in the 1950s. A Suburban Town Law was enacted in 1962 over the objections of cities and villages. Simply stated, as other forms of government acquired authority to provide general services and the legislature began a trend of "assigning new activities in local government to the counties rather than to the cities, towns, and villages," the need for and the number of new village incorporations declined dramatically (Moore 1967).

The 1950s–60s also saw a shift of population toward the suburban towns (outside villages) (Temporary State Commission on the Constitutional State Convention 1967, 31). These lower-density communities served as a reprieve from the problems of the cities; a progression that Judd and Hinze (2015) describe as the "romantic suburban ideal" (1815–1915), to the "automobile suburbs" (1918–45), to the "bedroom suburbs" (1946–70s) (171–77). Village incorporation post-1950s was most extensive in Nassau and Suffolk Counties, driven by city dwellers seeking to escape to a more idealized village life (Teaford 1979; 1997).[26] In some places, the influx of new residents was "traumatic . . . straining the fabric of community, the quality of life, the surrounding environment (Lingeman 1980, 447). Locals were priced out or revolted against rising taxation, complaining that their "way of life" had been destroyed. "The new arrivals' political demands inevitably clashed with the usually older, more conservative, and less improvement-minded local clique who ran things. Thus, was the stage set for newcomer versus old-timer conflicts" (Lingeman 1980, 450). Particularly in the downstate counties outside New York, villages

provided a quainter, more romanticized way of life—quieter country living—with proximity to the amenities of the central cities (Teaford 1979;
1997; Egleston 1878). Incorporation protected these communities from
the threat of annexation and allowed village residents sufficient control
to preserve their property values, maintain their desired level of services,
and enhance their democratic self-governance.

Tensions between towns and villages over a shifting tax base and
municipal boundaries also grew as a result of suburbanization. As new
areas were developed, additional infrastructure and revenue needs fueled a
desire for territorial annexation and the preemptive formation of new local
governments. The degree of strategic planning, investment, and land use
varied widely from town to town and between rural, suburban, and urban
areas. Some localities adapted to and managed commercial and economic
development, while others resisted economic growth. Development, in
other words, created winners and losers among municipalities jockeying to
harness or deter it through zoning and land-use authority. Teaford (1997)
situates village incorporation in Nassau and Suffolk Counties within this
context of suburban development. Village incorporation was not always
intended to facilitate suburbanization but to "preserve and protect" an
"idealized village form of government, a small-scale, non-partisan polity
characterized by volunteerism, cooperation, and consensus" (Teaford 1997,
15–16).[27] Indeed, this desire for "the benefits of village living can be seen
in the development of new urbanism, which promotes village-type amenities and atmosphere within cities" (O'Brien 2015).[28]

Boundary Establishment: Regulating Land Use and Defining Communities of Interest

Incorporation is, in the simplest terms, a form of municipal boundary
change (Smith 2018). By incorporating, residents gain a legally distinct
status from the surrounding township, vesting governing authority in their
own locally elected, independent governing body. This decision to incorporate is frequently defensive, undertaken to prevent annexation by adjacent
communities or to regulate membership in the community through the
drawing of municipal boundaries. Indeed, "municipal incorporation efforts
from 1920 to 1940 were often shrouded by exclusionary ambitions (Smith
2018, 8). Rice, Waldner, and Smith (2014) recently identified the major
reasons for new incorporations more generally, finding that four of the
top-five rationales are defensive: first is to prevent annexation, second is

to combat undesirable growth and development through zoning authority, third is to preserve the character and identity of the community, fourth is to provide or enhance services, and fifth is to control revenue (Rice, Waldner, and Smith 2014, 148–49). Thus, while earlier (pre-1950s) incorporations were largely about service provision, which arguably promotes the public (collective) good, modern efforts to incorporate tend to rest on political, economic, and sociological motivations in the private interest (Smith 2018, 44).

Teaford (1979) details the ways in which permissive state incorporation laws allowed communities to erect boundaries in the interest of creating tax havens, evading regulation, protecting preferred religious or moral practices, and defining their preferred community identity. The demarcation of boundaries and corresponding obligations separated suburban residents from urban places, and semi-rural residents from rural ones. Manufacturing interests could escape "heavy taxation by creating municipal fiefdoms" or promote their private interests through a more amenable municipality (Teaford 1979, 14). Powers granted under the General Village Law additionally allowed village governments to control housing density through zoning regulations, code enforcement, and the passage of local laws. Incorporations post-1950 were, in this sense, largely about boundary establishment—creating a separation and demarcation from urban areas and ensuring lower population density housing through local land-use powers (New York Department of State 2018b, 89).

Burns's classic work on the formation of local government (1994) argued that the formation of municipal governments translates private values into public institutions. The impetus generally involves a coalition of citizens, entrepreneurs, businesses, and private organizations to petition for municipal creation. For Trachtenberg (2007), the corporatization of the United States more broadly has transitioned of the inherently public purpose of municipal incorporations toward increasingly private ends. The zoning and taxing authority that attends incorporation allows the exercise of that local authority to be used in ways that can be intentionally less (or more) inclusive of diverse interests. Municipalities provide more than services; they serve a social function, offering amusement, educational opportunities, and social and cultural enrichment to the residents. Such amenities become *private goods* in the sense that they contribute to the quality of life for those who live in, or who are part of, the municipality.

Recent incorporation controversies suggest that the contemporary desire to incorporate is less about service provision and increasingly about ensuring localized control over land use, code enforcement, zoning, and development. New York "stands alone" in the degree of local government autonomy over land use and zoning (Kazis 2020). But while the authority of towns and villages to regulate land use is similar, village incorporation gives control to a smaller territory, or to a subset of the population within the town.[29] For example, residents in East Quogue (Suffolk County) filed an incorporation petition in 2019 to try to wrest control over a proposed golf-community project from the town. The proposal was for a "skinny-incorporation"—one that would transfer zoning authority to an unpaid village board even as the village continued to rely on the town for most of its services.[30] Incorporation was rejected by a vote of 889–642.

Incorporation can also preemptively prevent a community's falling subject to the land-use decisions of an embracing, adjacent, or even future municipality. In July 2019, residents in the town of Tuxedo (Orange County) voted to incorporate a new village of Tuxedo by a vote of 478–23 while simultaneously voting to immediately consolidate the new village with the town (under Article 17-A) by a vote of 615–22. The consolidation left the preexisting village of Tuxedo Park (incorporated in 1952) intact; its residents voted on the consolidation but not the incorporation question.[31] The benefit of the two-step incorporation-consolidation was that it prevented *any other, future village from being incorporated in the territory of the town*, because a village cannot be created within territory already otherwise incorporated. Tuxedo existed only as a "paper village," created to block a long-stalled, multiphase planned commuter-community, known as Tuxedo Farms, from perhaps eventually incorporating as a new village of its own.[32]

The ongoing battle over the proposed incorporation of a village of Edgemont illustrates how the desire for localized autonomy may clash with the interests of the embracing town or towns (Foderaro 2017; 2017b; Parshall 2020).[33] Residents in this affluent neighborhood have been trying to incorporate since the 1960s. In 2017, and again in 2018, the town of Greenburgh supervisor ruled the incorporation petitions insufficient, prompting legal challenges that were decided in favor of his authority.[34] Residents favoring incorporation wanted greater control over zoning and development and assessments. They also did not want to support town-outside-village (TOV) services, including minority-serving community centers, from which residents of the proposed village perceived no direct benefit. From the town's perspective, the shift of revenues from the town to the village would "leave behind" the more diverse and less affluent residents in the town-outside-the-village (Casey 2018).[35]

Discriminatory intent may not be necessarily overt or even present—those who favor creating a village are often seeking better services and amenities, enhanced political representation, more space, and less congestion. The instruments by which they create their ideal way of life (zoning and code enforcement) however, can operate with discriminatory effect, pricing many out of the community and enforcing homogeneity. In some cases, the formation or dissolution of a village is a very deliberate effort to carve out a separate community to accommodate a unique community identity or to defend against the feared encroachment of a growing minority population either by erecting a barrier of local authority or diluting their political control. In this way, municipal formation and dissolution become a means of preserving competing community values by separating an "us" from a "them."

The battle over dueling community identities is perhaps most dramatically illustrated by village incorporation and dissolution cases in Orange, Rockland, and Sullivan Counties, where clashes between growing ultra-Orthodox (or Haredi) Jewish populations and non–ultra-Orthodox residents have been contentious, litigious, and, occasionally, even violent. In short, the migration and growth of ultra-Orthodox Jewish communities in counties surrounding New York City has led to the creation of villages (and towns) to accommodate their needs as well as the proposed dissolution of villages to dilute, or constrain, their political power. Villages founded to constrain the impact and influence of non–ultra-Orthodox residents include Pomona (1967), Wesley Hills (1982), Chestnut Ridge (1983), Montebello (1986), and Airmont (1991) in Rockland County and South Blooming Grove (2006) and Woodbury (2006) in Orange County.[36] Villages created to accommodate Orthodox communities include New Square (1961) and Kaser (1990) in the town of Ramapo in Rockland County and, perhaps most famously, Kiryas Joel in the town of Monroe (now Palm Tree) in Orange County.

The incorporation of the village of Airmont (town of Ramapo, Rockland County) in 1991 is an example of an effort to guard against the anticipated impact of a sizeable influx of ultra-Orthodox neighbors. To deter the expansion of higher density, multifamily housing, in-home religious worship, or in-home schools, a village government was established to ensure more localized control over zoning and land-use decisions (Edmonds and Merriam 1996, 445; Smith 2000, 1163–64). Airmont's incorporation petition survived a series of legal challenges and a preliminary injunction (trying to prevent the election of village officers, thereby rendering the village inoperative) (Lefkowitz v. Reisman 1988; 1989; Leblanc-Stenberg v. Fletcher 1991). In 1993, members of the ultra-Orthodox community were joined by the US Department of Justice (DOJ) in a suit against the new village, alleging selective zoning enforcement and violations of the 1968 Fair Housing Act and the Religious Land Use and Institutionalized Persons Act (RLUIPA) (Laycock and Goodrich 2012; LeBlanc-Stemberg v. Fletcher 1995). Per judicial order, for a period of five years, village zoning ordinances were to be reviewed by the DOJ for discriminatory intent (U.S. v. Village of Airmont 1995). The DOJ filed suit again in 2005, launching six years of litigation that ended with the village entering a consent decree in 2011. New zoning disputes and the adoption of a building moratorium resulted in additional suits against the village in 2016 and 2018.[37]

In the tiny village of Bloomingburg (town of Mamakating, Sullivan County), residents tried to dissolve the existing village to dilute the voting power of the ultra-Orthodox residents and return planning and zoning control to the town. The controversy began in 2006 with a proposed housing development intended for ultra-Orthodox residents. After its initial approval, it was revealed that the developers had intentionally selected a smaller community, promising investors that upon full occupancy of the new development, the new residents could effectively control the local government and along with it the zoning power to approve new, even bigger housing projects (Bekiempis 2014). To prevent what some Bloomingburg residents saw as a "hostile takeover" of their village, they petitioned to dissolve under the Empowerment Act. Irregularities in the resulting referendum, including the false registration of voters, led to a federal investigation and criminal convictions against the developers for engaging in voting fraud in their attempt to defeat the dissolution effort. The development's permits were rescinded and the dissolution failed, but simmering tensions remain.

As noted, other villages have been created to accommodate growing religious communities. The village of Kiryas Joel was incorporated in 1979, its boundaries narrowly drawn to reflect the footprint of the ultra-Orthodox residents. In 1989, the New York State legislature approved the creation of the Kiryas Joel Union Free School District to better accommodate the education and special needs of the community.[38] As a modern version of the covenanted community—a community bound by shared religious and cultural value systems—the establishment of ultra-Orthodox enclaves as separate, self-governing municipalities is a relatively unique phenomenon, an effort to establish what Stolzenberg and Myers (2021) call an "American

Shtetl." Visitors to Kiryas Joel are greeted by a welcoming sign that advises visitors to abide by rules for dress and gender separation in all public places.

While having a separate municipal government and school district solves some problems, it has created others (Kahn 2018; Benjamin 2017; Foderaro 2017b; Samaha 2014; Roberts 2011). Ongoing acrimony between the village of Kiryas Joel (which now has a population of 26,800 residents) and the town of Monroe led to a municipal divorce of sorts through the creation of the town of Palm Tree in 2019 (made coterminous with the village in 2020).[39] The town of Monroe rejected a petition for the creation of a proposed village of Seven Springs in 2018, championed by a dissident faction of the ultra-Orthodox community seeking to break away from Kiryas Joel (Berger 1997; Berger 1997b; Speilman 2018).

The creation of separate villages for ultra-Orthodox communities has been both hailed as an exemplar of tolerance and condemned as a form of segregation. Benjamin (2017) questions whether the "creation and dissolution of local governments [should] be an available tactic for use in intra- and intercommunity disputes" (1384). Yet, as Myers and Stolzenberg have noted, the creation of ultra-Orthodox villages like Kiryas Joel is entirely lawful, using established private property rights, existing municipal incorporation laws, and the exercise of voting power to advance collective self-interests through the creation of municipal entities (Myers and Stolzenberg 2008; 2010). In this sense, the incorporation of "religiously homogeneous ultra-Orthodox communities is entirely of a piece with . . . broader American social, economic, and racial dynamics" (Myers and Stolzenberg 2008, 53). But for the non–ultra-Orthodox residents, control of a municipality or school district by representatives of a strict religious faction can feel threatening, and the disputes between the community factions have often turned bitter and ugly.

The creation of a new village does have an impact on embracing towns and adjacent municipalities, the residents of which have no say on incorporation. Indeed, New York's incorporation process does not require a study of the merits of the proposed incorporation or allow input from neighboring municipalities (Parshall 2020). The statutory requirements and petition elements are minimal and were adopted in an era of horses and buggies—when the primary question was whether residents of the proposed village were sufficient in number and willingness to bear the costs of a new village. As such, the state's incorporation process arguably does not adequately address the complex questions that surround the decision to incorporate.

Village Durability and the Narrative of Progress

New York has never provided a mechanism for orderly progression as determined by the organic growth or decline of a community. Classification as a town, village, or city is neither related to population size nor indicative of a significant difference in functions or powers. There is no legal requirement that a village reincorporate as a city upon reaching a certain population or that its corporate status is reviewed or revoked if population falls below a designated threshold. Rather, the decision to incorporate is one of local determination.

Nevertheless, village incorporation provides an important keyhole into explaining dissolution resistance and the durability of village government. There remains an unspoken narrative of progress that permeates the popular conception of municipal development: that communities naturally progress from a crossroads to a hamlet, from a hamlet to a village, and from a village to a city (Novak 1996). Once incorporated, there is, at minimum, an expectation of stable maturity or growth, such that the longevity of a village's incorporation is often equated with its success. Moreover, as will be seen in chapter 2, the thin thread of state oversight over local affairs and municipal formation, marked by a shift of control away from the state legislature into the hands of local residents, and then into the hands of local elected officials, is paralleled in the evolution of dissolution procedures.

Chapter 2

Dissolving Villages

Prior to the adoption of the General Village Law of 1847, village dissolution (like incorporation) was controlled by the legislature in response to local request. Thus, when dissolution formally occurred, it was by legislative repeal via special act. In a handful of cases, village residents abandoned their charter rights, ceasing to operate as a village with legislative approval. Once the General Village Law was adopted, dissolution was placed directly in local hands, initiated through a citizen petition process and subject to approval at a public referendum. Dissolution procedures were initially prescribed in §90 and §91 of the General Village Law of 1847 and were later recodified as §327 (in 1897) and §350 (in 1909). The 1972 overhaul law introduced an entirely new procedure with a new Article 19 of the General Village Law. In 2010, the procedures for municipal consolidation and dissolution were substantially revised with passage of the Empowerment Act and relocated to General Municipal Law Article 17-A.

Disincorporations from 1789 to 1972 reveal how changes in the process impacted the success of dissolution efforts and illustrate why residents sometimes eliminated village governments. From abandonment and remorse to discord and dysfunction, dissolution was often the consequence of decline or discontent. But village residents have also turned to dissolution to secure improved services, leverage revenue opportunities, revitalize their communities, or alleviate a growing property tax burden. The burgeoning interest in dissolution during the national anti-property tax movement of the 1970s coincided with the adoption of Article 19, which gave greater power over the process to local elected officials. Contemporary dissolutions (post-2010) reflect a desire for operational efficiencies and the impact of state-level policy and incentives in encouraging municipal reorganization.

The Evolution of Dissolution Procedures

New York's village dissolution law has evolved through four major paradigms, each of which may be distinguished 1) by the method (or statutory mechanism) by which dissolution occurs; 2) by the role assumed by the state in the process; 3) by the degree to which local (village) elected officials wield influence in the process; 4) by the degree of direct or indirect authority exercised by the citizens (village residents) and; 5) by the resulting locus of power in terms of which of these entities (state, local elected officials, or residents) control the decision to dissolve.

Under the Responsive Paradigm (1789–1846), the authority to dissolve village governments was exercised by the state legislature, generally in response to local request. In the Direct Command period (1847–1972), state legislative control was surrendered, giving the qualified electors of the village the power to directly command and implement dissolution through the ballot box. The Local Control model (1972–2009) delivered greater influence over the dissolution process into the hands of local elected (village) officials. The Empowerment Act (2010–present) sought to revitalize the citizens' role, restoring elements of citizen command. Transitions between the four approaches are marked by the major recodification of dissolution procedures in 1847, 1972, and 2009, signifying the legislature's adoption of a new paradigm. This evolution was the result of multiple factors including:

1. A trend toward local control, including a ban on incorporations by special act, the enactment of general municipal laws, and the expansion of municipal home rule authority.

2. Intermunicipal tensions over such matters as annexation, state aid, financing, and service provision, leading to varying degrees of cooperation and competition.

3. The competing demands of village, town, and county governments, as represented by their respective local elected officials and municipal organizations.

4. Fiscal and environmental pressures, including depopulation, service needs, rising property taxes, and regional concerns.

5. Specific dissolution controversies that required clarification or revision of the process.

The transition between these periods reflects the state legislature's evolving view of where the *locus* of control over the creation and dissolution of local governing units ought to rest, as well as its desire to disengage from internal, local affairs.

From Responsiveness to Direct Command

From 1789 to 1846, dissolving a village required action by the state legislature. Typically, locals appealed to the legislature, requesting that their municipal charter be revoked. As will be seen in later discussion of actual dissolutions, the reasons for such requests were varied and rarely explained in the legislation. Upon the adoption of the General Village Law of 1847, New York State legislature transferred the power to dissolve to residents amid concerns for the mischiefs associated with special acts. By then, there were 200 incorporated villages in New York State.

The first dissolution procedures established by §90 and §91 of the General Village Law of 1847 were relatively straightforward: the discontinuation of a village corporation could be initiated by a citizen petition (signed by "one-fourth as many persons entitled to vote for village officers, as voted for such officers at the next preceding election thereof"). A successful petition required the village trustees to schedule an election. If a majority voted "no" on the question of continuing the incorporation, the dissolution was effective at the expiration of six months. Within that six-month period, residents would determine disposition of property and discharge of village debt at a special meeting (L. 1847, Ch. 426, §90). After six months, all records and papers were to be transferred to the town (or one of the towns), and the town supervisor became the trustee of village property (L. 1847, Ch. 426, §91).[1]

The ban on special acts in 1874 (after sustained gubernatorial pressure) made direct local action the exclusive authority for both creating and dissolving villages, investing the preferred structure of local government in the "elective power of the people" (Lincoln 1909, 834, Governor Samuel

J. Tilden). In this way, it was thought that any "evils" in local governance could be "remedied by the people at home, upon whom the responsibility should rest" (Lincoln 1909b, 31, Governor Lucius Robinson).[2]

In response to the frequent and acrimonious attempts to dissolve newly incorporated villages (addressed in chapter 1), the state legislature amended the state's dissolution procedures by including a requirement that dissolution be approved in two successive elections (1880), by adding a new mechanism for the initiation of a dissolution proposition by the village board of trustees (1887), and by introducing a one-year ban on successive petitions following a defeat at the polls (1909). Amendments in 1919 introduced a higher threshold (two-thirds) for immediate approval at the initial submission (or, if passed by a majority, requiring resubmission and majority approval at a second election).

In this period of direct command (1847–1972), residents also exercised direct control over the implementation of the dissolution. The discharge of debt and disposition of property was determined by the voters at a separate election following the decision to dissolve. As the ruling in *Gebhardt v. Wilcox* (1935) clarified, propositions respecting the discharge of debt and property "in *no wise affect[ed] the validity of the legally attained determination of the village to dissolve*" (581, emphasis added). In other words, the role of local elected officials was to merely execute the dissolution proposition as directed by the voters.

Local elected officials, however, often tried to prevent dissolution by challenging the legality of citizen petitions. Such was the case in Nyack (Rockland County) in 1887, in South Floral Park (Nassau County) in 1941, and in Port Dickinson (Broome County) in 1959. They also sometimes either refused to schedule elections, as happened in Nyack in 1877 and Port Dickinson in 1959; or crafted unwieldy propositions, as in Old Forge (Herkimer County) in 1933. Frequently, elected officials withheld necessary information, including basic information as to the process, as happened in Pleasant Valley (Dutchess County) in 1925, in Old Forge in 1933, in Ossining (Westchester County) in 1934, in Downsville (Delaware County) in 1950, and in Port Dickinson in 1959. The ability of the village board to initiate dissolution by resolution (introduced into the General Village Laws in 1897) further allowed trustees to preempt or stall petition-initiated dissolutions with the promise that the matter was already under "study," as happened in Lewiston (Niagara County) in 1953 and Kenmore (Erie County) in both 1955 and 1962.

Judicial rulings upheld the authority of the state's dissolution procedures, including the voters right to *command* that dissolution take
place (Blauvelt v. Village of Nyack, 1876; Gebhardt v. Wilcox, 1935). A
complicated effort to dissolve the government of the village of Old Forge
(Herkimer) and the trustees' refusal to schedule the referenda led to
legislative revisions in 1933, which, because of the ban on special acts,
were made applicable to all villages of the fourth class (fewer than 1,000
in population) (L. 1933, Ch. 620, §350).

From Direct Command to Local Control

Documents from the Office of Local Government (OLG) in the late
1960s reveal growing concerns over village board resistance and the
limited information that existed to guide voters when considering dissolution. The reports outlined specific factors that ought to be considered,
including services, finances, and the need to preserve community identity
(Atkins 1969). These memoranda were a genesis of sorts for an eventual
study requirement, but did not specify who would collect or analyze the
relevant information. The several reports noted that the local consent
requirement was a barrier to municipal reorganization and that municipal
associations had become "strongly and aggressively representative" in their
anti-dissolution lobbying efforts. The OLG saw the need to enhance voter
information to counterbalance the control that local elected officials held
over information. The OLG's understanding was undoubtedly influenced
by dissolutions of the 1930s–50s (most notably in the case of Old Forge
in 1933, South Floral Park in 1941, and Downsville in 1950), in which
dissolution supporters were forced to seek state assistance when local
elected officials raised doubts about the process and the effect of dissolving.

Renewed attention to village dissolution procedures in the post-1930
period additionally reflected the growing rivalries between the town and
village forms of government. As service provision could now be accommodated by the creation of special districts, town officials increasingly
questioned the need for new villages. In many cases, town officials objected
to their incorporation as an effort to evade town planning regulations and
code enforcement, to engage in residential exclusion, and to wrest control
over the tax base or developed areas in which the town had made capital
and infrastructure investments. For many village residents, however, town
government was simply too distant and not sufficiently oriented to the

unique needs and interests of their community. Village government and dedicated representation for their smaller geographical area was thought to be more reflective and protective of their narrower interests.[3]

Because various state laws restricted some town services from being provided within village boundaries even as the costs were apportioned townwide, village residents argued that they suffered a form of "double taxation." At a 1969 hearing before the New York State Legislative Committee on Towns and Villages, the mayor of Mayville (Chautauqua County) pleaded for village exemption from key town budget items, alleging that the towns' padding of those line items to fund wages and benefits for town employees was a form of larceny. Assembly member John Beckman challenged the claim that villagers derived no benefit from TOV expenditures, arguing that "no one in the village lives entirely in a vacuum."[4] From the town government perspective, TOV services provided clear value and benefit to village residents. Moreover, because village incorporation is voluntary, they argued that villagers were responsible for their higher taxes as a consequence of their own choice and desire for augmented services.

Differences in state assistance and funding formulas between the municipal classes further fueled the simmering tensions. Among the more contentious of these issues was the allocation of highway expenses. State law required that newly incorporated villages stand as their own highway district, increasing operational costs and leading to feuds over road maintenance and distribution of the state tax on gasoline. Villages and towns routinely quarreled over the distribution of state tax revenues, highway funding, and the allocation of state aid. Formulas based on municipal classification, regardless of population size or capacity, produced inequities, particularly in unrestricted revenue sharing. For example, towns without villages might receive more aid to their town but less aid overall (or townwide) when compared to towns with incorporated villages (Feeney Commission 1975).

The practice and frequency of property tax assessment between jurisdictions adds to residential frustration and confusion as to what services one's property taxes funded. There are more than 3,700 taxing jurisdictions in New York State, each with its own authority to levy taxes on property (Office of the New York State Comptroller 2019b, 1). The various taxing authorities are responsible for determining their own rate (and frequency) of assessment, with some jurisdictions taxing lower and others higher than the full market value of the property. Under §1402 of the Real Property Tax Law (RPTL), villages have several assessment options, but roughly 75 percent rely on town assessments for the collection of village taxes.[5] Eighteen villages use the two property-class system of homestead (or primary residence) and non-homestead properties. To account for variations in assessment practices, as well the seventy or so villages that span multiple towns, the state applies an equalization rate—a ratio of total assessed value to total market value.[6] The Office of Real Property Tax Services (ORPTS) calculates an assessed full value tax rate, determined by dividing the levy by the total taxable value, expressed as an amount per $1,000 of assessed value. The assessed full value rate may not be the effective rate for homeowners because of the complexity of New York State's property tax system (homestead versus non-homestead jurisdictions, equalization rates, tax exemptions) and a variety of state laws that have tried to limit residential property taxes (Centrino and Benjamin 2014). The system is often confounding to property owners who tend to blame their growing tax burdens on whichever unit (or level) of government from which they derive the least benefit and therefore view as seemingly redundant.

Suburbanization, and the growth of cities and suburban villages, only exacerbated such rivalries. When and where the village populace was spatially segregated within a town, it was easier for residents to differentiate the level of services derived from each. With growth and development along municipal peripheries, the proliferation of special districts spanning multiple municipalities and the rise of shared service agreements made municipal boundaries increasingly fuzzy. Allegations that the residents of one class of municipality were subsidizing the service demands of the residents of another grew increasingly common. Suburbanization was the driver as well behind the consequential expansion of Town and Suburban Town Law powers that further blurred the functional distinctions between governing units and obviated the need for creating or maintaining villages. The rolling, simultaneous revisions of county, town, and village laws that were undertaken by a string of legislative committees revised the general laws of the different municipal forms independently rather than in relation to one another or the whole of the local government structure.[7]

The proliferation, overlap, and blurring of authority and taxing power that developed and ossified over time would be accompanied by growing calls for reform. Yet comprehensive reform was politically and practically infeasible as the various governing units, supported by their respective municipal associations, pleaded their own value and sought to redirect the sights of reformers toward the other classes. In some efforts, such as the push for expanded home rule authority, towns and villages were united in purpose. But shared interest sometimes cut across municipal types—pitting smaller or rural municipalities against larger and more urban ones and leading to accusations that legislative changes benefited some municipal units at the expense of others.

Between 1956 and 1968, various joint legislative committees were convened to separately study the recodification of Town and Village Law, focusing on the sources of conflict between these municipal units. Such conflicts, according to one report, were the inevitable result of municipal fragmentation (Legislative Document No. 25 1956, 25–36). The New York State Joint Legislative Committee to Study, Codify, Revise and Make Uniform Existing Laws Relating to Town and Village Governments had in 1956 recommended study on common subjects of dispute, including annexation, state aid formulas, and highway costs and proposed a variety of bills to prevent overlapping of taxes and inequities in service provision.[8] According to an interim report in 1967, there was "widespread dissatisfaction with the present structure of local government" that could be resolved only by a "drastic reorganization of the entire complex of county, town, village, and special district formations" (Legislative Document No. 24 1967, 16).

The ongoing tensions prompted representatives of the various units of government to point the finger of blame at one another in advocating for state-level policy reforms. In its 1968 report, the Town Law Committee, for example, took very direct aim at new village incorporations, recommending that General Village Law be amended to require the consent of the affected town (or towns) and be accompanied by a finding that the creation of a new village was "in the overall public interest" (Legislative Document No. 86 1968, 17). The committee had also entertained numerous proposals to make village dissolution easier.[9] Both recommendations were defensive, reflecting the unanimous consent of the Association of Towns and the consensus of town officials that village incorporations were often undertaken to evade town zoning regulations or retain residential and economic exclusivity (Legislative Document No. 86 1968, 18).

In stark contrast, the Joint Legislative Committee for the Recodification of Village Law, as a stand-alone entity, viewed the maintenance of robust village governance as paramount. Their report is a veritable ode to the integral role of villages as the "vineyards of democracy," closest to the people and "best qualified to solve such problems and to enforce locally adopted controls" (Legislative Document No. 21 1964, 10–11).

The Committee on Villages began its task by focusing on the first three articles of the General Village Law provisions (general corporate powers; incorporation and classification of villages; and elections), resulting in a revision and recodification of the first (now) four articles of the General Village Law.[10]

The separate committees were combined into a Joint Legislative Committee on Towns and Villages in 1969 that held hearings across the State (Joint Legislative Committee on Towns and Villages 1969; 1969b; 1969c; 1969d). Village dissolution was again introduced by town officials as a means of alleviating what they saw as the taproot of the problem— the excess of subcounty government.[11] William Sanford, the executive secretary of the Association of Towns, proposed formally studying dissolution, suggesting that smaller municipalities be justified, consolidated, or else eliminated and replaced by improvement districts (Joint Legislative Committee on Towns and Villages 1969, 16–17). The idea was echoed by Ross Kitt, the town of Ogden supervisor, who noted that there was no reason to maintain separate units that "could be easily combined" (Joint Legislative Committee on Towns and Villages 1969, 39). As long as the choice was left to village residents, he warned, meaningful change was politically and practically infeasible.

The committee chair, George Farrell, acknowledge the desire for streamlining local government organization but pointed out the obvious problem of coordination: "if you [the town] and your village cannot agree on the removal of snow or the joint project of removing snow, for instance—how in God's name are we going to get them to agree to dissolve the village and absorb it in the town unless we mandate it?" (Joint Legislative Committee on Towns and Villages 1969, 42). The answer, according to the testifying town officials, was adoption of improved legislative mechanisms to facilitate local consideration of the dissolution option.

NYCOM's counsel, Donald Walsh, warned that the focus of reform ought not to be exclusively on the villages. The state might also revise its consolidation procedures to ease the pathway of town-village consolidations. The disagreement between the Association of Towns and NYCOM was again evident at public hearings held in November 1969. In a turnabout, NYCOM's counsel pressed the committee to look toward town government as the more viable candidate for elimination: "we think that some villages ought to go, and we are willing to have them go, but our problem has always been with other people representing other units of local government that they are sacred, and not a one should be touched, and you can't operate that way. If villages ought to go, look at the other side and maybe some other units ought to go."[12]

As to dissolution procedures, NYCOM argued vigorously for "the creation of local committees" rather than state legislative action: "we think that you should provide the device, the statutory device where the people, locally, can make that decision" (Joint Legislative Committee on Towns and Villages1969, 72). The sparring between town and village representatives ultimately resulted in the Joint Legislative Committee's recommendation that the choice "*be left up to the local residents* to balance all of the factors involved in terminating a village or consolidating towns or making other adjustments in their units of local government" (Legislative Document No. 7 1970, 19, emphasis added).[13]

The 1972 recodification of village law and introduction of new dissolution procedures (Article 19) was thus the result of these developments. First were a number of legal challenges that had been filed in a number of dissolution attempts, prompting the OLG's determination that residents needed greater clarity and guidance in the process. Second were the simultaneous efforts of state legislative committees to recodify both town and village laws in response to growing rivalries. As town officials pressured the state to make dissolution easier, NYCOM pushed back, advocating for local study committees. By adopting Article 19 (with support from NYCOM), the legislature was ostensibly facilitating village dissolution but included within these provisions a mechanism (formulation of a dissolution plan) through which local elected officials *now exercised* the locus of control (Bill Jacket, L. 1972, Ch. 892).[14]

Article 19 changed the petitioning process to require signature by one-third of village electors (rather than property owners). A proposition could also be placed on the ballot by the board (N.Y. Vill. Law, Article 19, §1900[1]). In either case, however, a public hearing (with specified notice requirements) had to be held prior to the submission at the ballot box (N.Y. Vill. Law, Article 19, §1902). Most critically, §1904 required that the contents of the proposition "contain a plan for the disposition of property, the payment of [the village's] outstanding obligations including the levy and collection of the necessary taxes and assessments therefore, and such other matters as may be necessary" (N.Y. Vill. Law, Article 19, §1904[1]).

The law no longer separated the vote to dissolve from a subsequent vote on an implementation plan. Instead, the proposition to dissolve had to include an implementation "plan" on which the residents voted. It also made dissolution (upon approval of a majority) effective as of December 31 of the following year (N.Y. Vill. Law, Article 19, §1900[3]). As before, administration of the former village was transferred to the town, which was statutorily directed to "continue to provide the services theretofore provided by the village" (N.Y. Vill. Law, Article 19, §1914[1]).[15] If dissolution was rejected, there was a two-year moratorium on subsequent citizen-initiated petitions (N.Y. Vill. Law, Article 19, §1900[2]).

Despite Article 19's requirement that an implementation plan be included as a part of the proposition (§1904), it is a misnomer to characterize this as requiring a binding plan prior to the vote. As explained by the Division of Local Government, while

> all or any part of such a plan *can be* made the subject of a contract between the village and the town, the primary object of this plan is not to legally bind the village or the town. Rather it is a document which will educate and inform the resident village electors as to the consequences of their vote. By outlining an orderly program for the transfer to the town of village functions, assets, and properties, and for the disposition of any outstanding debts, obligations or taxes, the plan will provide the village residents some picture—*incomplete though it may be—of the tangible effects of dissolution.* (New York Department of State 1983, 11, emphasis added)

Plans developed under Article 19 are thus better characterized as implantation guidance, as there was no guarantee that town officials would adhere to the plan as approved by the voters, absent a binding contract.

Article 19 was subject to minor revisions in 1973 and again in 1997, when a 120-day time limit on the collection of petition signatures was added. More significant changes were made in 2003, with the additional requirement for the formation of an official study commission (L. 2003, Ch. 62, Part W, §34). Under a new §1901, the board was required to appoint a study commission consisting of at least two representatives from each town (or towns). That committee had to hold at least one public hearing and make a report according to a timetable established by the board. That report had to "address all topics included in a plan for dissolution," including "*alternatives to dissolution*" (N.Y. Vill. Law, Article 19, §1901 as added by L. 2003, Ch. 62, Part W, §35). Section 1903 expanded the items to be addressed to include the disposition of village property, the discharge of village debt, the transfer or elimination of village employees, any agreements entered into with the town(s) related to implementation of the dissolution, the effect on local laws (other than as provided under §1910), the continuation or termination of services under town administration, and the fiscal impact of the dissolution on both village and TOV residents, along with any other matters "desirable or necessary to carry out the dissolution" (N.Y. Vill. Law, Article 19, §1903 as added by L. 2003, Ch. 62, Part W, §36). These additions cemented the ability of local elected officials to exercise discretion, allowing the village board to determine when, and if, dissolution would be put to a public vote.

A few examples illustrate the point. After a year of study, the trustees of Liberty (Sullivan County) declined to advance a proposition (village of Liberty Joint Study Committee Report 2008, 1). Similarly, despite a study projecting "significant cost savings" from a village-town merger, the trustees of Lewiston (Niagara County) failed to put dissolution to a vote, citing a lack of resident demand (Mattera 2010). In 2008, the village of Cherry Valley declined a study grant, declaring it a "waste of time" (village of Cherry Valley 2008). In Macedon (Wayne County), officials rejected their own study findings and actively campaigned against dissolution in 2010 (Curry 2010; 2010b). The study for the village of Tupper Lake (Franklin County) was indefinitely tabled by village officials, the same fate that had been met by earlier studies (Resnek 2008). In Schuylerville (Saratoga County), local officials added ballot wording that warned residents that dissolving would leave fire services in question (*Glens Falls Post-Star* 2011; Dimopoulos 2011). After receiving a $49,999 state grant in 2008, the village board of Lake George (Warren County) opted not to put dissolution on the ballot, citing lack of certainty from the town (Roman 2010). The board of Victory (Saratoga County) passed a local law stripping the mayor's power after he was elected on a pro-dissolution campaign (McCarty 2011).

Article 19 procedures had shifted power, giving greater influence over the process to local elected officials and diminishing direct citizen command. The role of citizens was transformed: while they could still force consideration of dissolution by petition, the study itself (both in process and outcome) was largely controlled by the village board. Rather than commanding their representatives to draft a workable plan, citizens were now in the position of ratifying (with a yes or no vote) the proposal as crafted by the local study committee.

The infrequency with which villages formally dissolved was determined to be at least partially attributable to the complexities of Article

19. The petitioning process with a substantial signature threshold (33 percent of resident electors qualified to vote in the last general or special election, signing not more than 120 days prior to the petition's filing) was susceptible to "hyper-technical" legal challenges that often resulted in the disqualification of petitions. The mandatory pre-referendum study process (required whether initiated by the village board or citizen petition) further allowed for obstruction by local officials: in many cases the study process was truncated, or stalled, and the matter was never put before the voters at the polls.

Dissolution in Historic Perspective (1789–1972)

An examination of actual dissolutions helps to further illuminate the impetus behind the various revisions (as well as the consequences of the established procedures on the outcome), revealing broad trends in the history of New York's village dissolutions. The New York Department of State and State Comptroller's office provide official data for dissolutions since 1900. To identify pre-1900 disincorporation, the list of incorporations was compared against the list of villages still in existence and checked against village incorporation files housed at the New York State Archives and spanning the years 1886–1988. This comparison revealed several errors in the post-1900 data as reported by the state (including unreported and incorrectly reported dissolutions). To locate dissolution activity that did not make it to vote, online historical news databases were used. This list is not guaranteed to be comprehensive given the sporadic digitization of historical newspapers. However, a sufficient number have been identified to provide additional insight and to demonstrate that dissolution is considered far more often than the number of successfully dissolved villages would otherwise suggest.

In the pre-1900 period, village dissolutions tended to result from what may be deemed incorporation remorse: dissatisfaction with the cost of the new village government or an extension of the original fight over incorporation. The spate of dissolutions in the 1920s consisted primarily of villages that had peaked and declined, once thriving communities that, as a consequence of depleted resources, industry closures, or changing transportation routes, became depopulated. The 1930s ushered in dissolution as a response to fiscal stress. It was in this period that the number and proliferation of municipal entities came under intense scrutiny by the state. The 1970s witnessed the dissolution of village government as a means of alleviating the growing property tax burden—a trend that has continued and appears to have accelerated markedly in the last twelve years. More recently, the elimination of village government has been more directly linked to progressive reforms—the downsizing and restructuring of local governments to promote regionalism and encourage more efficient governance (Parshall 2011).

Dissolution and Remorse

Recall that, prior to the adoption of a General Village Act in 1847, the incorporation of villages was by state special act. Of the fourteen once-in-corporated villages that ceased to exist prior to 1900, six (or 43 percent) had their charters legislative repealed. The repeal acts themselves do not provide reasons for dissolving, but it was generally at local request. The repeal of Ovid's charter (Seneca County) in 1849 provides an illustrative case. When Seneca County was created in 1804, there was disagreement as to whether Ovid (sometimes called Verona) or the nearby village of Waterloo should serve as the county seat. Ovid had an early population advantage, but with the influence of a state senator who hailed from Waterloo, it lost the battle. Ovid's population declined after it was bypassed by the Erie Canal, and its charter was legislatively repealed (L. 1849, Ch. 387). Ovid was reincorporated under General Village Law in 1852—one of only two villages to dissolve and later reincorporate (Parshall 2012).

Rather than request legislative action, some villages simply ceased to exercise their corporate rights. Brewerton's (Onondaga County) 1872 incorporation was abandoned in 1878 when it was discovered that its incorporation paperwork had never been properly filed with the state (Hamlet of Brewerton Strategic Revitalization Plan 2008, 4). Ebenezer's (Erie County) charter lapsed in the 1860s when its nearly 1,200 residents, members of a religious society, relocated to another state. Details are missing on Clintonville and Constantia (both in Clinton County), the postmasters of which replied to the state's survey that their incorporations were discontinued years ago. In the four other cases of pre-1900 dissolutions, the disincorporation mechanism and circumstances are unknown, but it is likely their charters too lapsed when the village government ceased operations.[16]

Pre-1900, several villages successfully dissolved under the provisions established by the General Village Law, including Nyack (Rockland

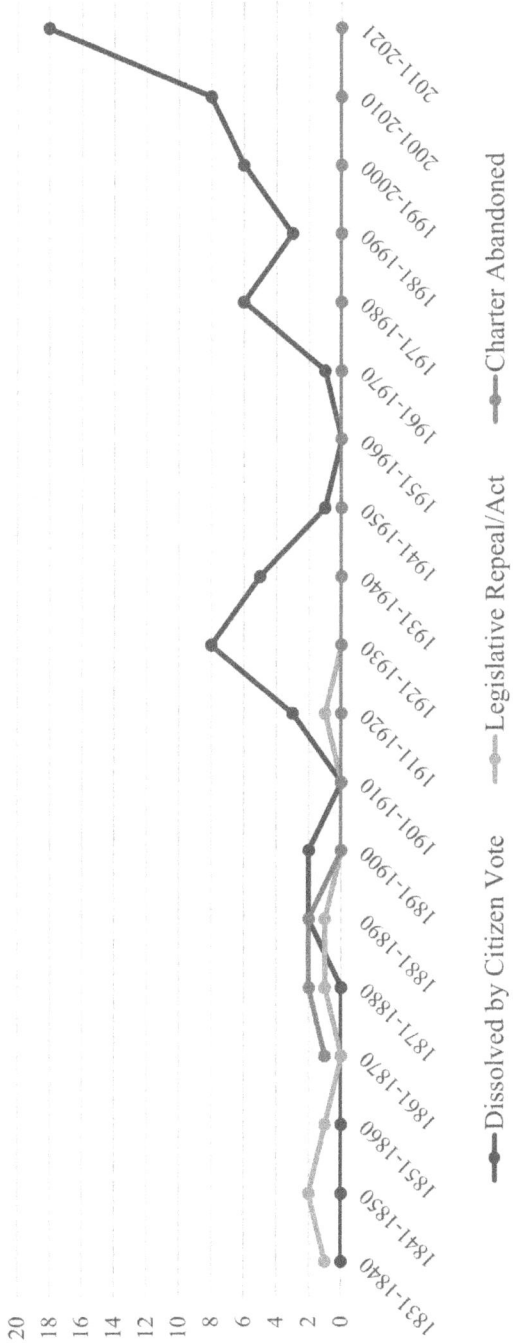

—Dissolved by Citizen Vote   —Legislative Repeal/Act   —Charter Abandoned

Figure 2.1. New York Village Dissolutions by Decade (1831–2021). *Source:* Author created graphic.

County) in 1877, Roxbury (Delaware County) in 1899, and Prattsville (Greene County) in 1899. The short interval between incorporation and attempted dissolution efforts suggests that the original fight over incorporation never subsided or that residents of the new village very quickly felt incorporation remorse. The dissolution of Nyack (Rockland County), incorporated in 1872, is illustrative. Within a few years of incorporation, disgruntled residents petitioned to dissolve, sparking a legal battle with the trustees who directly appealed to the New York State legislature to preserve the village charter (*New York Times* 1877; 1877b). A measure to block dissolution passed both chambers on its second attempt but was vetoed by Governor Robinson (*New York Times* 1877). After a two-year legal battle, the residents of Nyack finally got to vote, officially approving dissolution in 1877 (*New York Times* 1877b).[17] The continued growth of the community, however, soon led to worries about the town government's responsiveness to the former village's needs (*New York Daily Graphic* 1878). Such worries, along with fear about possible annexation by the nearby village of Upper Nyack, prompted Nyack residents to reincorporate the village in 1883 (Archives, N-AR 13243, Village Incorporation Files and Maps, 1886–1988, Box 6, Village of Nyack Folder).

The 1870s–90s witnessed several failed dissolutions, including the attempted disincorporation of the villages of Edgewater (in 1881), Holland Patent (in 1887), Northport (in 1896), Southampton (in 1896), Mount Kisco (in 1898), Pleasantville (in 1899), and Mamaroneck (in 1897 and 1898). In Holland Patent (Oneida County), dissolution was put to a vote just two years after its bitterly disputed incorporation. The fight was so heated that, after dissolution was defeated, the local paper desperately pleaded for peace. Patchogue and Amityville (both in Suffolk County) similarly faced dissolution within a year: the petition effort "fizzled" in the former, while Amityville's residents rejected dissolution at the polls (in 1895) (*Brooklyn Daily Eagle* 1895; *Suffolk County News* 1895). In Southampton (Suffolk County), angry village residents who resented the unexpected costs championed rejoining the town (*Brooklyn Daily Eagle* 1896).

That same year, residents in neighboring Northport (Suffolk County) petitioned to dissolve their two-year-old village government (*Brooklyn Daily Eagle* 1896e; 1896f). The effort was rejected but was back on the ballot (and voted down again) in 1899 (*Brooklyn Daily Eagle* 1899b). Accusations of a town plot to bond the village to pay for sewer services led to an 1898 failed effort to disincorporate the eighteen-month-old village of Pleasantville (Westchester County)—an outcome that inspired an impromptu victory parade (*New Rochelle Pioneer* 1899; *New York Sun* 1899). The cost of progress (in the form of new sewage system) likewise prompted a failed dissolution vote in Mount Kisco (Westchester County) that same year (*New Rochelle Pioneer* 1898). After its incorporation in 1893 (with only five votes to spare), dissolution was twice put to a vote in Babylon (Suffolk) and "very nearly triumphed" (*Brooklyn Daily Eagle* 1899). Efforts to disincorporate Sea Cliff (Nassau County) in 1896 and then again 1900 were also fueled by frustration with the new village's expenditures (*Brooklyn Daily Eagle* 1896b; 1896c; 1896d).

Just two years after Mamaroneck's (Westchester County) incorporation, a "war" over dissolution set the "Progressives, who want[ed] to boom the village even if it does cost a little more in taxes," against the "Conservatives or Reactionaries, who d[id]n't want any village at all and [were] working to effect a disincorporation" (*New York Sun* 1897). This colorful, journalistic account painted a vivid portrait of the clashing views between those who considered incorporation to be costly "da-dude nonsense" and those who considered its opponents to be penny-pinching "fossilized trilobites" (*New York Sun* 1897). Disincorporation was voted on again in 1898, when a twenty-eight-person majority once more voted to maintain the incorporation (*Mount Vernon Chronicle* 1898).

Even in these early cases, there was an emerging recognition that it was far easier to go forward (incorporate) than to go back (dissolve). The fear that incorporation might be an irreversible mistake doomed the attempted incorporation of Carmel (Putnam County) in the 1890s, where one of the "chief and most persistently used arguments of the anti-incorporators" was "that the people of incorporated villages now regret their act" (*Putnam County Courier* 1897). Conversely, incorporation advocates argued that the number of failed dissolutions confirmed the wisdom of forming a village government. The choice between incorporating or foregoing services was not a false one in that era, but these cases also revealed a popular belief that incorporation was indicative of progress, while dissolution was a "backwards step." The *Suffolk County News* wrote: "It is very hard to find a village that has tried incorporation that is willing to go back again to old-fashioned, slow-coach methods. . . . We do not favor anything like reckless extravagance, but we do look upon incorporation as the only means of acquiring these needful things," like street lighting (*Suffolk County News* 1895).

The dissolution saga of St. Regis Falls (Franklin County) is not reported in the state data and illustrates substantial confusion over the dissolution process. In 1887, residents voted to incorporate. At their first meeting, trustees were presented with a petition to dissolve (*St. Regis Falls Adirondack News* 1913). Residents voted to dissolve, but because village law at that time required that dissolution be approved at *two* successive elections, citizens had six months to reconsider (*St. Regis Falls Adirondack News* 1887). On March 24, 1888, voters reaffirmed the dissolution. Under §90 and §91 (then in effect) the corporation was to cease in six months, requiring its officers to conclude the village' affairs. But village officials failed to duly file proper notice of the dissolution with either the town or the state. Thus, St. Regis Falls remained on the state's list of municipalities, causing ongoing and frequent confusion, particularly over the distribution of state aid. In 1905, a prominent business owner wrote the state requesting that the incorporation be officially annulled. He explained that no official village business had been conducted, nor had village elections been held after dissolution had been approved a second time. In the meantime, the former (and only) village clerk had passed away, and the related paperwork had since been "lost or destroyed," leaving St. Regis Falls standing on "on the books as incorporated when it should not be so." His letter was marked by the secretary of state's office as "filed" (NC-AR 13243-81, Village Incorporation Files, Box 1, Letters to Incorporated Villages Folder). In 1909, a dispute over liquor license (requiring the approval of a village president) sparked an unsuccessful petition to reestablish the incorporation (*St. Regis Falls Adirondack News* 1909). At last, New York State Assemblyman Alexander MacDonald sponsored legislation to affirm the dissolution (L. 1913 Ch. 184). The local newspaper rejoiced: "This matter that has been dragging along for years, is now settled (*St. Regis Falls Adirondack News* 1913b).

Disagreement over the legality of its corporate status was also an issue for Tottenville (Richmond County), incorporated in 1869. Responding to the state's 1886 inquiry, the local postmaster R.W. Wood noted a "difference of opinion" as to whether Tottenville was a still-functioning village or not. He explained that the board had given up, although there were some " 'old timers' who continued to serve as elect trustees" (New York State Archives, N-AR 13243, Village Incorporation Files and Maps, 1886–1988, Box 8, Letters to Incorporated Villages Folder). Tottenville, along with roughly twenty other villages, would be eventually annexed as part of New York City.

Several dissolutions in the 1920s may also be attributed to a failed experiment in self-government and resident remorse. La Fargerville (Jefferson County), for example, incorporated and dissolved in the same year (1922). Sound Avenue (Suffolk County) incorporated in 1921, changed its name to Northville in 1927, and dissolved in 1930, and thus is incorrectly double counted in the state's data. The village simply "did not last long, especially when the founding fathers discovered how expensive the distinction was" (Young 2011).[18] The desire to share revenue from the state gasoline tax (not applicable to roads in villages) also explained Northville's decision to surrender village status (*Suffolk County News* 1930).

Pine Valley's (Suffolk County) incorporation as a village was similarly short-lived. In 1988, residents of the poorest areas within the town of Southampton sought to preserve its rural character through a dedicated village board and planning committee. Although their vote to incorporate was judicially upheld against legal challenge, things did not go well: residents were hit with higher-than-anticipated taxes, and the new village board was plagued by constant squabbling between trustees and between pro- and anti-development residents (Lyall 1989). Lacking a sufficient tax base, the new village was rather quickly deemed a failed experiment and castigated as a nothing short of a "joke" (Lyall 1990). Its residents voted to dissolve 165–142 in 1990.

DISSOLUTION AND DISCORD

In at least one early case, dissolution was pursued as a weapon in a highly personalized and bitter political rivalry. In the tiny village of Hillside (Westchester County), an unpopular local justice used his judicial authority to arrest the sheriff, his arch political rival (whose jailbreak using his very own key was joyfully reported in the local papers). When the magistrate's political opponents were unsuccessful in ousting him from office, they turned to dissolution of the village as "the only way they [could] see to get rid of the justice" (*New York Times* 1911). The dissolution of Hillside was approved by its citizens in 1914. Hillside is not, however, included in the state's data, likely because of its convoluted corporate history. Originally incorporated as Sherman Park in 1906, the name was changed to Hillside in 1909, pursuant to public referenda. On the same day dissolution was approved, residents voted to change Hillside's name to Thornwood. Notice of both actions was simultaneously received by the state. The state secretary had to ask the attorney general for clarification on whether it was legally permissible for voters to dissolve and change the name of the incorporation through separate propositions submitted at the same election. The attorney general's response blamed the confusion on the ambiguities of §350 (the dissolution provision) of Village Law, noting that dissolutions had to be submitted at successive referenda. If approved a second time, the village "*is to be regarded as dissolved six months after the second election*." From the "meager facts" provided, the attorney general concluded that the dissolution had been lawfully approved, but until dissolution was finally implemented, the village retained the "right to do anything an existing village may lawfully do, including changing "its name for the duration of its corporate existence" (N-AR 13243, Village Incorporation Files and Maps, 1886–1988, Box 3, Village of Hillside Folder).[19]

DISSOLUTION AND DECLINE

Among the spate of dissolutions in the 1920s were several cases attributable to economic decline and population loss (*New York Times* 1990). Often the seeds of decline were sown in the overly ambitious vision of a community founder. Oramel (Allegany County) followed a similar story line to that of Prattsville (discussed in chapter 1). In pioneering spirit, Oramel Griffin had purchased a large tract of land on which to create a new community. In short order, Oramel boasted the county's largest public house and all manner of businesses, from mercantile stores to shingle factories and sawmills. The bustling village was heralded as the "Syracuse" of Western New York." But by 1906, the timber supply was depleted, and the community was struggling. When the last of the village's eleven sawmills closed, its founder disinvested his properties. Oramel was officially dissolved in 1925 and was a "ghost town" even before a fire devastated what little was left in 1937 (Parshall 2012).

With the closure of its once prosperous mills, the village of Rifton (Ulster County) lost more than half of its population in a single decade (1910–20) (Wick and Wick 2003). In 1920, a bill to dissolve Rifton passed the state legislature (*Kingston Daily Freeman* 1920). Pleasant Valley (Dutchess County) was another community that, by the early 1900s, was already past its prime (Wick and Wick 2003, 89). By 1920, only 384 residents remained. Unhappiness over high taxes and a bitter dispute over the purchase of a new fire engine prompted residents to demand the board's resignation (*Poughkeepsie Daily Eagle* 1924). A bid to dissolve Pleasant Valley failed, just six votes shy of the two-thirds then necessary (*Poughkeepsie Daily Eagle* 1926). A year later, the village was again in turmoil after the election of two trustees was deemed null and void and its president abruptly resigned. The village was forced to seek out the opinion of the attorney general as to how to proceed, suspending all village business in the interim of a special election (*Poughkeepsie Daily Eagle* 1925; 1925b). In 1926, disincorporation was again placed on the ballot. In an unprecedented turnout, a majority of twenty-six voted to dissolve (*Poughkeepsie Daily Eagle* 1926b).

The economic decline of other communities can be inferred by their depopulation. The village of Newfield (Tompkins County), which dissolved in 1926, lost 28 percent of its residents between 1880 and 1920; Belleville (Jefferson County) lost more than 34 percent in that same period and dissolved in 1931 (Schupe, Stein, and Pandit 1987). There is little information on the dissolution of Henderson (Jefferson County). Incorporated in 1886, it fell from a peak population of 374 (in 1900) to just 262 (in 1930) and dissolved in 1932. The village of the Landing (Suffolk County) lasted only eleven years. By 1939, its residents dwindled to 140. Only seventeen of the Village's thirty-eight qualified voters (a property ownership requirement was then in effect) participated in the referendum to dissolve (the vote was 17–3 in favor) (*Suffolk County News* 1939). The outgoing mayor (chosen in an election in which only six residents voted) diagnosed the reason as "lack of interest" (*New York Times* 1939; *Patchogue Advance* 1938). In 1986, Pine Hill (Ulster), once famous for its bottled spring water, surrendered its incorporated status, its population having declined to under 300.

A cluster of dissolutions in the early 2000s can also be attributed to dwindling populations insufficient to support continuation as a village. The Villages of Pike (Wyoming), Limestone, Randolph, East Randolph, and Perrysburg (in Cattaraugus County) were tiny places, struggling with the effects of depopulation and economic stagnation after being bypassed by new railway routes. The latter three villages, all in the town of Randolph, already received most of their services from the town, making their merger a natural progression toward unification. With substantial public support, the dissolutions were not controversial; support for maintaining the village had gradually faded away.

DISSOLUTION AND PROGRESS

Popular and scholarly discussions of municipal disincorporation are dominated by an unspoken metanarrative in which incorporation is viewed as progress and dissolution is generally equated with municipal decline, or death. A review of historical cases offers a more complex and nuanced view of why villages dissolve. Indeed, there are progressive elements in several of these historical dissolution cases wherein dissolving was seen as a positive, forward-thinking development. The village of Roxbury (Delaware County), for example, surrendered its incorporation in 1899, after just two years in operation. Birthplace to conservationist John Burroughs and railroad financier Jay Gould, this quaint Catskills village was a popular summer resort for the New York City elite. One of its most prominent citizens, Helen Miller Gould (daughter of Jay Gould), emerged as a benefactress. Her generous donations constructed a memorial church, partially funded the main roadway, supplied teaching staff for the local school, and built a gas plant "large enough to supply gas for the streets, business places, and residences" (*New York Times* 1894; 1903; 1903b).

Roadway improvement was another motivator for dissolution. When, for example, the Reverend Shumway steered his trusty Ford toward Brookfield (Madison County) in 1919, encountering one mudhole after another, he wondered what purpose incorporation served. His dismay was so great that not only did it challenge his religion, it also prompted him to pen an editorial in the local paper exhorting residents to "take pride enough" to maintain the roads (*Brookfield Courier* 1919). As the *Fairport Herald* explained, state law restricted villages from receiving state and county highway aid (*Fairport Herald* 1922). Such funding, however, was available for towns. For Brookfield, the choice literally came down to staying incorporated or building a road, and the voters chose the road (*Brookfield Courier* 1922; 1923; *Oswego Farmer* 1922).

Not enough has been recorded about the dissolution of Belfast (Allegany County) to determine whether its dissolution was for the purposes of local improvement, but it seems likely. Although not among the dissolutions reported by the state, a 1920 law authorized the transfer of property of the "former Village" to the town (L. 1920, Ch. 292). The town issued more than $6,000 in bonds in 1924 for the creation of a roadbed, further suggesting that its corporate status was traded for road improvements. "Believing that better road construction and more efficient government [could] be gained by the town than by the village," the residents of Marlborough (Ulster County) voted to dissolve by two "practically unanimous votes (*Poughkeepsie Eagle News* 1922). Marlborough was originally incorporated in 1906 under the alternative spelling of Marlboro; thus its dissolution is reported twice, as different communities, in the state data.

Residents of Old Forge (Herkimer County) also saw dissolution as the pathway to public improvements and greater regional coordination

(*Utica Daily Press* 1932; 1932b; *Utica Observer Dispatch* 1935). Downsville's (Delaware County) residents voted to dissolve to "take advantage of the lower [town] taxes" following construction of the Pepacton Dam by New York City (*Monticello Republican Watchman* 1947; *Binghamton Press* 1950; 1950b). Because the dissolution procedures under the General Village Law were "ambiguous," the State Department of Audit and Control recommended validation of the referenda by the state legislature, which legalized the dissolution in 1951 (*Binghamton Press* 1951a; 1951b; L. 1951, Ch. 5).

Three state-reported dissolutions in the 1920s were the result of consolidation or annexation. The Villages of Union and Endicott (Broome County) were consolidated by special election in 1921 (New York State Archives, N-AR 13243, Village Incorporation Files and Maps, 1886–1988, Box 2, Village of Endicott Folder.) And Eastwood (Onondaga County) was annexed to the city of Syracuse in 1926. Eastwood remains a vibrant and recognizable neighborhood that has been dubbed the "Village within the City" by its neighborhood association.[20]

DISSOLUTION AND TAXES

Concern over high taxes led to several unsuccessful dissolution efforts in the early 1900s.[21] Dissolution was voted on and failed in East Bloomfield (Ontario) and South Corning (Steuben) in 1923 and 1925, respectively (*Corning Evening Leader* 1923; 1925). Fiscal disarray in Old Forge (Herkimer) prompted a complicated effort to dissolve that led to clarification and revision of the General Village Law in 1933. An audit by the Office of the State Comptroller (OSC) revealed "laxity which bordered on extravagance," resulting in substantial village debt (*Lowville Journal Republican* 1932). A petition to dissolve backed by local businesses was submitted. Village efforts to step up the collection of back taxes owed was insufficient to resolve the financial pinch. An official delegation traveled to Albany, returning with the pessimistic news that there were few precedents to follow and no clear guidance from the Department of State. More importantly, they confirmed that dissolving would not discharge village debt.

In January 1933, the dissolution of Old Forge was rejected, just nine votes short of the necessary two-thirds, but was resubmitted at the next annual election. Again, village officials stalled and fussed over the scheduling of the vote, arguing that resubmission (if approved) would wreak uncertainty with an effort to collect back taxes through a "tax sale" (*Utica Observer Dispatch* 1932; 1932b). Dissolution supporters appealed directly to the state legislature to force their local leaders to schedule an earlier date. The legislature obliged. Because of the ban on special laws, the change was made applicable to *all villages of the fourth class* (i.e., fewer than 1,000 in population) (L. 1933, Ch. 620, §350). The amendment provided that any proposal to dissolve that did not have the requisite two-thirds support at the special election had to be resubmitted at the next annual election not fewer than six months *or more than eight* months following. It further required the separate submission of a proposition for the disposition of village property and raising of taxes necessary to discharge debt, including the creation of special taxing districts. Under these provisions, existing village improvements would be carried out by the town (creating town improvement districts); all taxes would be collected as town taxes, including uncollected village taxes (to be re-levied and collected by the town board).

When resubmitted in July 1933, Old Forge residents voted 117–96 to dissolve (*Geneva Daily Times* 1933). Under General Village Law, the village was to cease at the end of six months, but things once again took considerably longer. The propositions on the disposition of debt and property were said to be as "complicated as Deuteronomy." Moreover, the village attorney argued that, under §350 of the General Village Law, all outstanding debt had been fully discharged prior to dissolving. But he pointed out that the commissioners of the fire districts (which had to be created to bond over the village's remaining debt) did not have the legal authority to issue such bonds until *after* the village was officially dissolved—creating a dissolution catch-22.

Despite the complicated wording and lingering questions, the proposition on the disposition of village property and assets was carried (by a mere thirteen votes). Another legal challenge resulted in a temporary injunction and sent the matter to court (*Utica Daily Press* 1934; *Utica Observer Dispatch* 1934). On appeal, the court affirmed the principle of direct citizen command, holding that confusion in implementation did not negate the citizens' decision to dissolve (Gephardt v. Wilcox 1935, 581). Old Forge was officially terminated on April 1, 1935 (*Geneva Daily Times* 1935). Even then, closure took additional time and legislative effort, as dissolution opponents sought to derail the process with legal challenges to the town's authority over affairs of the former village (*Amsterdam Daily Democrat and Recorder* 1936; L. 1936, Ch. 204).[22]

Henderson's (Jefferson County) dissolution in 1933 was uneventful; others in the 1930s continued to produce confusion.[23] Residents of North Bangor (Franklin County) approved dissolution in successive referenda in

1936, but no certificate was filed. Mistakenly interpreting §350 (then in effect) to require two-thirds passage, the board continued to hold elections for the selection of village officers. Reviewing the matter in 1939, the village attorney filed proper (albeit belated) notice with the state (New York State Archives, N-AR 13243, Village Incorporation Files and Maps, 1886–1988, Box 6, Village of North Bangor Folder).

Forestport (Oneida County) hired a Utica-based law firm to handle its dissolution proceedings (*Utica Observer Dispatch* 1938b). But this otherwise smooth dissolution hit a bump when the town board—after initially complying with terms of the proposition for the disposition of village affairs—rescinded authorization for the necessary bonds. A state trial court ordered the town to proceed as directed by the voters according to the terms of the approved proposition (*Utica Daily Press* 1940).

The smaller number of dissolutions and dissolution attempts spanning the 1950s were also largely related to rising tax burdens and fiscal pressure. The villages of Lewiston and Barker (both in Niagara County) studied the consolidation of village and town services in 1953 and 1958, respectively (*Niagara Gazette* 1953; 1958). Dissolution was proposed in Port Dickinson (Broome County) and voted down in Rosendale (Ulster County) in 1959 (*Binghamton Press* 1959; 1959b; *Kingston Daily Freeman* 1959; 1959b; 1959c; 1959d; 1959e; 1959f). Downsville (as previously discussed) was the only successful dissolution in that decade.

In the 1970s–80s, another wave of dissolution resulted from residents seeking to lower their taxes through reorganization and consolidation. A report by the Office for Local Government Services noted that some seventy municipalities in twenty-two counties were considering some form of merger (*Oswego Palladium* 1972). In the village of Prattsburg (Steuben County), dissolution was initiated by the board and approved by residents (157–139) in March 1972. A study had estimated a 25 percent savings in taxes through the merger with the town (*North Tonawanda Evening News* 1972). A study by the same organization (Kinglsey Associates of Albany) recommended the dissolution of Fort Covington (Franklin County), finding "no disadvantages" and a 32 percent decrease in taxes for its residents (*Fort Covington Sun* 1974). Residents approved the dissolution by a vote of 223–15.

An effort to dissolve Rosendale (Ulster County) was defeated in 1959 (156–133). But in 1976, its residents approved dissolution (179–87) after it was put forward by the village board in the interest of the "greater good." Rosendale's trustees had formally concluded that they could "no longer do an adequate job of providing services at a reasonable cost" (Brandon 1976).

Concerns over the potential costs of a new sewer system led residents in Savannah (Wayne County) to petition for dissolution in 1977. By a vote of 134–75, they decided to dissolve their incorporation, anticipating savings by elimination of duplicative services. Although the issue was divisive, implementation went smoothly. At their last meeting, the soon-to-be former mayor joked that, in the final implementation plan, officials needed to include "50 cents in there for a death certificate" (Heveron-Smith 1979). When Woodhull (Steuben County) dissolved in 1985, it was the result of a citizen-initiated effort to lower taxes. The mayor explained, "it would have been done earlier except for sentimental reasons. Now it's economic reasons" (*Medina Journal Register* 1985).

Four Essex County villages dissolved between 1980 and 1993 in an effort to reduce the local tax burdens. For residents of Elizabethtown (Essex County), "duplication of services and 100-percent assessment in the village" were the major reasons the board placed it on the ballot (Wright 1981). The idea of dissolving the neighboring village of Bloomingdale (Essex County) had circulated for nearly twenty years (*Adirondack Daily Enterprise* 1983). Voters had rejected the effort in 1951 (by a vote of 85–26). After a study committee concluded that dissolving would reduce taxes, residents voted to jettison the incorporation in 1985. The village of Westport followed suit in 1992. Ticonderoga had been flirting with dissolution for years: dissolution was rejected there by 517–139 in 1961. By the 1980s, the village had been pronounced to be "on its death bed" (Wright 1981). A dissolution study was renewed in 1989 on the initiative of the village board, but the effort again stalled out. At last, a citizen's petition (legally challenged and settled) brought the issue to ballot in March 1992 when residents voted 443–344 to disincorporate (McKinstry 1992).

It was a tax increase that prompted the board to launch a dissolution study for Shenevus (Otsego County) in 1992. Residents approved dissolution by a vote of 96–81 the following year. Citizens pushed for a vote on dissolution in Mooers (Clinton County), arguing that their tax rate was higher than neighboring communities. Their efforts started in 1984, stymied by resistance of the board in the preparation of a plan and the scheduling of a vote. A 1988 petition was similarly turned away, and the board refused to enact a resolution to move it forward. The matter made it to referendum in 1994, when residents approved dissolving by a vote of 123–41. Residents in Andes (Delaware County) similarly had to battle the village board to put the matter to a vote (*Daily Star* 2002). The vote in favor of dissolving was 81–63. As elsewhere, the pro-dissolution coalition residents had been motivated by a combination of reduced services, unpaid taxes, and poor fiscal management.

Lessons and Context for the Passage of the Empowerment Act

Although in many of the cases (particularly in the early 1900s–20s) dissolution was a consequence of economic decline and depopulation, the rationale for village residents to consider and approve disincorporation is more complex: incorporation remorse, political discord, and (most notably of late) the desire to alleviate fiscal stress and the property tax burden are all reasons why citizens propose and sometimes approve dissolving. Yet, historically, far more village governments have been "lost" to growth than to decline, either through annexation by a neighboring community or by reincorporating as a city.

As dissolution procedures evolved, state legislative authority over local government structure and organization was never surrendered. Rather, enacting a General Village Law giving direct control over incorporation and dissolution decisions to village residents was thought to be the best means of minimizing state-level interference in the internal affairs of local governments and reducing growing discrepancies between villages in terms of functions and powers. The changes to dissolution procedures with the enactment of Article 19, particularly through the introduction of mandatory study provisions, however, meant that local elected officials could exercise informal veto authority through newly enacted study requirements. Rather than facilitating local government reform, Article 19 procedures had "made it literally impossible" for citizens to pursue village dissolution (Sampson 2010).[24]

As attorney general and aspiring gubernatorial candidate, Andrew Cuomo would seize on the need to revise the state's processes for consolidating and dissolving local units of government as a policy priority. To reduce the overall growing property tax burden, he advocated a long-standing suggestion for reform—eliminate inefficiencies and duplication in the local government structure. Villages, as both the smallest unit of general service government and the only form of local government that can be created and dissolved through local action, proved the easiest target for the state's reorganization efforts.

Chapter 3

The Empowerment Act

Hailed as a "transformational moment in New York history," the Empowerment Act (L. 2009, Ch. 74) was championed and drafted by then Attorney
General Andrew Cuomo. It was presented as the culmination of decades
of research linking New York's outdated local government structure to
the state's high property tax burden. That idea was neither a new nor an
uncontested one.[1] Indeed, such claims could be traced at least as far back
as the Mastick Commission of 1935, which noted that there were "too
many" units of local government (Mastick Commission 1935, 15–16).[2] The
2008 Commission on Local Government Efficiency and Competitiveness
(the Lundine Commission) had likewise concluded that New York's local
government structure was unnecessarily complex, layered, and outmoded,
estimating a potential savings of more than $1 billion through restructuring
reform alone (Lundine Commission 2008, 2).[3]

When introduced in early 2009, the Empowerment Act received
little legislative vetting or scrutiny, moving from introduction to passage
in just thirty-five days.[4] Per its name, the intention of the law was to
empower citizens. By lowering the petition threshold and removing the
required pre-vote study requirements in citizen-initiated proceedings,
the Empowerment Act made it easier for residents to put dissolution on
the ballot. After its passage, the Cuomo administration continued and
accelerated the trend of using state assistance to incentivize and pressure
local governments to explore functional or structural reorganization. By
wedding state aid to the search for local efficiencies, New York set about
forcing the hands of local officials to consider municipal reorganization
more seriously.

In the fourteen years since its passage, The Empowerment Act has undeniably increased the pace and number of village dissolutions. But with more villages voting on the issue, the rate of success under the Empowerment Act is somewhat lower than it was under Article 19. An examination of those villages that successfully dissolved under the revised process, as well as those that rejected dissolution at the polls, demonstrates how the Empowerment Act has made it easier for residents to put dissolution on the ballot, even as perceived deficiencies in the process have been effectively used by dissolution opponents to persuasively argue against dissolving.

The New Dissolution Process

The Empowerment Act revised the processes for consolidation (applicable to towns, villages, and special districts) and dissolution (applicable to villages and special districts similarly), providing two avenues for consolidations and dissolutions to proceed: either through the self-initiation of the governing body or via a citizen-initiated petition. The Empowerment Act also retained the authority of counties to reorganize or abolish local governments (including cities, towns, villages, or districts; or the offices, departments, or agencies within those local governments) via local law, contingent on the approval of a triple majority (voters within cities, voters outside the cities, and voters living within affected villages) in a countywide referendum.[5]

Consolidations are procedurally more difficult than dissolutions insofar as they require the approval of *all* affected municipalities and their residents. The provisions of the Empowerment Act thus have primarily impacted the pace of dissolutions, making it easier for residents to force dissolution onto the ballot. Table 3.1 summarizes the distinctions between dissolution and consolidation, lists the local government entities to which each applies, and provides a brief synopsis of the processes and petition requirements (which are similar).

Board-initiated dissolutions require the development of a proposed dissolution plan prior to a public vote. Once a resolution is adopted, the board has five days to post the proposed plan and must hold public hearings within thirty-five to ninety days. Approval of a final plan is required no more than 180 days after the final public hearing. The law requires the scheduling of a referendum date within forty-five days, which must be held sixty to ninety days thereafter. If approved by a majority, dissolution will

Table 3.1. The Empowerment Act summary (General Municipal Law 17-A)

	General Description:	Applies to:	Process Synopsis:	Petition Requirements
Dissolution	The unilateral dissolution of the governmental entity. Requires approval of voters of the entity to be dissolved.	Villages and Special Districts	Board-initiated: board resolution to initiate and endorse a dissolution plan; approval in a public referendum. Citizen-initiated process: citizen petition, public referendum; development of a dissolution plan; final board approval; plan is implemented unless petition forces a permissive referendum. Rejection of dissolution at referendum (whether board or citizen-initiated) triggers a 4-year moratorium.	10% of number of electors or 5,000 signatures, (whichever is less). In villages fewer than 500 in population, 20% of number of electors or 500 signatures (whichever is fewer). For permissive referenda, within 45 days of approved plan, 25% of number of electors or 15,000 (whichever is fewer).

continued on next page

Table 3.1 (*Continued*)

	General Description:	Applies to:	Process Synopsis:	Petition Requirements
Consolidation	The consolidation of two or more entities into a new municipal government (successor) or a surviving (absorbing) municipality. Requires approval by voters of the entities being consolidated in simultaneous referenda.	Towns, Villages, and Special Districts	Board-initiated: concurrent board resolutions to initiate and endorse a consolidation study and plan; public hearings and simultaneous referenda. Citizen-initiated: citizen petitions in each affected municipality; public referenda; development of a consolidation plan; final board approvals; plan is implemented unless a petition forces permissive referendum. Rejection of consolidation at referendum by voters of anyone of the municipal units to be consolidated triggers a 4-year moratorium.	10% of number of electors or 5,000 signatures, (whichever is fewer). In villages fewer than 500 in population, 20% of number of electors or 500 signatures (whichever is fewer). For permissive referenda, within 45 days of approved plan, 25% of number of electors or 15,000 (whichever is fewer).

Source: Author's own material.

be implemented. If rejected by the voters, dissolution fails, and a four-year moratorium is in effect. Figure 3.1 depicts the process and timeline for board-initiated dissolutions.

For citizen-initiated dissolutions, the Empowerment Act lowered the petition threshold (from 33 percent under Article 19) to 10 percent of the number of electors or 5,000 electors, whichever is less (for municipalities with fewer than 500 electors, the requirement is 20 percent) (N.Y. GML Article 17-A, §779[1] and [2]). The filing of a valid petition requires that dissolution be put up for a referendum, giving officials thirty days to set the date of the election (§779([1]), which must be held within the following sixty to ninety days (§780[1]). If approved by the voters, the board is then required to develop a proposed dissolution plan. The Empowerment Act gives the governing body 210 days, requiring a meeting within thirty days of the vote and 180 days thereafter, to prepare and approve a final plan (§782[1] and §780[1]). A public hearing (or hearings) on the plan must be held within thirty-five to ninety days of the board's initial approval, with a final resolution endorsing the final plan due within sixty days of the last public hearing (§784[3]). Within forty-five days of that approval, a second permissive referendum may be compelled upon submission of a valid petition signed by 25 percent of village electors (or 15,000, whichever is less) (§785[2]). The permissive referendum must be held within 120 days (i.e., following verification of the second petition, the governing body has thirty days to adopt a resolution for a permissive referendum, which must be held sixty to ninety days after its adoption) (§785[4] and [5]). If approved, the dissolution becomes effective on the date specified in the final dissolution plan (§785[1]). Defeat of a dissolution proposal at referendum triggers a four-year moratorium on the filing of another petition; however, the ban would not apply in the event the dissolution plan was defeated in the permissive referendum (§781[4]). The citizen-initiated process is graphically represented in figure 3.2.

Because the Empowerment Act expressly exempts towns from dissolution (N.Y. GMU Law, Article 17-A, §773[1]) and places practical restrictions on elimination of special districts (insofar as the dissolution of such entities requires that its services be either eliminated or continued on a townwide basis (N.Y. GMU Law, Article 17-A, §750[5]), villages were the primary target of the revised dissolution procedures.

The Empowerment Act "anticipates the possibility that the governing boards may be unable or unwilling to comply with the requirements imposed on them during the course of a citizen-initiated consolidation

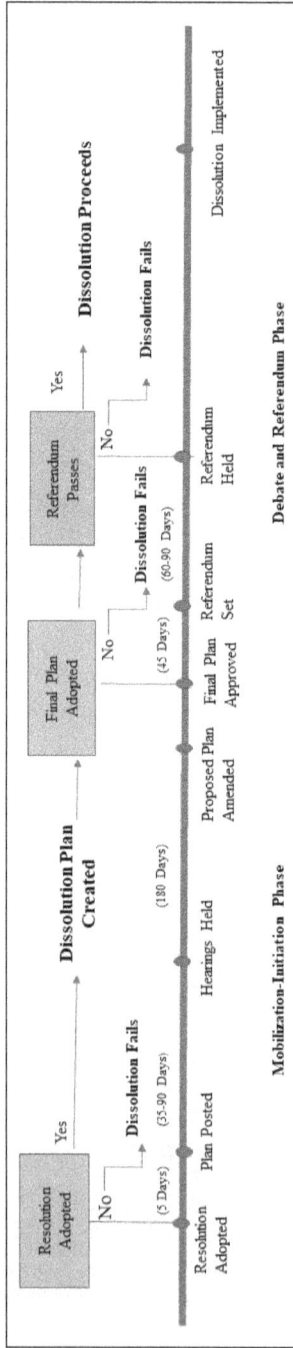

Figure 3.1. The Board-Initiated Dissolution Process. *Source:* Author created graphic.

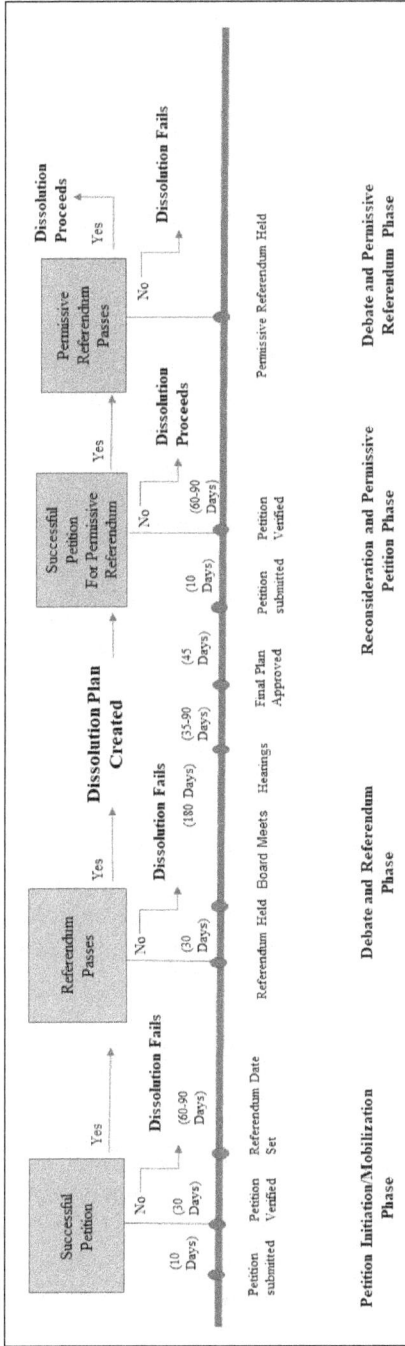

Figure. 3.2. The Citizen-Initiated Dissolution Process. *Source:* Author created graphic.

or dissolution."[6] Either the invalidation of a petition or a failure to abide by the timeline established under the statute is grounds for an Article 78 motion in dissolution disputes. In such circumstances, citizens may bring an Article 78 motion before the courts (N.Y. CPLR Article 78 §§7801–7806). This is a special proceeding under New York's Civil Practice Law and Rules to compel compliance with the law or to challenge a government decision that is made in violation of lawful procedure, is "arbitrary and capricious," or constitutes an abuse of discretion.

The New York Conference of Mayors and Municipal Officials (NYCOM) along with the Association of Towns of the State of New York voiced "vehement opposition" to the law (New York Association of Towns 2009). The Empowerment Act, they complained, had been forced through the legislature with limited consideration of the merits and no public hearings (Beltramo 2009). NYCOM attributed the low rate of success under Article 19 to minimal savings found in most dissolution studies after expensive and time-consuming efforts. Indeed, NYCOM had advised local officials to "avoid costly dissolution studies that waste the time and effort of village officials and cost the taxpayers money" (Beltramo 2008).

NYCOM insisted that, far from clarifying the process, the Empowerment Act added even further confusion. They objected to the lowering of the petition threshold and the removal of the 120-day restriction for signature collection. The requirements to trigger a permissive referendum, by contrast, were far too restrictive in NYCOM's view. Taken together, the provisions that allowed dissolution to proceed to a vote without a formal study were tantamount to "dissolution by default"—requiring dissolution to proceed "even if the arguments for dissolving that were asserted at the beginning of the process are found to be without merit after dissolution is actually studied and a plan is formed" (Beltramo 2009).[7]

NYCOM's objection that the citizen-initiated process does not mandate study of the issue by a formal dissolution committee or the drafting of a dissolution plan *prior* to the public vote would become critically important in future dissolution debates. Even before petitions could be filed under the provisions of the new law, local officials were similarly attacking the revised process, warning that "there's nothing about the law that compels implementation of a developed plan" (Johnson 2010).

The Empowerment Act had eased the pathway for consolidations and merger. For Cuomo, the "next step" was "to come up with financial incentives to actually encourage governments to consolidate, merge, come together" (New York State Gubernatorial Candidates Debate 2010). To that end, the Cuomo administration enacted several additional measures designed to substantially step up the pressure on local municipalities. Key among these was the creation of Citizen Reorganization Empowerment Grants (CREG) in 2009—noncompetitive, high priority grants to study and implement reorganizations under the Empowerment Act (providing up to $100,000 in funding).

This was followed in 2011 by the Citizens Empowerment Tax Credit (CETC) awarding additional state funding to municipalities that undertake a successful merger. The surviving local government(s) of a dissolution or consolidation receive additional annual aid equal to 15 percent of the combined amount of real property taxes levied by all the municipalities involved in the consolidation or dissolution not to exceed $1,000,000. The program mandates that at least 70 percent of such aid be used to provide property tax relief for the residents.

New York also created a Financial Restructuring Board (FRB) for Local Governments, a ten-member board that can assist fiscally distressed local government entities. Eligible municipalities may request FRB review of their "operations, finances, and management structure." Based on their findings, the FRB may make recommendations, including potential restructuring options. Review and recommendations of the FRB are thus designed to promote fiscal stability for struggling localities as well as to encourage reorganization and improved efficiency.

The signature accomplishment of Cuomo's first term was the passage of a property tax cap in 2011 (Centrino and Benjamin 2014). Introduced in 2011 and made permanent in 2019, the property tax cap limits a municipality's increase of its annual tax *levy* to 2 percent or the rate of inflation, whichever is less, following a formula that includes limited exclusions.[8] It is not a hard cap in that municipalities, with 60 percent approval of their governing board, can pass a local law to override the cap (albeit at the risk of angering taxpayers).[9] Further incentive to stay within the cap was provided through a 2015 "tax freeze" and the creation of tax credits (to offset property tax increases) directed to property owners in municipalities where school districts and local governments stay within the tax cap for consecutive years (introduced in the FYE 2015 budget). Because the cap applies to the *levy*, moreover, rising assessments or reassessment may require lowering the tax rates to stay within the levy. The dollar value of real property taxes and assessments of all villages have risen nearly 96 percent between 2012 and 2020, although the property tax cap has kept the year-to-year percent change in the tax level under 2 percent in most years (given the low rates of inflation in that period). Politically popular, it has been touted as a win for New Yorkers, but for local officials, limitations on review raising capacity, along with the press of state mandates, contribute to the sense of fiscal pressure.

Critics of the cap argue that it places an arbitrary restriction on the ability of local governments to generate the necessary revenue to support service needs. Property taxes are the primary source of local revenue on which local governments can rely, particularly during times of emergencies or economic downturns. Citizen feedback, they argue, provides a more meaningful and efficient mechanism for checking property tax growth. Moreover, the mechanism for override arguably favors wealthier communities that are more willing to support the override to maintain the preferred level of services. The Center on Budget and Policy Priorities suggests that such state-level taxation limits force localities to adopt more regressive forms of taxation, including fees for services and licensing, cost-shifting the savings to property owners from non–property-owning taxpayers, which exacerbates racial and income inequality (Lav and Leachman, 2017, 1–2). Rivera and Xu (2014) report that local governments have coped with the cap by cutting services.

Cuomo unveiled two additional incentive programs, aimed at increasing shared services and consolidation, in 2016 and 2017. The Municipal Consolidation and Efficiency Competition allowed local government consortiums to compete for a $20 million award by demonstrating how government consolidations and innovative restructuring initiatives will yield reductions in property taxes. The recipient of this award was the town of Brookhaven, made eligible by the dissolution of the village of Mastic Beach in 2016. The Countywide Shared Services Initiative (CWSSI) (L. 2017, Ch. 59, Part BBB) requires the chief executive office of the fifty-seven counties outside New York City to create a countywide shared service panel to identify, propose, and implement shared, coordinated, and more efficient services to reduce property taxes. Plans that create savings are eligible for an equal match of state funding.

These incentive programs must be understood against the backdrop of declining or flat local government assistance from the state and federal governments. New York has long provided some form of revenue sharing with its local governments that has targeted municipalities by class (Office of the New York State Comptroller 2008; 2015). The Aid and Incentives for Municipalities (AIM) program was created in 2005 to overhaul and consolidate the various local government assistance programs, with three major implications for the trajectory of municipal reorganization. First, the formulas for assistance remained keyed off base levels for villages and towns that were set in the 1960s, with additional assistance based on indicators of fiscal stress.[10] As a consequence, the AIM program continued to award more funding to cities that exhibited higher levels of stress and for which base-aid formulas were readjusted in the early 2000s.[11] The transition to AIM thus locked in a formula that disadvantaged villages (and towns), particularly as AIM funding levels became stagnant.[12] In nominal dollars, AIM funding has remained flat since 2011. When adjusted for inflation, AIM "has declined by $153 million or 24 percent since 2011, when the state real property tax cap was enacted" (Office of the New York State Comptroller 2022, 11).

As importantly, the transition to AIM was accompanied by a new emphasis on finding local efficiencies and encouraging shared services. The impetus was both the trends of increasing fiscal stress and concerns about the inefficiencies of local governments, particularly the duplication of services. The 2005 budget had also created the Shared Municipal Services Incentive (SMSI) program, renamed the Local Government Efficiency Program (LGEP) in 2008. These programs provided grants to municipalities to study and adopt a variety of restructuring options, including consolidation, dissolution, mergers, cooperative agreements, and shared services (L. 2005, Ch. 50). CREG was split off from these programs in 2009, but the LGEP continues to exist as additional incentive for local governments to pursue efficiency opportunities.

The 2019 executive budget introduced a permanent change that eliminated direct AIM payments to 1,326 towns and villages where AIM funding was less than 2 percent of their budget revenue. Direct AIM payments for these municipalities were replaced with AIM-related funding subtracted from the county share of the sales tax to close the gap for eliminated towns and villages (L. 2019, Ch. 59).[13] Counties, the class most dependent on sales tax revenue, protested the state's interception of sales tax to replace state AIM payments as well as to create a fund to assist distressed hospitals and nursing homes. Cities thus remain the primary recipients of traditional state-funded AIM (receiving about 99 percent; only 137 towns and villages continued to receive direct AIM payments, generally accounting for between 2 and 5 percent of their budget). Whereas AIM-related payments will remain funded at the statutorily set amount (unless amended), the direct AIM program remains contingent on annual appropriations and is subject to change in funding levels. This shift to AIM-related payments was touted as saving the state $59.2 million.

When viewed as a piece with the Empowerment Act, these various incentive programs, along with the property tax cap, stagnating AIM, and the transition to AIM-related payments, have combined to pressure local governing units to engage in more shared services, increase their charges to other local governments, and consider functional and structural reorganization (Warner 2015; Hakim 2012). Despite local government complaints, Cuomo remained unsympathetic: "we've been talking, we've been asking, we've been beseeching. . . . If you don't want to, don't do it. But then the people in your district don't get their tax credit, and you'll have to explain to them why they didn't" (Carleo-Evangelist 2014). As Cuomo viewed it, "everybody has their own little political fiefdoms, but we can't afford it anymore and they are going to have to tighten their belt." (Goodman 2008). Local governments, however, have been resistant. And when they push back, "municipalities have a two-word mantra: 'local control'" (Goodman 2008).

Evaluating the Empowerment Act's Impact

The number of communities putting village dissolution to a vote has increased since 2010 when the Empowerment Act went into effect. Table 3.2 summarizes the number of village dissolutions that have been put to a public vote under Article 19 and the Empowerment Act. (A full list of historic village dissolutions and dissolution votes can be found in Appendix A on page 213). Between 1900 and 1972, only twenty-four villages had surrendered their incorporated status (.33 a year on average). From 1972 to 2009 there were twenty-nine dissolution votes (including both successful and unsuccessful) for an average of less than one per year; from 2010 to 2015 there were 2.6 dissolution votes per year on average under Article 19, .59 per year on average successful dissolutions. Under the Empowerment Act provisions, an average of 4.6 communities per year have voted on dissolution (excluding the six permissive referenda), and 1.63 per year have dissolved (on average between 2010 and 2021). It is important to note that several post-2009 dissolutions were initiated and completed under Article 19 procedures and thus are included under Article 19 successes. Indeed, an additional thirteen votes were initiated and conducted under Article 19 procedures, including a spate of 2010 dissolutions in Western

New York—Randolph, East Randolph, and Perrysburg in Cattaraugus County; and Seneca Falls in Seneca County.

Of the forty-seven villages to hold referenda under the procedures of the Empowerment Act, eighteen (or 38 percent) have voted to dissolve. In six of these eighteen successful cases, dissolution was subject to permissive referenda (and reapproved in all six). The board-initiated procedure was used in five of the eighteen successful cases (28 percent) and in four (14 percent) of those twenty-nine failed votes (representing twenty-seven villages, as Macedon in Wayne County and Brockport in Monroe County voted twice under the Empowerment Act).

The Empowerment Act thus has succeeded in at least four ways: 1) by making it easier for dissolution to get on the ballot; 2) by facilitating an increase in the number of communities studying and considering village dissolution; 3) in shortening the length of the study process (which could drag on for years or stall out indefinitely under Article 19 procedures); and 4) by increasing the number of successful dissolutions. But the success rate for dissolutions was higher under Article 19 procedures, which the Empowerment Act replaced: 64 percent of attempted dissolutions (put to a public vote passed under Article 19 relative to only 38 percent under the Empowerment Act). As a caveat to the success rate for Article 19 procedures, however, it should be noted that dissolution only made it to the ballot when there was substantial support from local elected officials to move the process forward. Where that support was lacking, or when local village officials were overtly hostile to the proposal, dissolution was less likely to make it to a public vote. Another explanation for the lower success rate under the Empowerment Act is that, while the law made it easier for citizens to force dissolution to a vote, the process became vulnerable to the counternarrative that voters were being asked to make a uniformed choice by having to vote before a study had been conducted or a plan developed.

The Empowerment Act's record on consolidation is far more meager. Indeed, village-town consolidations have always been relatively rare and a less politically feasible option than dissolution because they require approval in simultaneous referenda.[14] As noted in chapter 1, in 2019 the village of Tuxedo was incorporated and consolidated with the town of Tuxedo in simultaneous referenda. Rather than a consolidation of a functioning village, Tuxedo was a paper village (one that existed only as a legal construct that was created and dissolved in the same election). In 2020, a citizen-initiated effort to consolidate the village and town of

Table 3.2. Village dissolution votes in New York State (1972–2022)

Article 19 (1972–2015)		Empowerment Act (2010–22)	
Approved at Referendum	Defeated at Referendum	Approved at Referendum	Defeated at Referendum
23	15	18	29
64.3%	35.7%	38.3%	61.7%
Average Dissolution Votes Per Year (1972–2010)	.61 (23 over 38 years)	N/A	N/A
Average Dissolution Votes Per Year (2010–15)	2.6 (13 over 5 years)	Average Dissolution Votes Per Year (2010–15)	4.3 (47 over 11 years)

Data collected by author. Excludes village consolidations.

Pawling (Dutchess County) was defeated with 72 percent of the village and 87 percent of the town residents voting in opposition.

Successful Dissolutions Under the Empowerment Act

The individual case studies offer lessons for evaluating the impact of the Empowerment Act and provide clues as to the factors contributing to dissolution success. While the presentation of cases here is chronological rather than thematic, all the familiar themes of remorse, discord, decline, and concern over taxes that were seen in the historical cases are present in the contemporary debate. Most of the villages that have dissolved since 2010 have been small and provided limited services or were already engaged in extensive service sharing. In many instances, voter apathy, declining services, or frustration with the current administration reached a tipping point in overcoming the residents' desire to remain a village. Receptivity or resistance by village officials was often a critical variable influencing the outcome. Likewise, the stance of town officials played an important role in intensifying or assuaging voter uncertainty, as have consulting and municipal organizations in framing the debate and providing (or not) information that is critical to the voters' choice.

Altmar (Oswego County): "Everybody for Themselves"

Altmar's story of a declining population and stagnant economy is familiar for many of New York's small, upstate villages. A dissolution attempt in the 1980s had been derailed by opposition from the village board and fire department (Groom 2010; 2010b). After sparring with the mayor over a street curb, a local business owner launched a petition drive in 2010, taking advantage of the newly enacted Empowerment Act and arguing that taxes were too high given the low level of services and general apathy toward village operations: "We have no water, no sewer, and the village doesn't maintain the streets. . . . [Altmar] used to be quite a place at one time . . . And now nobody's working for anybody. It's everybody for themselves" (Mattison 2010).

By a vote of 80–74, Altmar became the first village to successfully dissolve under the Empowerment Act (Vielkind 2011b). As required after the vote, a draft dissolution plan was prepared by a local dissolution committee with the assistance of the Rochester-based Center for

Governmental Research (CGR). The plan projected "substantial savings" for former village residents and a minimal increase in taxes for those living in the town-outside-the-former-village (Groom 2011). The public hearing on the draft plan produced no controversy, lasting all of twelve minutes (Vielkind 2011b).

After the final plan was approved by the village board in August 2011, the mayor and village clerk-treasurer (who both had been members of the dissolution committee) pushed for a permissive referendum, warning residents, "you're not going to save money, you're going to lose services" (Mattison 2010b). A petition for a permissive referendum was filed, forcing a revote. Residents again voted to dissolve, this time by a vote of 54–50. On its last day of operation, the village of Altmar was given a sendoff, complete with "a funeral procession, coffin cremation, and, of course, a tombstone" (Blazonis 2013). But not everyone viewed its "passing" as mournful. "It's evolution," remarked one longtime resident. "We went from a village to a fire company" (Blazonis 2013).

The merger uncovered problems that were previously unknown to the voters. Unable to gain access to village finances from uncooperative village employees, town officials sought state intervention. The resulting OSC audit revealed that the village's clerk-treasurer had stolen $117,000 from the community, "going so far as doubling her own salary without detection" (Resila 2014). The embezzlement had consumed more than 66 percent of the village's tax levy (in both the 2011 and 2012 fiscal years) and escalated as the dissolution efforts progressed. Her conviction added a sad coda to the story of Altma's last days as a village. A donation jar placed on the counter of one business was accompanied by a sign reading "The 'old' Village Board needs your help. They owe the taxpayers $117,000" (Carey 2014).

Lyons (Wayne County): "Out of Hand" and Into Court

When it comes to local government reform, "change isn't easy" (Vielkind 2011b). This was especially true for Lyons, the first case to test Article 78 as the judicial remedy specified in the Empowerment Act for noncompliance with its provisions. Residents had grown frustrated by the board's failure to enact a stalled shared services plan and for alleged violations of state open meeting laws. Tax increases and an unfavorable audit of the village's water and sewer management spurred a citizen-led dissolution effort. In 2012, an organization calling itself "OneLyons" presented the village clerk with a petition to dissolve the village. The group's name was an effort to frame dissolution not as a divorce but as unification of the village and town. After a contentious debate, residents voted 619–585 in favor of dissolving (51.4 percent in favor). Both prior to and immediately following the vote, Lyons' outgoing mayor lamented the lack of a plan: "Basically the decision was made on I don't know. That's *how we tried to portray it to the voters in the village*, that you are making a decision on no studies and no facts" (Tucker 2012, emphasis added). The controversy spilled into the mayoral race, in which the losing candidate attributed his loss (by just four votes) to his pro-dissolution stance (Anderson 2013b). The winner penned editorials warning residents against dissolving, while village police predicted an increase in drug activity and violence without a dedicated village force (Vanstean 2014; Tulis 2014).

When the board missed the statutory deadline for the approval of a final dissolution plan, they blamed the delay on a lack of guidance from the state. OneLyons immediately filed an Article 78 proceeding with the state supreme court (Anderson 2013). Their petition alleged a lack of good-faith compliance, unnecessary delays, and official displays of opposition (Order to Show Cause, Bailey et al. v. Village of Lyons 2013). The petition also singled out NYCOM for its advice that village officials "give 1st priority to developing a thorough understandable plan, rather than rushing the process merely to comply with the 180-day time period," and for assuring the board that "As long as village officials work diligently and in a good faith effort to complete the proposed dissolution plan, it is unlikely a judge will interfere in the process" (New York Conference of Mayors 2010). Such directions, they argued, established "an official belief that the statutory deadlines were not mandatory because a judge would grant leniency in the process" (Order to Show Cause, Bailey et al. v. Village of Lyons 2013). OneLyons further argued that the consulting firm with which the village had contracted for the study (MRB Group Consultants) had a conflict of interest, as it was composed of the former Seneca Falls officials and a past president of NYCOM, all of whom had "officially opposed dissolution in that capacity" (Appellants Brief, Bailey et al. v. Village of Lyons 2013, 12). Freedom of Information Act (or FOIA)–obtained communications between the consulting firm and village officials had revealed the consultants' antipathy toward dissolution in OneLyons' view (Order to Show Cause, Bailey et al. v. Village of Lyons 2013).

At the hearing, the village respondents assured Supreme Court Judge John Nesbitt, that the dissolution was proceeding in good faith. Although he warned that "judicial leniency should not be the norm and [should be] justified only on a case-by-case basis supported by good cause," Judge Nesbitt granted the board an extension (Memorandum Order, Bailey et al. v. Village of Lyons 2013). OneLyons appealed, arguing abuse of judicial authority. The village motioned for dismissal, describing its "herculean efforts" and claiming the issue was now moot, as a plan had since been developed and approved—a position with which the appellate court agreed (Reply to Motion, Bailey and DeWolfe v. Village of Lyons 2013; Memorandum Order, Bailey et al. v. Village of Lyons 2013).

As soon as a plan was finalized, the anti-dissolution coalition immediately set to work to discredit its validity, warning that implementation was up to the town and that there was no guarantee that the promised savings would materialize. "We're still in a situation . . . where you still don't know what you're voting for," the mayor warned (Miller 2013). The Lyons' own supervisor, in turn, offered only vague assurance to residents: "I believe that the Town Board will look at that dissolution plan, and I think we would respect and do as much of it as possible . . . that would definitely be a starting point . . . I know the plan is definitely not just to throw it out" (Miller 2013).

Dissolution opponents also rallied to force a permissive referendum spearheaded by the citizen group "Save the Village of Lyons." OneLyons challenged the validity of their petition in a second legal proceeding, alleging that it failed to comply with technical requirements and that the number of valid signatures fell below the required 25 percent threshold (GML 17-A, §§785 and 779). They also argued that there had been official pressure and intimidation in securing signatures by uniformed law enforcement officers going door to door. As one resident explained, "it's a small community. I know these people. And . . . two police officers are knocking and asking me to sign the petition . . . I felt that if I didn't sign, I will be a target" (Anderson 2013c). OneLyons again challenged NYCOM's involvement, arguing that the organization works against citizens' interests "and does so using elector tax dollars" (Reply to Motion, Bailey and DeWolfe v. Village of Lyons 2014). A motion to dismiss the challenge for lack of standing was rejected, but on the merits Judge Nesbitt found substantial compliance with petitioning requirements. The court made no finding as to voter intimidation in the absence of a sworn allegation by any of the signatories (Memorandum Decision, Bailey and DeWofe v. Village of Lyons 2014).

OneLyons responded to the judicial setback by noting that the Empowerment Act entrusted village officials to "perform statutory required duties, even while they may be reluctant and hostile participants to a process which seeks to completely dissolve the entity they serve" (Order to Show Cause, Bailey and DeWolfe 2014, 13). By deferring to those same officials, the court had "left citizens without further options" by giving "license to municipalities undergoing dissolution to ignore the clearly written law with impunity." In their view, "the ordinary citizen still has no standing to fight entrenched politicians" (OneLyons Press Release 2014). But rather than appealing, OneLyons put its energies into winning the permissive referendum. Dissolution was once again approved by the voters, to the obvious frustration and dismay of village officials. For many observers, the level of rancor was lamentable: "People are literally fighting, name calling. It's gotten so out of hand, and it's so sad," observed a former village trustee, who blamed pro-dissolution residents for not regularly participating in village affairs: "I've always thought of us as a close-knit community, and people are coming out of the woodwork, people I've never seen, and causing all this havoc" (Miller 2013). Lyons received a $50,000 grant to assist implementation. For proponents, the outcome has been largely positive, resulting in service levels that were unchanged or even improved. For opponents, the loss of village policing and the refusal of the Wayne County Sheriff's office to hire some former village police officers were unsatisfactory outcomes that have left lingering resentments.

KEESEVILLE (CLINTON AND ESSEX COUNTIES): "A SLAP IN THE FACE"

Dissolution efforts had been percolating in the village of Keeseville for at least fifteen years (Henson 2013). Keeseville's backstory is also one of decline and economic stagnation following the loss of its once-prosperous timber and tanning industries (Williams 2014). In 2011, the village secured a $45,000 grant to study merging with the surrounding towns of Ausable (Clinton) and Chesterfield (Essex). Although not required, a draft study was commissioned by the village board. As the study (assisted by the Roundout Consulting and Fairweather Consulting firms) neared completion, a citizen-led petition was filed under the provisions of the Empowerment Act. As the mayor at the time explained, the board "was very pleased the petition came in because now the weight [of moving forward on dissolution] is off their shoulders" (Kittle 2012). However, as the voted approached, elected officials, including the mayor, urged the voters to retain the village government. By a margin of 268–176 (62.6 percent support), Keeseville's voters approved the dissolution. The board approved a final plan within the deadlines established by the Empowerment Act (Lobdell 2012). A petition to force a permissive referendum, reportedly led by the mayor, was successful. As part of that campaign, residents received anti-dissolution messages in their water bills sharing the board's unanimous opposition and questioning the readiness of the towns to respond to village needs (Lobdell 2013).

Chesterfield's town supervisor responded with frustration that village officials "talked like our town governments are foreign government," reminding voters that "we are in your community and our officials are elected by all of the town of Chesterfield residents, including those who live inside the village." Whereas many town officials eschew any involvement in the debate over dissolution, both affected town supervisors were actively involved in the study process from the outset. "Usually, we do not have anyone on the committee that is formally representing the towns," one consultant noted, explaining that in many ways, "the best people to hear from are the ones that will be in charge afterward because it will be their butts that are put on the line if this goes forward" (Lobdell 2012).

Chesterfield's supervisor reassured residents as to the feasibility and benefits of dissolving. The town, he pointed out, had already "taken over several departments from the village, and we have always been able to do the same work, if not more, for less. . . . We have done it with the courts, building inspectors and assessors. I am on record as saying if the town taxes were to increase because of the potential dissolution, then I would resign, and I will not cut services to do that" (Lobdell 2013b). When Keeseville's voters returned to the polls in October, they again voted to dissolve. Village officials were resigned: "I just hope they are happy about it" (Lobdell 2013c).

Keeseville's dissolution was complicated by the fact that the village straddles two townships in two different counties. By mutual agreement, the town of Ausable assumed responsibility for the Keeseville wastewater treatment facility, leaving Chesterfield to take over the water plant. Keeseville had several water woes that posed challenges for town officials, who actively began seeking state grants to assist with the necessary upgrades. The Chesterfield supervisor commented: "I have a file marked 'Problems Inherited from the Village.' They aren't our problems but we're going get to [fix] them" (McKinstry 2014). Village officials too reported working closely with the towns to make the transition as painless as possible: "We could just put the key on the desk and walk out on the 31st, but we don't like that. That's not consistency for the taxpayer" (McKinstry 2015). But the bitterness was evident. In the final hours before its dissolution, Keeseville's last mayor described the loss of the village government as nothing less than "a slap in the face for those who died for democracy" (DeMola 2015).

BRIDGEWATER (ONEIDA COUNTY): "NO INTEREST"

A thriving community some fifty years ago, the village of Bridgewater had been on a gradual, even inexorable, track toward dissolution. With only 470 residents, Bridgewater struggled to keep within the property tax cap and from a stark lack of interest on the part of its residents: only ten people voted in the 2013 village elections. The mayor explained, "There's really no interest in village residents in stepping up and following after us in running for election or assuming a position . . . It's as much that as it is financial issues" (Fries 2013). Because so many of Bridgewater's services were supplied by the town, residents were not confronting significant changes in their existing service levels (Cooper 2013; Geruntino 2014; Rose 2014). Dissolution was forwarded to a public vote by a resolution of the board. In March 2014, its residents voted 40–8 to dissolve. The village received a $49,950 grant from the state to assist with implementation.

SALEM (WASHINGTON COUNTY): "CUT-AND-DRIED"

The dissolution of Salem also proceeded with relatively little fanfare. Incorporated in 1803, the community of 946 residents had already dissolved its fire department and other services: "We have been moving that way for years," explained a resident leading the petition effort, "there are fewer and fewer village services now, I think our situation is pretty cut-and-dried" (Toscano 2014). The dissolution was citizen-initiated and broadly supported: the petition was submitted with 116 valid signatures and approved by a vote of 192–49 (Toscano 2014b; Gardiner 2014). Although not required, Salem had initiated a self-study prior to the vote. Voters thus had a fair idea of what to expect before approving it at the polls. The Hartford town supervisor observed that "as long as we get the state money, it's a no-brainer" (Toscano 2014c).

Local officials had also learned from failed dissolution in the neighboring village of Greenwich, and village and town officials had already ironed out the stickiest issues (the fate of the town library and responsibility for sidewalk snow removal), prompting one observer to call it the "politest" dissolution process the state had ever seen (Scanlon 2015; Toscano 2014b). There was little hyperbole and few attempts to magnify the sense of loss. The outgoing, recently elected mayor summarized: "Your neighbors are still your neighbors, your streets are still your streets. Life goes on. I don't think [citizens will] notice the change other to see some of the services may be stronger or better organized" (Willard 2015).

As the deadline for filing a petition for a permissive referendum approached, however, tensions escalated. The village board retreated into executive session to debate the final plan without the presence of the consultants, sparking public condemnation (Scanlon 2015b). The mayor lobbied in support of a revote, reminding residents that they "have a chance to reverse the dissolution" (Scanlon 2015c). Local media shared citizen anger over the board's disregard for open meeting law and their failure to respond to requests for more information (Scanlon 2015c; *Glens Falls Post-Star* 2015). Town officials, in contrast, were proactive, promising transparency and that the consultant organization would be duly compensated for its work (Scanlon 2015d). In the end, Salem's trustees approved the final plan (unanimously), and no petition to force a permissive referendum was filed. One trustee resigned before the end of his term, citing his lack of agency in closing out the affairs of the village: "I feel like there's not much more to do that would make a difference" (Scanlon 2015e).

PROSPECT (ONEIDA COUNTY): "OUR ONLY OPTION"

The disincorporation of the tiny village of Prospect was precipitated by a financial crisis in the form of two separate worker's compensation claims, the settlements of which were beyond its financial capacity. The claims totaled $685,000, and the settlement allowed just six months for the taxpayers to pay the debt. By dissolving, residents were able to reduce that amount to $577,000 through the sale of assets and to extend repayment to twenty years (Cooper 2015c). A study by CGR urged the board to take quick action to further avoid impending insurance premium increases. As one of the trustees explained, dissolution was the only option (Cooper 2015b). By a vote of 91–7, residents agreed to dissolve. Because a substantial number of services were already provided by the town, the transition was undramatic, although many citizens expressed deep remorse to see their village government dismantled (Cooper 2015c). The town of Trenton supervisor urged residents not to regard the town "as the boogie man . . . [d]on't think we will take anything from you" (Cooper 2015). In 2015, Prospect received a $50,000 implementation grant from the state (*Utica Observer Dispatch* 2015).

MACEDON (WAYNE COUNTY): "A POSTER CHILD FOR GOVERNMENT DYSFUNCTION"

Macedon had a long history with dissolution that was driven by years of personal animosity and bitter disagreements between village and town officials (Sherwood and Whitacre 2014). A 2002 dissolution study, undertaken at the initiative of the village board, had stalled out without being put to a public vote. In 2008, dissolution made it to the ballot but was defeated by a vote of 257–228. In 2010, a first attempt under the Empowerment Act was similarly rejected, 295–199, resulting in a four-year ban on the effort.

In 2014, a surprise board-initiated resolution was rejected 4–1, setting the stage for a citizen-coalition, "One Macedon," to file a citizen-petition (*Times of Wayne County* 2015; Taddeo 2015; 2015b). Pro-dissolution leaders cited the record of town-village discord and resulting litigation fees, along with the costly duplication of services, as their motivation. Local news editorial boards agreed that the town had "diminish[ed] the village's relevance," making "Macedon a poster child for government dysfunction" in the process" (*Daily Messenger* 2015). The *Henrietta Post* sounded a similar note: "Some would probably support a dissolution effort to put an end to the endless and mostly childish bickering between the two governments that has put Macedon in the headlines for all the wrong reasons. But the real issue is whether the village can justify its existence given its diminished role" (*Henrietta Post* 2014).

An anti-dissolution coalition, Village Pride, joined their elected officials in the campaign to save the village, warning that "once the village is gone, it's gone" (Moule 2015). A study, prepared by CGR, found potential savings of up to 40 percent for village residents and 12 percent for TOV taxpayers once state incentives were applied (Curtis 2015). Macedon voters approved the dissolution 300–246. A second petition forced a permissive referendum that affirmed the decision and left many residents feeling exhausted by the process (Hudak 2016).

The acrimony between village and town officials permeated the implementation process. Town officials accused village officials of prematurely abdicating their responsibilities, of creating problems in the transfer of records, and for a host of inherited problems like a former village hall that was noncompliant with disability law requirements. Implementation was further complicated by different budget cycles. Town officials struggled to absorb village expenditures into the less flexible town budget and admitted that the answers they needed from the state were not always forthcoming, forcing them to muddle through on their own. Yet they reported that resident complaints were surprisingly few once the transition of services to the town was complete.

HERMON (ST. LAWRENCE COUNTY): "WHY CAN'T WE?"

The dissolution of Hermon was a board-driven process. The village and town already shared a municipal space, working only "five feet apart from each other'" (Mende 2015). Residents had watched the dissolution of the neighboring village of Edwards and asked, "'if Edwards can do this, why can't we?'" (Mende 2015). In 2014, Hermon received a $10,000 state study grant. With the consulting assistance of the Development Authority of the North Country (DANC), a board-appointed joint village-town committee studied the impact of dissolution. The meeting minutes demonstrate collaboration and transparency, and frequent consultation with the Office of Local Government Services. A plan, sent to both boards for official approval in advance of the referendum, estimated a 52 percent decrease in village property taxes and a potential 1 percent increase for the TOV after state incentives.[15] Voters approved dissolving by a vote of 95–15. As one explained, "I realized we'd still have the same sense of community. We just won't have a village. It's been a struggle to keep the village going and financially, this will certainly help." Another agreed, "we get along well with the town. We've been sharing services for quite a few years now. We help each other out" (Mende 2015b).

PORT HENRY (ESSEX): "HEARTACHE"

Despite being a long time in the making, the debate over dissolving Port Henry was an emotional one. An attempt to dissolve the village (under Article 19) had been narrowly defeated five years earlier when, despite a failed petition effort, the village board put the matter up for a public vote. In June 2015, a citizen petition was filed. The organizers pointed to a 10 percent increase in village taxes and a pending purchase of new fire equipment (McKinstry 2015). With the assistance of a state study grant and the Laberge Group consulting organization, a draft study was prepared, and three public forums were held. Many residents feared losing their community identity, expressed "heartache" at the prospect of losing the village, and worried over the loss of services (Mann 2015). The town of Moriah supervisor pledged that 100 percent of state incentives would be dedicated to the reduction of property taxes and promised continuation of the services that villagers had come to expect: "We're all residents of the Town of Moriah," he said. "Is the town prepared to take this on? Absolutely" (McKinstry 2015b).

Port Henry voters approved dissolution 190–71 (72.8 percent in favor). Local editorials urged collaboration and speed: "Port Henry will get through this. And if life in the now-hamlet of Keeseville is any indication, they'll come out stronger in the process" (*Sun Community News* 2015; *Plattsburgh Press Republican* 2015). The dissolution was upheld in a permissive referendum in which turnout rose and dissolution support fell to 52.63 percent in favor. Anti-dissolution residents were resigned: "We lost. I'm good with it. I just hope things prosper." (Mann 2016). Two years post-dissolution, local media reported that taxes were indeed lower and residential complaints were few, but the jury was still out on whether dissolving had sparked economic renewal (Roland 2018).

Forestville (Chautauqua County): "We Are a Sinking Ship"

Forestville's dissolution was prompted by a fiscal crisis. In 2014, a $250,000 loan (borrowed five years previously to fund a demolition project) was recalled for nonpayment, and an unexpected expenditure for a new water line resulted in a 445 percent increase in operating costs and a 110 percent spike in village taxes (Chiappone 2014). With little other recourse, the village appealed to the Chautauqua County legislature for assistance. The county provided a low-interest emergency loan contingent on the requirement that Forestville study reorganization options and submit to fiscal review. A citizen petition filed in August 2015 forced the measure onto the ballot.

A study by CGR estimated that there would be minimal increases for TOV taxes and a substantial reduction for village residents.[16] The subsequent debate sharply divided Forestville residents. Dissolution committee members pleaded with the public to dissolve an "inept government that is going to bankrupt us," warning, "we are a sinking ship" (Chiappone 2015; Bittinger 2015). The editorial board of the *Post News Journal* agreed: "the village is a mess—and sometimes corrupt—and needs to go away" (*Post*

News Journal 2015). In November 2015, the voters of Forestville approved dissolution with 58 percent in support and again, in a permissive referendum, by a vote of 195–125.

HERRINGS (JEFFERSON COUNTY): "IT'S TIME"

In the tiny village of Herrings, with a population of ninety, talk of dissolving was frequent. In 2015, internal discord led to the resignation of the village clerk and one of the trustees, who explained, "I can't put up with the arguing and fighting anymore" (Avallone 2015). Another frustrated trustee and former mayor presented a citizen petition before he too resigned. "I think it's time," he said. "The village is in bad shape, and I see no other way than to dissolve" (Avollone 2015). There was no time for a preliminary study of the matter, although a Department of State (DOS) staffer was present for the November 1 meeting of the board to answer residents' questions about the process. Two days later, by a vote of 19–9, residents voted to dissolve.

MASTIC BEACH (SUFFOLK COUNTY): HERE AND GONE

Mastic Beach, incorporated in 2010, is a modern case of incorporation remorse. Residents of this beachfront community wanted greater control over zoning and stricter code enforcement for rental properties, concerns they believed were not being adequately addressed by the town of Brookhaven (Bolger 2016; Powell 2009). Incorporation supporters believed a village government could "crack down on absentee landlords and quality-of-life problems associated with the high number of vacant and seasonal properties." They had promised that the incorporation would be "tax neutral," leading the new village's administrators to "lowball" startup costs and operating expense estimates (Whittle 2011; Smith 2017).

From the outset, the new village was beset with problems. Board meetings were so contentious that the first mayor quit midterm. Indeed, Mastic Beach went through three mayors, six treasurers, five attorneys, and three clerks in just a six-year span (*Newsday* 2016; Hampton 2016). The village also suffered external environmental challenges. Hurricane Irene struck a week after its incorporation. Two years later, Superstorm Sandy ravaged its beachfront, creating new sewer and environmental issues and exacerbating ongoing issues with abandoned ("zombie") properties. Despite federal assistance, many residents struggled to bring their properties up to code. In 2016, an overexpenditure on roadwork—explained as an "accounting error"—resulted in a 125 percent increase in the tax rate (WCBS 2016). The mayor admitted to overspending, but blamed previous administrations for having made false promises about costs: "A village, especially a new village, cannot be tax neutral" (Smith 2017). The board made deep budgetary cuts to vital services and eliminated code officers, creating an estimated two-decade backlog of existing code violations (Smith 2017). In 2016, Moody's Investor Services downgraded the village's fiscal rating, citing "financial instability, a declining tax base, and an operating deficit for three straight years" (Hampton 2017). As if all this were not enough, the village faced several lawsuits alleging housing discrimination, one of which claimed that the "incorporation was based primarily on the desire to turn Mastic Beach into a more upscale rental community . . . by forcing low-income and minority residents out of town" (Lawyers Committee for Civil Rights Media Release 2015). A *Newsday* editorial characterized Mastic Beach as a "cautionary tale about local control" (*Newsday* 2016).

Fed up, residents petitioned for dissolution, calling the experiment a "nightmare and disaster" (Hampton 2016). A study by the Laberge Group projected that, once dissolved, taxes would *rise* for village residents who retained the debts of the former village—but the increase would be even higher if the village remained. In November 2017, residents of Mastic Beach voted to disincorporate, making it the largest village to date to dissolve under the Empowerment Act.

Town of Brookhaven representatives had been active participants in the planning, pledging close consultation with residents of the former village (Smith 2017b). Despite previous dissatisfactions, returning administration to the town was hailed as the "right move" (Newsday 2016). An anti-dissolution former mayor acknowledged the promise of tax neutrality was unrealistic, that the town had the "advantage of economies of scale in carrying out services" (Hampton 2016). Post-dissolution, Brookhaven made significant progress in the demolition of abandoned properties to the benefit of adjacent home values and development (Hampton 2018).

In 2018, the town of Brookhaven was awarded $20 million under the state's Municipal Consolidation and Efficiency Competition (MCEC) grant program. Working with state officials, the town also secured federal funding for the biggest water-sewer in Suffolk County in thirty years, with direct economic benefit to the former village of Mastic Beach (Hampton 2018).

CHERRY CREEK (CHAUTAUQUA COUNTY): FAREWELL

Cherry Creek, incorporated in 1893, was once the center of a bustling farming community, boasting canneries, creameries, inns, and businesses, all with easy railway access. But as its agriculture declined and jobs departed, Cherry Creek fell into a downward spiral. The village commissioned a dissolution feasibility study in 1995, but with no state-level incentives or tax credits at the time, it projected only modest savings (Bridges 1995). When offset by the corresponding loss of services, support for the idea dissipated.

Interest was reignited in 2016 when the tax levy increased by 68 percent in response to anticipated bonding for a municipal project. Concerned residents presented the board with a petition to call a dissolution vote (*Dunkirk Observer Today* 2016). The board weighed commissioning a study. "If we don't do this before the vote," the mayor argued, "we're asking for people to vote in the fog" (Dedie 2016). CGR was hired and presented a preliminary report projecting a reduction in both village and TOV tax rates (Center for Governmental Research 2017, 8; *Dunkirk Observer Today* 2017). Cherry Creek's residents voted 70–32 to dissolve in December 2016. Village officials were resigned to the process, acknowledging that there was a "lot of work" to be done (*Post News Journal* 2017). The Chautauqua County legislature approved funds ($36,303) to assist in the dissolution efforts, praising the voters for being "aware that in order for small communities to survive and prosper, unnecessary layers of government must be eliminated" (*Dunkirk Observer Today* 2018).

As the official dissolution date approached, the *Buffalo News* featured a story titled "Farewell to . . . a Farming Community That Will Exist No More" (Sommer 2017). It explained how depopulation, fiscal stress, and the loss of agriculture left the community unable to afford maintaining the incorporation. In both tone and content, the story read much like an obituary.

BARNEVELD (ONEIDA COUNTY): NO QUESTION

Barneveld was settled in the 1790s under the name of Olden Barnevelt. In 1819, it was incorporated by legislative charter as Oldenbarneveld. It was rechartered as Trenton in 1833. In 1908, the residents petitioned the federal government to rename its post office and rail crossing as Barneveld to avoid constant confusion with Trenton, New Jersey. In 1970, the village reincorporated under General Village Law, formally changing its name to Barneveld in 1975 as the more popularly used identifier. At its peak, Barneveld never surpassed 500 residents. By 2010, its population had fallen to 284. Between 2011 and 2016, real property assessment had fallen from $20,156 to $7667 and village expenditures from $657,603 to $138,238. Indeed, most of the village's services, including streets, plowing, zoning, and code enforcement, were administered by the town of Trenton. In 2017, residents submitted a petition and made the decision (by a vote of 54–12) to dissolve, a step viewed as not much more than filing the necessary paperwork to make the phase-out of the village official (WKTV 2017; Thomas 2017). The town assumed the costs of upgrading sewers and (nonexistent) sanitation systems, noting that "they need something done there, no question" (WKTV 2017).

Van Etten (Chemung County): Village versus Town

As with many small communities, Van Etten struggled with financial challenges and internal political problems. Burdened by debt on its water system and high tax rates, the village regularly sparred with the town over fire and emergency services (Lantz 2018). For most of its history, the village's fire department (VEFD-Department 17) had provided fire services to the town. But then the controversial firing of the fire chief splintered village and town volunteers, leading to the creation of a separate Community Fire and Rescue company (CFR-Department 24). In 2011, the town switched its contract to CFR, renewing with them in 2013 after a bidding war between the two fire departments. According to the town supervisor, the VEFD "slapped us in the face by padlocking the (expletive-deleted) door in June." He reasoned, "If we take this . . . contract with the village, three months down the road they have a bug up their (expletive-deleted) and padlock the door again. I am not ever going to do that" (Hicks 2013).

In April 2017, at a joint village-town meeting, town officials voiced support for dissolving, citing the tax savings from state-level incentives. Village officials, however, were cold to the idea (Paz 2017). Residents were split, with some angry at the board's reticence, while others warned that the "town board was organizing a hostile take-over," making the debate "the village versus the town" (Altieri 2017; Marx 2017).

A citizen petition, for which the town officials disavowed any involvement, was filed in August (Marx 2017). The village hired CGR to conduct a study ahead of the referendum, although the study was slowed by a delay in receiving state incentive funds (Hice 2017). Chemung County legislators, several of whom attended the dissolution study meetings, provided temporary funding to support the dissolution process (Freeze 2018d). When CGR's study was released, town officials felt vindicated by the projected tax savings, concluding it was a "no-brainer, really" (Mearhoff 2017). The referendum was delayed by a failure to publish timely notice per the Empowerment Act, but when it was held, residents voted 103–76 in favor of dissolving.

In the crafting of a final plan, tensions flared. Fire services were transferred to CFR, "an emotional blow during an already tumultuous time" (Cone 2018). Problems with village finances were uncovered, including budget shortfalls and alleged discrepancies in water billing. The town supervisor accused village officials of "dragging their feet" in the process (Platsky 2018, May 14). Some residents vented frustration at the village for putting forth a "bad dissolution plan," while others directed complaints at CGR, the consultant group, for a supposed bias and an "'over-simplified' plan catering to the wishes of the town'" (Freeze 2018). Although the village administration had left room for a permissive referendum, the petition for such "narrowly failed" (Cone 2018; *Elmira Star Gazette* 2018; Freeze 2018b; 2018c).

Van Etten dissolved effective December 31, 2018. The final handoff of the former village's affairs to the town was (surprisingly) anticlimactic given the earlier rancor (Freeze 2018e). The decrease in tax rates was in line with study projections (Freeze 2018f), One county legislator concluded it was "a learning experience," predicting that other communities were likely to follow suit (Platsky 2018b).

Morristown (St. Lawrence County): "Logical and Sensible"

Morristown began informally studying dissolution in 2008 (Robinson 2016). Encouraged by the dissolutions in Edwards (under Article 19) in 2011 and Hermon (under the Empowerment Act) in 2015, the village received a $15,000 CREG award and contracted DANC for a yearlong study. For village residents, dissolution would equalize the tax rates of the village and town given the town's larger tax base, higher assessments, and regular use of village amenities. They felt it was simply "'not right' that village residents, who constituted only twenty percent of the town's population) pay so much more for the same benefits the town uses freely and for free" (*North Country This Week* 2018; Robinson 2018b). DANC estimated 60 percent savings for village residents and a 6 percent increase for TOV upon dissolution (Robinson 2018). The mayor's public stance was neutrality, declaring that her goal was to ensure a fair vote and avoid creating divisiveness in the small community: "It's still a community no matter what way the people vote" (*WWNYTV News* 2018). Dissolution overwhelmingly passed 130–47. For most voters, the decision came down to economics as expressed in one editorial: it was "only logical and sensible to consolidate" (*Ogdensburg Journal* 2018).

Harrisville (Lewis County): The Bottom Line

With a population of just under 700, Harrisville was the fourth-largest village in Lewis County. In 2016, citizens submitted a petition that was deemed invalid by the village clerk. Concerned that a successive, successful petition would move the process forward without an adequate study, the village board-initiated the process. A joint village-town study committee was assisted by DANC and funded by a $15,000 grant from the state (Virkler 2018; 2018b; New York Department of State 2017). Their report estimated sizable savings once state credits and incentive were factored in (Virkler 2017). The mayor, however, remained skeptical. "My number-one concern is that we're going to lose services and there's no two ways about it" (WWNYTV 2017). Ahead of the vote, the mayor sent mailings to village residents, decrying the study as flawed and alleging that DANC had an interest in taking control of the village's water system and that Cuomo's reorganization efforts were geared toward a presidential run (Cook 2018). Harrisville voters approved dissolution by a vote of 112–70, As the village moved toward dissolution (effective January 1, 2019), indications were that the resulting savings would be more than 50 percent for former village residents.

South Nyack (Rockland County): The Elephant in the Room

A stagnant tax base, deteriorating finances, and dissatisfaction with village administration were ongoing concerns for many South Nyack residents. The village regularly operated on a deficit and had substantially overridden the property tax cap in 2020. Proponents argued that dissolution would reduce personnel costs and provide for more efficient services. The pending sale of the former Nyack College property to a Ramapo-based yeshiva raised new concerns that village officials were not up to managing the potential land-use controversies that were likely to result as developers sought rezoning for the site.[17]

A citizen-initiated dissolution petition was filed in August 2020. While much of the public debate concentrated on the potential tax savings and implementation options, the subtext of the debate was community discord over the pending purchase of the former college. Some residents faulted the village board for not being more proactive in finding a non–tax-exempt commercial developer. Many feared that the already cash-strapped village simply was not prepared to deal with lawsuits or legal settlements from possible Religious Land Use and Institutionalized Persons Act (RLUIPA) disputes (Staff 2020). Having observed land-use battles in other communities, some considered what had happened in "villages like Airmont as the canary in the mine shaft," and believed that dissolving was "an insurance policy" against similar litigation costs (Traster 2020). Still other residents expressed frustration that the referendum had been forced by a "vocal minority" who were using unfounded fears to rush dissolution to a premature vote. Village officials initially opposed dissolving, unwilling to cede land use and local law authority to the town planning board (on which there were no South Nyack residents), warning that, once the village dissolved, its residents would have a diminished voice in influencing town decision-making.

A preliminary study, contracted to and conducted by CGR, did not directly address the sale and development of the college property, but projected potential tax savings from dissolution. Just days after the college's sale was finalized, South Nyack residents voted in support of dissolution by a vote of 508–292. South Nyack contracted the LaBerge Group to assist with the creation of the implementation plan. The idea that South Nyack could reincorporate or reincorporate or join with adjacent villages (creating a so-called mega-village with more power to deal with impending land-use dispute) was part of the public discourse as a possible next step. No petition for a permissive referendum was filed, and the dissolution is proceeding as scheduled, effective March 31, 2022.[18] The dissolution plan included paying down outstanding debt through the sale of the former village hall and department of public works complex (Lieberman 2022). If sale of the properties is not finalized prior to the effective date of dissolution, the assets will transfer to Orangetown, which has no legal obligation to apply the proceeds against the legacy costs of the village, meaning former village residents face a potential increase in their projected post-dissolution property taxes. Thus far, the town supervisor has been "noncommittal" on the issue, taking a "wait and see" approach (Kratz 2022).

Unsuccessful Dissolutions Under the Empowerment Act

Of the forty-seven dissolution referenda conducted under the Empowerment Act, twenty-nine votes resulted in rejection of dissolution at the polls. Most of these failed attempts (83 percent) were sparked by the desire for greater operational efficiency as one of the primary motivators. Several cases were unique circumstances in which internal dysfunction or discord were motivating factors. This includes water woes in Champlain (Clinton County) as well as political infighting in Macedon (Wayne County) (which rejected dissolution in 2010 but approved it in 2015) and Fleischmanns (Delaware County). Several cases (six cases or 20 percent) were motivated by fiscal stress in relation to dwindling populations (a factor in 28 percent of failed cases). Given the similarities in motivating factors and characteristics, it is impossible to discern why dissolution outcomes differ in similarly situated communities, although chapter 6 addresses the importance of the narrative persuasion tactics used by the dueling coalitions.

What then can be concluded from these failed dissolutions generally? First, the change in the legal mechanism for putting dissolution on the ballot matters. Because the Empowerment Act lowered the petition threshold, more villages are voting on the question, perhaps without sufficient support (or time to build the support necessary) to carry the question successfully. Moreover, in most of these cases, the perceived deficiencies of the Empowerment Act (particularly the lack of a pre-vote study) have become persuasive anti-dissolution talking points. In case after case, members of the anti-dissolution coalition stress that residents are being asked to vote without full knowledge of the impact on service delivery and taxes and warn that state incentives are not guaranteed indefinitely. What appears to doom most dissolution efforts is uncertainty over its likely impact on services and taxes—a factor that looms large in the narrative policy debates.

Second, smallness or rural character does not provide a satisfactory explanation for why some villages dissolve and others do not. Most small, rural villages never consider dissolving, and many that do reject it at the polls—often by substantial margins. The village of Odessa (Schuyler

County), for example, voted on and rejected (154–74) a citizen-initiated dissolution motivated by costs and voter apathy. A self-study provided a "portrait" of the community without its village government, noting that, whatever the outcome, the "buildings, landscape, and people" would remain. But so too, it warned, would the common problems, including poor water quality and a "depressed business environment" (Village of Odessa Scoping Report 2010, 13). Dissolution, in other words, was not regarded by a majority of residents as a reliable solution to the village's myriad problems.

In Leicester (Livingston County), a citizen-led effort was met by the resistance of local elected officials, who turned what was supposed to be "facts only" public meetings into pro-village "pep rallies" that focused on the potential loss of services (*Livingston County News* 2011). Claiming that "most villages that dissolve do so because of financial hardship," the mayor declared Leicester financially stable (Garragazzo 2011). Despite Leicester's small size and its reliance on the town for several key services, residents voted to keep the village by a vote of 135–48.

The village of Chaumont (Jefferson County) rejected dissolution three times—in 1999 and 2012 (under Article 19) and in 2020 (under the Empowerment Act). With only 625 residents (accounting for 29 percent of the town of Lyme's population), the board reinitiated dissolution efforts in 2012. "We didn't go into this knowing it was going to be a big tax savings. The biggest thing was because our equipment was low, our DPW was small, and we were lacking in resources. And duplication of services—that was pretty much the biggest thing" (Richards 2012). A study by the consulting group CGR projected healthy (nearly 50 percent) savings for village residents. Still, its voters said no. In 2020, the village hired DANC for an updated review. Once again, the consultants projected village residents could reduce their taxes by half. To the surprise of elected officials, voters yet again rejected dissolution by a vote of 136–119.

Victory (Saratoga County) considered dissolution (board-initiated under Article 19) after an OSC audit revealed fiscal mismanagement problems. The village of 600 had voted against dissolving in 2013 by a vote of 143–82. Similarly, residents of Champlain (Clinton County) rejected disincorporation of their community of 1,000. And in the tiny village of Fleischmanns (Delaware County), with a population under 350 and less than one square mile of territory, residents turned down dissolving by 70–46 in 2019. Being small, rural, or having a history of fiscal or administrative problems does not guarantee dissolution support.

At the same time, the case studies suggest that dissolution is a much harder sell in communities that are larger, relatively affluent, or visibly appealing and vibrant. Residents are willing to pay associated costs of maintaining the village to secure the amenities and quality of living that it provides. Consider the case of Richfield Springs (Otsego County), a once prosperous and popular sulfur-spring resort destination for New York City's elites in the Victorian era. Although the springs have long since dried up, the village retains significant charm. As the site of three national historic districts, Richfield Springs boasts exceptional architecture and historic estates that keep it something of a tourist attraction. As importantly, the buildings are a visible and eye-pleasing testament to an illustrious past and a rallying point for cultural and historical organizations. Dissolution was overwhelmingly rejected in 2013 with 86 percent of its residents opposed, fearing that disincorporation would diminish services and daily quality of life.

Indeed, the attempts to dissolve larger villages often fail at the petitioning phase or are defeated, as was the case with Johnson City (Broome County, population 15,174) and Potsdam (St. Lawrence County, population 9,428) under Article 19 and Depew (Erie County, population 15,303) under the Empowerment Act. In larger communities, service delivery is typically more complex and often includes village fire and police services—a complicating factor in the debate. Their operating budgets and capacity are larger and the populations are more heterogenous. As importantly, the anti-dissolution coalitions are typically better organized. In addition, a large population is typically popularly associated with municipal stability and fiscal health, even if village finances are strained. With more businesses and development, the scope of conflict in such cases may also be broader. And when a village is the population center of the surrounding town (or towns), its service demands are not only typically higher but also less readily transferrable to the town, requiring more complex implementation. Suburban, or metro-adjacent, villages, moreover, have a stronger motivation to maintain a separate identity and localized control over land-use regulations. In short, the politics of dissolving are more complicated in larger villages. Indeed, the two largest villages to dissolve are arguably explained by their somewhat unique circumstances. Seneca Falls (Seneca County)—which dissolved in 2010 under Article 19 procedures—is often used as an exemplar of a progressive dissolution undertaken in the cooperative spirit of community development and renewal. With a population of over 7,000, the picturesque community claimed itself as inspiration for the fictional Bedford Falls in the classic film *It's a Wonderful Life*. The village board had spearheaded the effort to find efficiencies and savings through service sharing with the town. Most significantly, the merger allowed former village residents to benefit from revenues generated by Seneca Meadows landfill—a circumstance that dissolution opponents elsewhere argue negates its value as an example. Similarly, Mastic Beach (Suffolk County)—the largest village to dissolve to date—was a modern case of incorporation remorse. Its incorporation lasted just six years and was beset by cost overruns, fiscal mismanagement, and internal political strife from the outset. The precedential success of these cases is, understandably, generally caveated in subsequent dissolution debates.

But villages do not need to be large, or visibly vibrant, for their residents to feel the pull of the past or the desire for continuity. Indeed, smallness can enhance the sense of neighborliness and shared identity, making it easier for elected officials and anti-dissolutionists to rally support through personal outreach to neighbors. The case studies demonstrate that, regardless of community size, the debate plays out in much the same way: even when potential savings are demonstrated, residents express concern over a potential loss of services and tout the intangible benefits of incorporation, including preservation of village history and identity. Several of the cases in which dissolution was rejected are examined in greater depth in the following chapters, which explain the political and social contexts of the dissolution debate and the power of narrative persuasion.

Part II

The Political and Social Context

Chapter 4

Fiscal Incentives and Pressures

Renewed attention on the structure of local government in 2010 was, in part, precipitated by worsening trends in municipal fiscal stability. Even prior to the Great Recession of 2008–9, the signs of fiscal pressure were starting to mount for New York's localities. Between 1994 and 2004, municipal debt and debt service doubled for all classes. The Office of the State Comptroller's (OSC) *Annual Reports on Local Government* noted an increase in operational deficits and bonding, ever-increasing expenditures for employee salaries and benefits and growing Medicaid costs for counties. At the same time, the property tax burden began to grow along with other revenue sources for local governments, such as fees and charges for services. The annual reports and audits conducted by the OSC flagged key indicators of concern for towns and villages in 2003, including low fund balances and cash liquidity, operational deficits, and increased debt service. Tax and debt limits (originally characterized as an issue of "little or no concern" for towns and villages in the 2004 *Annual Report*) had trended upward by 2010 (Office of New York State Comptroller 2004; 2011). Because constitutional tax and debt limits are expressed as a percentage of property value, when property values fall, struggling communities with declining tax bases start to run up against their limits. By 2012, the number of local governments ending their fiscal year in a deficit had grown to nearly 300 (Office of New York State Comptroller 2013). The signs of persistent municipal fiscal stress hit counties and cities more severely than it did towns and villages, but the new reality for all local government, as described by the OSC, was continually learning how to do more with less.

Although escalating financial pressures are one reason that residents may consider municipal restructuring, the popular linkage between stress and dissolution is not supported by the evidence. Indeed, there appears to be little correlation between indicators of fiscal stress and village dissolution activity in New York State. That is, fiscal stress does not provide a satisfactory explanation as to when and why residents consider or approve village dissolution.

Identifying Aggregate Costs and Savings

An underlying rationale behind the Empowerment Act was that the number and overlap of local governments contribute to the state's high property tax rates.[1] This argument assumes that it *is* the *aggregate* cost of maintaining nearly 560 villages alongside some 990 towns that overburdens New York's taxpayers. Yet demonstrating the aggregate county or statewide savings to be had from dissolution has proven a difficult task.

In 2006, a local civic activist and regionalism advocate in Western New York, Kevin Gaughan, undertook a five-month study, *Paying Our Politicians: What 439 Elected Officials Cost Us* (hereinafter the Cost Study) to try to assess the collective burden of the local government structure. Gaughan argued that the excess of local elected officials in Erie County (ten times the number of any like-sized community in the United States by his count) created multiple veto points and erected self-interested barriers to regional policy solutions (Gaughan 2009b; Chandler 2009; Miles 2009).

The Cost Study found the highest concentration of politicians in suburban communities. Village government accounted for 25 percent of Erie County's elected representatives, serving just 9 percent of the population at an annual operating cost of nearly $6 million and another $7 million in state assistance. His proposed solution was to downsize government by eliminating two seats on every town and city board and to dissolve all villages countywide. "Once we downsize local government, we will vest ourselves and our local servants with the moral authority to compel Albany to change too. And in one fell swoop, we'll forever end the shell game of town governments complaining about school districts; county executives whining about state excess; and everyone lamenting public authorities" (Gaughan 2009). Previous reorganization efforts had failed, in his view, not because they required local citizen consensus, but because the route of implementation ran right through the layers of local elected officials

(Gaughan 2006). In the end, his petition campaign successfully placed dissolution on the ballot in three villages. Resounding defeat in all three cases ended the reform effort (see chapter 5).

The *Albany Times Union* also sought to answer the question of whether more layers of government lead to greater costs through a comparative analysis of three villages to assess the level of services relative to their respective property tax rates (Vielkind 2011). The report compared budgets for the Villages of Green Island (Albany County), Mechanicville, and Clifton Park (Saratoga County). Green Island (the smallest and one of only six coterminous town-villages) received the most state assistance on a per-resident basis but also had the highest property tax burden.[2] When varying community amenities were factored in, any meaningful conclusion as to relative value for cost became increasingly "murky." As a political scientist, Gerald Benjamin noted, it is "a very treacherous task to get to an apples-to-apples comparison" in any intermunicipal evaluation (Vielkind 2011).

Another way of trying to assess the aggregate costs of overlapping government is to add up the savings produced by its elimination. Yet using individual village dissolution studies is also problematic, as there is no consistency in the metrics or methodologies across studies. Rather, each community appoints its own study committee or hires a consulting firm to design a study to identify potential areas of savings. Implementation then falls to the town officials, who are not bound to adhere to the plan. In other words, what was planned and what is executed may be subject to alteration—and how a plan is ultimately implemented matters (Boyd 2008). Projected savings may also dissipate over time and are offset by cost shifts to the town(s).

Moreover, dissolution studies generally focus on a pre- and post-dissolution comparison of village and TOV tax rates (per $1,000 of assessed value) based on assumptions as to the transfer, reduction, or elimination of services after a line-by-line review of the village budget. Caution is warranted insofar as every dissolution study is an *estimate* of potential savings based on the unique factors of each case. How substantial the actual savings are, how the relief is distributed, and for how long can only be projected. Most dissolution studies find some potential savings in the form of reduced taxes for the former village residents, commonly accompanied by a (usually modest) increase in TOV taxes, along with some (usually minor) reduction or alternation of services. New York State has not yet funded studies to evaluate whether those savings are lasting or to assess the impact of dissolution in the years or decades to follow. Once dissolved, villages fall out of the OSC system, and their data is aggregated with the surrounding town(s), making the impact for the former village and TOV harder to track.

The basic argument supporting dissolution is that, if dissolving a village produces potential savings (even if modest), then the elimination of a substantial number of villages will result in county or statewide benefits. But when residents vote on dissolution, their immediate concern is for *its impact on their own property tax burden and services*. The broader questions of county or statewide benefits are less central to their decision. The Empowerment Act eases the pathway for citizen-initiated efforts, but coordination of those efforts across multiple villages (to maximize area or countywide savings) is rare.

Figure 4.1 depicts the various categories of potential savings associated with village dissolution.[3] Of these, the Cost Study focused primarily on just one, "Wages and Benefits," with the presumption that savings would materialize by replication across multiple communities and counties. In other words, while the wage-related savings from the dissolution of one village government would be minimal, the elimination of multiple village units would accrue to substantial savings countywide. Employee benefits are the fastest-growing item of expenditures for all classes of government (Office of New York State Comptroller 2017, 8). Such savings, however, are offset by the transfer of at least some former village personnel costs to the town. While village mayor and trustee positions would be eliminated, the number of town employees may need to be increased to accommodate the shift of services from the former village. The Cost Study was thus critiqued for being too simplistic in its assumptions, particularly when accompanied by the promise that existing levels of service would not be disrupted or diminished.

Boyd (2008) focused on the more elusive category of "Efficiencies and Savings" that derive from the merging of services, the elimination of redundant efforts and personnel, joint usage of facilities and shared equipment, economies of scale in procurement and contract negotiation, and so forth. He wrote: "It is possible that layering creates inefficiencies that are difficult to measure—the complications and expense that may come from numerous meetings, phone calls, and other forms of communication and coordination among multiple layers of local government serving the same general population. However, there does not appear to be research examining or quantifying the extent of this" (Boyd 2008,

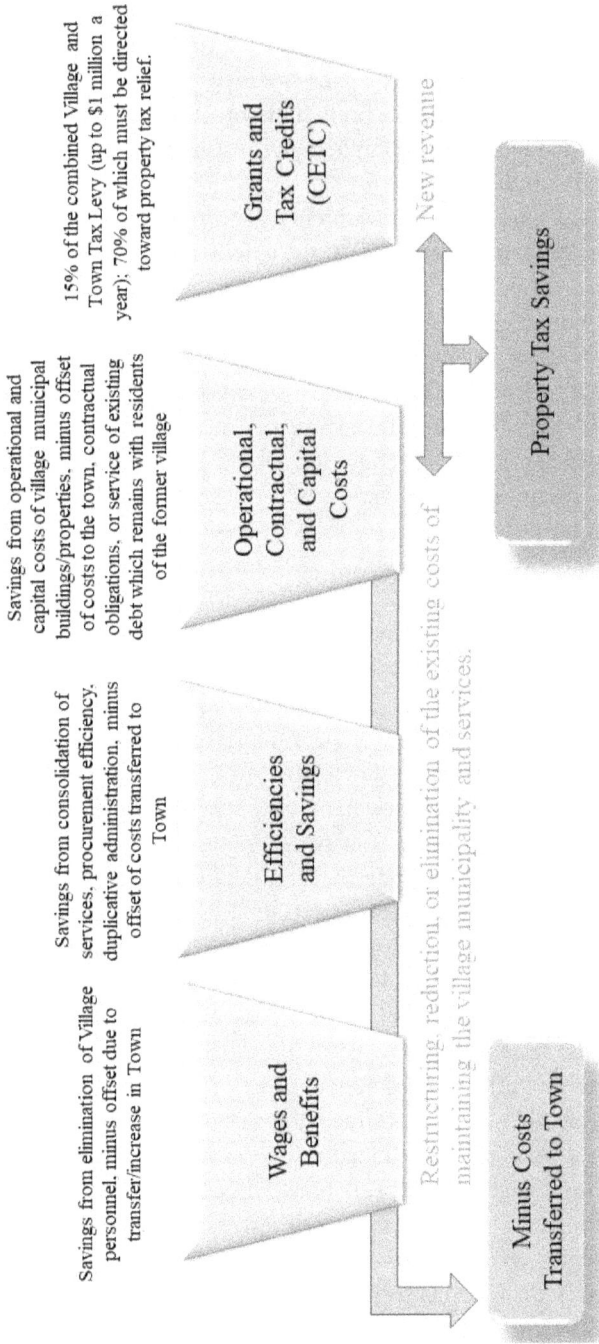

Savings from elimination of Village personnel, minus offset due to transfer/increase in Town

Savings from consolidation of services, procurement efficiency, duplicative administration, minus offset of costs transferred to Town

Savings from operational and capital costs of village municipal buildings/properties, minus offset of costs to the town, contractual obligations, or service of existing debt which remains with residents of the former village

15% of the combined Village and Town Tax Levy (up to $1 million a year); 70% of which must be directed toward property tax relief.

Wages and Benefits

Efficiencies and Savings

Operational, Contractual, and Capital Costs

Grants and Tax Credits (CETC)

Restructuring, reduction, or elimination of the existing costs of maintaining the village municipality and services.

New revenue

Minus Costs Transferred to Town

Property Tax Savings

Figure 4.1. Village Dissolution: Categories of Savings. *Source:* Author created graphic.

7–8). Moreover, Boyd noted that the layering is not consistent throughout the state. "Denser, more urban areas tend to have fewer governments per hundred thousand population than do sparsely populated areas" (Boyd 2008, 11). Calculating the costs (and therefore the potential savings) is exceedingly difficult given the complexity of "mismatched and overlapping boundaries" (Boyd 2008, 13).

Studies undertaken by the Municipal Financial Restructuring Board (FRB) provide illustrative examples of the extent of the functional overlap between municipal units in close geographic proximity. For example, the villages of Herkimer, Ilion, and Mohawk, all within the town and county of Herkimer, overlap in all but two of twenty-two service areas (tax bill printing and foreclosure). The village of Amityville, town of Babylon, and county of Suffolk similarly overlap in all but one of twenty-two services (wastewater/sewer). Dissolution would reduce duplicated efforts and effectively *force* the consolidation of these services by eliminating an entire governing unit.

Empirical evidence on the cost savings produced by the increased service sharing between municipal units is mixed (Warner 2014). Kay and Corrigan (2016) argue that, rather than looking at the savings to the specific municipalities (the focus of most shared service studies), it is more appropriate to look for an aggregate reduction to overall cost of local government at the county (or potentially regional) level. Their preliminary research found small, but statistically insignificant, reductions in local government spending, which suggests that shared services do not dramatically reduce the costs of providing local services. Indeed, the linkage between interlocal service sharing, performance, and savings has not been clearly established in the literature (Bromberg 2015). Aldag and Warner challenge the assumptions that intermunicipal cooperation will always produce savings that will remain stable over time. In their examination of sharing in twenty-nine service areas, cost savings were achieved 56 percent of the time on average, with improved service quality emerging in only 50 percent of the cases (2018; 2019). Cost savings materialized in only some service areas, remained the same in others, and in a few cases, costs increased as a result, leading the authors to conclude that cost savings tend to be a short-term outcome, while noting that coordination and quality concerns require longer-term assessment and maintenance.

This category of efficiency savings also must be offset by the transfer of services to the town. As Hattery (2015) explains, residents must consider the service activity (whether the same things covered), the cost (per unit and total, including transition costs), service characteristics (frequency, response times, quality), and continuity (any gaps or future loss of service provision). Ensuring that those who benefit from the services bear the expense additionally means that in dissolutions, special service and taxing districts may need to be created. NYCOM similarly cautions that the level of services, as well as the rate at which the service is provided, may also change post-dissolution. Shared services also impose their own transactional costs (time and monetary cost of negotiating, monitoring the agreements), coordination problems (complexities in coordinating, communicating, and allocating relative benefits and burdens between units), and noncommitment problems (defection or adversarial frictions) that offset the potential efficiency gains (Hawkins and Carr 2015). Opponents of consolidation argue that, in the long run, smaller local governments are more efficient in the tailoring and delivery of services (Haber 2008; Germa and Warner 2015).

The third category of potential savings from village dissolution includes "Operational, Contractual and Capital" expenses of separately maintained facilities or services, offset by any obligations, services, or debt that remains with the former village residents. The extent of the savings will vary by community. The sale of properties and equipment can be used to pay down debt or for the reduction of taxes. Not having to maintain separate facilities, utilities, and equipment, along with greater economies of scale, can translate into an overall cost savings that, in turn, can lower the local property tax burden on residents.

The last category of savings is new revenue from "Grants and Tax credits" that New York provides to communities that undertake dissolution or consolidation. The Citizen Empowerment Tax Credit (CETC) provides 15 percent of the combined levy of all municipal entities involved in the dissolution or consolidation, with a maximum award of $1 million annually. Per the law, at least 70 percent of such amount must go toward direct property tax relief. In addition to CETC, towns continue to receive the AIM funds of the former village. The 2022 fiscal year ending (FYE) executive budget indicates that, to date, twenty-six local governments have received more than $18 million in CETC funding. CETC funding is contingent on annual reappropriation. In the public debate, elected officials and residents voice concern that the CETC funding may be reduced or eliminated at some point in the future and are often skeptical that state-level incentives will be funded indefinitely.

The Department of State (DOS) is required to report the annual LGE and CREG-related grant expenditures and estimated savings under state finance law.[4] Between 2005 and 2018, the state awarded $94.2 million to fund 531 efficiency awards. Altogether, the DOS reported that the 531 awards were estimated to produce a savings of $639 million, or a $6.79 return for every $1.00 spent (New York Department of State 2018).

As summarized in figure 4.2, grants for the study and implementation of consolidation and dissolution account for 19.4 percent of the total awards at $4.8 million in state funding (excluding the $20 million MCEC grant to the town of Brookhaven) but only 1.6 percent of the *estimated savings*. The annual projected savings for some awards, such as Hermon's 2014 award of $50,000, have produced a small annual savings of only $7,402 (New York Department of State 2017, 4). Other projects result in more substantial savings: the implementation grants for the village of Keeseville in the towns of Chesterfield and Ausable, for example, produced a savings of $183,344 for a $100,000 investment of state grants (New York Department of State 2017, 4). Projects involving capital or infrastructure-related projects, on the other hand, produce a larger return on the investment. As the DOS notes, "consolidation and dissolution awards are often focused on developing the planning to meet statutory compliance and have not reported the savings accrued from reorganization implementation" (New York Department of State 2018, 8).

Assessing the tax impact is more complicated. The DOS divides the cost savings by the equalized value of the municipal tax base to produce a cost-savings rate per $1,000, which is then multiplied by the median home value of the municipality (New York Department of State 2010). State incentives and AIM increases are not factored into the analysis. By this calculation, the 2010 annual rate of return on the LGE program (for all categories of grants and awards) was 89 percent on onetime investments. From 2005 to 2007, the DOS reported an 824 percent return on all categories of grants and awards (New York Department of State 2007, 17). State data specific to dissolution and consolidation grants have not been clearly or consistently reported.

The fiscal impact in the years or decades after a village is dissolved is a question that New York has not tracked, studied, or funded. Once a municipality has dissolved, it drops out of the OSC financial reporting system, and its data are aggregated with the surrounding town (or towns). Aggregated data, even where performance benchmarks are tracked, make it difficult to determine whether all areas of the municipality are equally well served (Ammons 2012).

One could argue that when residents reject dissolution at the ballot box, it is prima facie evidence that they perceive the benefits of

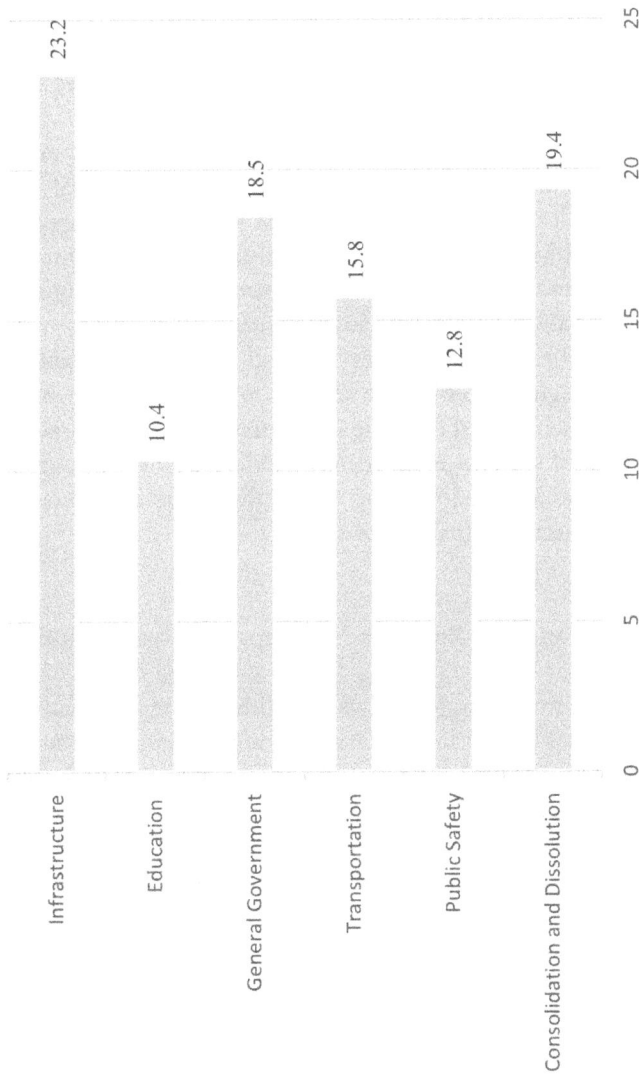

Figure 4.2. Local Government Efficiency and Citizen Reorganization Empowerment Grant Awards by Function: (2005–2018). *Source:* Author created table using data from New York Department of State. 2018. "SFY 2017–2018 Annual Report: Administration of Local Government Efficiency Program." October 2. Albany, New York: New York Department of State.

maintaining the incorporation as outweighing the costs. Even when the focus is on the value for services received, the costs may seem quite reasonable. For example, the mayor of the village of Perry broke it down for his constituents: the owner of a median-value home pays $32 a year for public works, $28.40 for public safety, $12.60 for village administration and management, and so forth (Hauser 2018). In Brockport, dissolution opponents compared the $.92 per day for village police services to the daily cost of a cup of coffee or cable television.

Brunori argues that "the logic of localism is grounded on two interrelated virtues that resonate with citizens." The first is that "local governments are efficient providers of the most visible, and many of the most important, public services." Second is that they "enhance and foster democratic values and civic participation" (Brunori 2007, 3). Consistent with public choice theory, then, residents arguably view their property tax burden as a deliberate choice in services and values. Simply put, they are willing to pay higher taxes for the services and perks that living in a village provides. When viewed from the local perspective, the tax rate may be worth the level of services received. When viewed through a broader statewide or regional lens, maintaining duplicative layers of general-purpose governments arguably makes less sense.

Fiscal Stress and the Push for Municipal Reorganization

State approaches to managing local fiscal conditions vary (Berman 2003, 113; Coe 2008). In New York, the OSC has long monitored the fiscal conditions of local governments by providing risk assessment of localities, by offering technical assistance and consultations, and through auditing and field visits to localities that they have flagged as problematic on key indicators. Special OSC reports have highlighted key issues or have focused on trends for a certain class of municipality, while routine auditing has singled out individual localities for in-depth review. Generally, New York's approach has been ad hoc, aiming to address local fiscal instability *before* it reached crisis proportions. In cases of acute stress or crisis, New York State has occasionally intervened through the appointment of hard fiscal control boards, as was the case of New York City in the 1970s and Erie County in 2005. In this way, New York has prevented localities from sliding toward municipal insolvency.

THE OSC FISCAL STRESS MONITORING SYSTEM

New York has generally defined fiscal stress as the inability of a locality to generate enough revenue to meet its service obligations on a continuing basis.[5] A healthy municipality should be able to maintain reasonable fund balance, to enact policies that will cushion it against variations in cash flow, to repay interfund transfers, to avoid short-term borrowing to fund operations or infrastructure, and to adopt multiyear financial planning that monitors and accounts for changing revenue and expenditure trends. Stressed municipalities, by contrast, struggle to stabilize their budgets, have low fund balances, and have an insufficient cash flow to pay their bills as they become due (Henderick 2011; Office of the New York State Comptroller 2013).

In 2012, the OSC systematized its monitoring efforts to offer early detection, joining thirty-seven other states in providing an early warning system for localities (Chapman and Ascanio 2020). The Fiscal Stress Monitoring System (FSMS) is an informational tool, compared with state intervention, that is designed to identify problems *before* they reach a crisis point (Shankse 2017). The FSMS evaluates and weighs multiple indicators in the calculation of scores, assigning designations of no stress (44.0 points/percent and below), susceptible to stress (45 to 54.9 points/percent), moderate stress (55 to 64.9 points/percent), and significant fiscal stress (for localities scoring 65 to 100 points/percent on the stress scale). The classification "no designation" indicates that the municipality does not meet the criteria to be assigned a stress rating but does not "imply that the entity is free of all fiscal stress conditions" (Office of New York State Comptroller 2017e, 5). The classification "susceptible to fiscal stress" was developed to identify units that are exhibiting conditions that may lead them into fiscal stress in the short term. Moderate and significant stress designations indicate that the locality is currently experiencing stress according to the indicators monitored. The FSMS defines communities in chronic stress as those earning a stress designation for three or more years.[6] Revisions were made to the FSMS scoring system for 2015 and again starting in 2018, which means that the reporting of data is not comparable across years.[7]

A 2013 OSC report identified some common themes for village governments. Among their frequent fiscal woes were low fund balances and operating deficits (Office of the New York State Comptroller 2013b).

Of the fifteen villages identified as fiscally stressed that year, most had low liquidity and heavier reliance on short-term debt. McDonald (2017) affirms that the New York FSMS fiscal scores are heavily impacted by three primary drivers: low fund balances (FSMS indicators 1 and 2), operating deficits (indicator 3), and low cash levels (indicators 4 and 5). The fund balance provides an indication of how well a locality can handle revenue shortfalls and expenditure overruns. Fund balances can be restricted or unrestricted and include resources remaining from prior fiscal years that can be used as funding sources in the next year's budget to reduce the amount of revenues needed.[8] Adequate fund balances also provide sufficient cash flow to allow for timing differences between revenue receipt and expenditure disbursements, contain a reserve for unforeseen expenses, and ensure that service levels can be maintained during shortfalls. Fund balances thus should be utilized per policies that reflect short- and long-term fiscal planning strategies. Proper management ensures that property tax levies reflect current funding needs (i.e., are not higher than necessary). Because villages tend to have smaller budgets, their fund balances are smaller than city or county governments. "Consequently, the sharp decrease in these nominally small rainy-day reserves means towns and villages generally have fewer financial choices when faced with rapid increases in regular costs, constraints on raising revenue, or unexpected events" (Office of the New York State Comptroller 2017d, 6; 2017c).

The operating deficit indicates whether the municipality was able to meet its expenditures in that budgetary year—a significant operating deficit is more than 10 percent of expenditures. Multiple years of operating deficits signal those revenues are not sufficient to support recurring expenditures. The cash ratio measures whether the locality has enough cash flow to cover its ongoing expenditures while awaiting revenue or whether short-term borrowing is required each year or as a trend. Stressed communities are more likely to rely on short-term debt (RANS, TANS, budget notes) and tend to over-rely on borrowing when they have small fund reserves and operating deficits). Other OSC indicators (FSMS Indicators 8 and 9) capture the fixed costs of the municipality, including revenues required for personnel services, employee benefits, and debt service. Higher fixed costs reduce fiscal flexibility in responding to variable pressures. Overall, the fixed costs (staffing and debt service), particularly salaries and employee benefits when measured as a percentage of village revenue, have been growing steadily.

The FSMS also calculates environmental scores, indicators that may "pose challenges to the fiscal health of a municipality," including declining property values, population loss, population age, poverty rates, unemployment, state aid, and other "demographic and resource-related measures" (Office of the New York State Comptroller 2017c, 9). Localities are assigned the same designations categories used for fiscal stress (i.e., no designation, susceptible to environmental stress, moderate environmental stress, or significant environmental stress) based on the OSC scoring system. Environmental scoring has also been revised, and substantially so for FYE 2017 data. It is important to note that the environmental scores *are not factored into the fiscal warning designations*. But understanding environmental stressors does provide insight for local budgeting context and the economic challenges that villages face.

Population loss, for example, is recognized as a major environmental factor contributing to fiscal stress. Depopulation is associated with the loss of industry, declining economic opportunities, the deterioration of housing stock, declining property valuations, and a residential base that is smaller, older, poorer, and has higher service needs. Changes in median age and child poverty rates are also included as indicators of environmental stress. Population demographics are directly related to the community's property tax base and property values. The "root cause of municipal fiscal crisis is the decline in personal and corporate income, retail sales, and property values, all of which comprise the main tax bases" for municipal government (Ingram and Hong 2010, 23). Population loss and demographic challenges may lead to an erosion of the property tax base and loss of revenue even as expenditure needs rise.

Environmental risk scores do not correlate with the fiscal stress scores as calculated by the OSC: "The results indicated only a .13 correlation coefficient between the fiscal stress score and the environmental variable score for the cities and a lesser amount of correlation (.015) for the group of counties" (Bronner 2016). The data for villages from 2018 and 2019 replicate Bronner's (2016) finding, with a correlation coefficient between fiscal and environmental stress scores of .028 and .036 for 2018 and 2019, respectively. The lack of correlation suggests that environmental factors do not account for the differences in the fiscal stress experienced by local municipalities. As the OSC explains, while "villages in fiscal stress rate highly on many environmental stress indicators, they do not always differ dramatically from villages that have no stress designation. For example, *nearly all villages are struggling with high unemployment and job losses, and more than half are experiencing population loss*" (Office of New York State Comptroller 2013b, 4). The same is true for growing child poverty rates.

Where the OSC did find a difference between stressed and non-stressed villages in 2013 was with respect to property value: "Two-thirds of fiscally stressed villages have low and/or declining property values (measured as a trend in full value and full value per capita) compared with fewer than half (44.6 percent) of villages with no designations. This is mostly a downstate occurrence." (Office of New York State Comptroller 2013b, 4). Stressed downstate villages are growing at a slower rate than are their non-stressed peers. But the OSC has concluded that the "environmental factors driving stress downstate appear to be more related to their relatively low property wealth and relative high poverty rates compared with other neighboring villages" (Office of New York State Comptroller 2013b, 5). Of those upstate villages with stress designations, only four had higher property values and lower child poverty rates than their no-designation counterparts (Office of New York State Comptroller 2013b, 5).

THE FINANCIAL RESTRUCTURING BOARD FOR LOCAL GOVERNMENTS

The state provides a variety of resources for training and assistance aimed at improving local capacity, including opportunities for state-level review for communities that register as stressed. In 2013, the Financial Restructuring Board (FRB) for Local Governments was created to help distressed local governments restructure and regain solvency before the strict enforcement of a control board is needed. The FRB assesses the local government's operations, finances, and management structure to make recommendations to improve the local government's finances and efficiency and may offer grants and/or loans through the LGE program to implement the recommendations. To receive the aid, the local government must agree to fulfill the terms of the recommendations.

Local governments are automatically eligible for review if they have either an average full value property tax rate that is greater than the average full value property tax rate of 75 percent of other municipalities or if they have an average fund balance that falls below 5 percent. The FRB may include municipalities not automatically on the eligibility list on a case-by-case basis. Additionally, non-automatically eligible localities can request to be reviewed. The eligibility metrics for FRB are less refined than FSMS designations. For the period of 2011 to 2015, almost one-third (177) of villages automatically qualified for review: 171 of these qualified on full property tax criteria and 8 on the fund balance. Three villages automatically qualified on both metrics (Amityville, Catskill, and Solvay). Another forty-seven villages did not report the data necessary for the calculation. For 2013–2017, 31.9 percent of villages automatically qualified, compared to only 13.3 percent of towns, 49.1 percent of counties, and 73.5 percent of cities. Another three qualified on both criteria (Amityville, Andover, Catskill). A total of 7.6 percent of villages were missing data, including several with dissolution activity.

Despite the high number of eligible villages, only seven villages (as of this writing) have undergone FRB review. Collectively, the comprehensive review of those seven villages does not support a direct connection between fiscal stress and dissolution. Of the seven villages to request review, only Potsdam (board-initiated) and Wilson (citizen-initiated) had dissolution activity, with both rejecting dissolution in 2011 and 2014, respectively. Indeed, the FRB's recommendation to consider dissolution appears to be a default and perfunctory recommendation in all cases, lacking the detail of a full-blown dissolution study.

THE INTERNAL CAPACITY OF VILLAGE GOVERNMENTS

The fiscal and environmental scores calculated by the FSMS do not directly measure internal capacity of village governments—whether there is adequate fiscal skill or oversight for sound fiscal management. The audits routinely performed by the OSC provide a keyhole into municipal functioning.[9] Collectively, their findings suggest that necessary skills and training may be lacking, particularly with respect to clerk-treasurer roles and lax board oversight.

OSC audits are generally preceded by a risk assessment process and may take one of three forms: 1) internal control, or accountability audits, which review and test adherence to policies and procedures; 2) performance, or financial condition audits, which identify potential cost savings; or 3) budget reviews, which examine whether the local government's preliminary budget is supported, reasonable, and balanced. The audit period can span months or years and involves field work investigation by OSC staff. Localities may respond with a Corrective Action Plan (CAP) to address specific recommendations in the OSC report.

Huefner (2011) reviewed more than 300 village and town audits from 2003 to 2009, finding that "all but a handful of these public entities exhibit numerous governance and control issues" (21). Villages averaged 26 percent more deficiencies than towns ("an average over the seven years of 7.89 findings for villages compared to 3.27 for towns" (26). He argued that the rate of errors represents a preventable cost to the community, suggesting "substantial room for improvement" (27).

Village audits spanning 2013–21 reveal a similarly high rate of adverse findings for village governments.[10] Of 255 audits (excluding nineteen budget reviews and five follow-up audits), only seven concluded without any findings warranting a recommendation for improvement. In other words, *97 percent of the village audits resulted in at least one deficient finding.* The reports identify several common themes, including insufficient oversight by the village boards of trustees, poor record keeping by clerk-treasurers, a lack of segregation between the clerk and treasurer's duties, failures in reporting that result in inaccurate fiscal projections, and fund imbalances to the detriment of sound long-term planning. Six cases (2 percent) reveal a lack of training and capacity that belies the romanticized view of local governance.

Heufner (2011) further found little evidence of a "learning effect" in the seven-year span of his study. Data from 2013 to 2021 support that finding as well.[11] Of the twenty-three communities that were audited more than once, only one (Voorheesville) had a clean audit (albeit the first, but not the second time around). There were another five follow-up audits conducted in that time span. Ballston Spa (2017) made modest progress, implementing in full or part nine of thirteen recommendations resulting from its earlier audit (2017M-256-F). In South Glens Falls, only one of two recommendations was partially implemented (2014M-102-F). Victory made less progress: of its eight recommendations, two were implemented, four partially implemented, and two were not (2010M-35-F). Harriman, on the other hand, succeeded in implementing two of the four OSC recommendations in full, and the other two in part (2001M-182-F). And, finally, Webster managed to implement seven of its eight recommendations, with the other partially implemented (2012M-110F).

Devas, Blore, and Slater (2014) identify four classes of municipalities: those that are dynamic (having both strong leadership with the requisite skills base), challenged (having strong leadership but with weak skills), frustrated (strong skills but weak leadership), and failed (both weak leadership and skills) (2004, 14). Findings from the OSC audits suggest that few villages meet the dynamic category. Shanske (2017) identifies the lack of fiscal expertise and training generally as a significant concern for local governance. He writes: "Local democracies are an excellent means of having communities decide for themselves what kind of places they wish to be, but they are not an excellent means of deciding on all the financial details required to achieve their vision" (825).

Fiscal Stress and Village Dissolution Activity in New York

Villages and towns are overall in less danger of fiscal stress than are city and county governments, as detailed in table 4.1. Indeed, the number of local governments in fiscal stress has declined in the last few years (even as the pace of dissolution has increased). Despite improvements in overall fiscal health, the OSC urges caution as local governments continue to face multiple risks and uncertainties (Office of New York State Comptroller 2017). Moreover, survey-grounded research confirms that municipalities self-report far higher rates of stress than is captured by the FSMS designations (Aldag, Warner, and Kim 2017, 2).[12]

FISCAL STRESS DESIGNATIONS AND DISSOLUTION

FSMS stress designations do not correlate with dissolution activity. Of the sixty-seven villages to hold a referendum on dissolution since 2000, only two (Potsdam and Cherry Creek) received a designation under the FSMS in the years 2015 to 2017. As detailed in chart 4.2, a simple correlation

Table 4.1. Percentage of municipalities with OSC Fiscal Stress designations (2013–2020)

	2013	2014	2015	2016	2017	2018	2019	2020
Villages	3.2%	4.4%	3.7%	1.8%	2.0%	1.6%	1.5%	.01%
Towns	1.9%	2.4%	2.3%	1.3%	1.1%	.82%	1.3%	0%
Cities	13.5%	25.9%	20.0%	18.5%	14.5%	22.6%	11.5%	.5%
Counties	18.5%	21.4%	18.5%	15.1%	17.9%	14.3%	12.7%	0%

Data source: Office of the New York State Comptroller (2020b).

Source: Author created table using data from Office of the New York State Comptroller. 2020b. Fiscal Stress Monitoring System: Municipalities Fiscal Year 2019 Results; Fiscal Year 2020 Risks." Albany, New York: Office of New York State Comptroller.

test shows no relationship between various OSC indicators and dissolution activity since 2010 (where cases in which a petition drive was initiated, public meetings on dissolution were held, a study was undertaken, or the village received a New York State study grant are coded as 1; a formal vote rejecting dissolution is coded as 2; and a formal vote to approve dissolution is coded as 3). In other words, there is no correlation between a village's fiscal stress or environmental scores (captured in the period of 2017 to 2020), nor is there a correlation between fiscal stress measured as a continuous variable and dissolution activity ordinally ranked in the period between 2010 and 2021.

Nor is there a relationship between post-2010 dissolution activity and a village exceeding 75 percent of its constitutional tax or debt limits or registering as eligible for FRB (all of which were coded as simple dummy variables). The constitutional tax limit restricts the total amount of taxes levied each year and is calculated by multiplying a municipality's five-year average full valuation by 2 percent (Office of the New York State Comptroller 2020c). The tax limit differs from the property tax cap (which restricts year-to-year increase in tax levy). Villages are subject to both the constitutional taxing limit and (since 2012) to the property tax cap.[13] Fewer than 3 percent of all villages, on average, exceed 75 percent of the constitutional tax limit. Of these twenty-nine villages, 51 percent had chronic tax limit issues (three or more consecutive years), and 48 percent had dissolution activity in this same period. Six of the twenty-nine voted on dissolution, with only two voting in favor (Lyons and Hermon, the latter of which exceeded the limit only once, in 2010).

Approaching the constitutional debt limit is similarly viewed as an indicator of poor fiscal condition.[14] Between 2005 and 2018, sixty-six villages exceeded the constitutional debt limit. Only 9 percent exceeded their limit for three or more consecutive years. Of these, only five had dissolution activity (Alexander Bay, Cayuga, Ellenville, Portville, and Whitehall), and one (Cuba) voted on the issue, rejecting dissolution in 2010.

Casting the net even more broadly to include all post-2000 dissolution activity (this time coded as a simple dummy variable) increases the correlation coefficient for the 75 percent of the tax limit variable but still produces only a weak positive correlation of .28753. This exploration of a possible linkage between fiscal stress and dissolution activity is searching *only* for a correlation between various metrics of stress and dissolution activity and is not conditioned on the indicator data *preceding* the dissolution activity, so one also cannot infer causation (that one was the direct temporal cause of the other). Rather, it is broadly looking for any possible correlation between the two (i.e., does registering on any of these indicators at some point correlate with having dissolution activity at some point?) (see table 4.2).

Table 4.2. Correlation coefficients between dissolution activity and OSC fiscal indicators

	Dissolution Activity (Dummy 1/0) From 2000–21	Dissolution Activity from 2010–21 (1=activity, 2=Failed, 3=Successful
2017–20 Average Fiscal Stress Score (Continuous Value)	.03775 (Pearson)	.02306 (Pearson)
2017–20 Average Environmental Scores (Continuous Value)	.12063 (Pearson)	.06119 (Pearson)
75% Debt Limit Exceeded (2005–18) (Dummy 1/0)	−.04542 (Pearson) −.045 (Tau) −.045 (Rho)	−.05387 (Pearson) −.039 (Rho)
75% of Constitutional Tax Limit (2005–19) (Dummy 1/0)	.28753 (Pearson) .224 (Tau) .224 (Rho)	.12256 (Pearson) .158 (Tau) −.162 (Rho)
MRF Eligibility (2013–17) (Dummy 1/0)	.15788 (Pearson) .158 (Tau) .158 (Rho)	.10893 (Pearson) .114 (Tau) .118 (Rho)

Dissolution Activity: the issue of dissolution was considered (a petition drive was initiated, public meetings held, a study undertaken, or a state grant received) but there was *insufficient mobilization or support to proceed to formal action* (there was not a successful petition or resolution to move it to a public vote). There are 69 such cases in the data set (35 of which are post-2010).

Unsuccessful (Failed) Dissolutions: dissolution was put to a formal vote and was defeated in a public referendum or else in a permissive referendum.

Successful (Approved) Dissolution: dissolution was put to a formal vote and approved by village residents and was not subject to, or survived, a permissive referendum.

N=550. Original data set by author.

Although dissolution is frequently linked to fiscal stress in the public discourse, there is no significant correlation between the most frequent metrics of fiscal stress and dissolution activity or success, or to municipal bankruptcy (McDonald 2017, 1, 11–12). In some cases, mismanagement or fiscal concerns certainly do drive the effort to dissolve. But the point at which fiscal stress reaches crisis level is neither well understood nor clearly demarcated in the literature on municipal finance. Moreover, there are many fiscally stressed villages in which dissolution has never made it onto the public agenda, much less the ballot.

The data from New York State suggest that *fiscal stress alone* is not sufficient to spark dissolution activity. It should also be noted that villages can move in and out of stress designations quickly, and several villages swung more than thirty points in their FSMS scoring within a three-year period. "Towns and villages, especially if they are small, are particularly susceptible to large score changes, since even relatively small changes in revenues or expenditures from year to year may cause them to run operating deficits or experience a decline in fund balance, which are both major factors in determining fiscal stress" (Office of the New York State Comptroller 2016, 8).

RELATIVE TAX BURDENS AND DISSOLUTION

Experts at the Office of Local Government Services suggested that dissolution occurs when the village government is essentially moribund (provides few, if any, services) or where property taxes are higher than in adjacent municipalities so as to be perceived by residents as out of line.[15] In other words, it is the perception of relative burden compared with neighboring villages or the relative level of services received. However, an examination of the full-value tax rate of villages from 2009 to 2019 finds only a weak correlation between dissolution activity and property tax burdens that are above the county average (as measured by the full-value village tax rate per $1,000). There is dissolution activity in 29.3 percent of those villages in which the full-value tax rate average is above their county average for the 2009–19 period. In villages that fall below their county average, 18 percent have had some type of dissolution activity.

County rank in village taxes also does not correlate with dissolution activity or success. For example, there was no dissolution activity in Yates County and only one dissolution in Wyoming County, despite those counties having the second- and third-highest county averages for village full taxation rates, respectively. There are examples, of course, of dissolution activity in a few villages that rank toward the top for their county in terms of their full-value tax rates. For example, two of the ten villages in Allegany County had dissolution activity in the period of 2009 to 2019. Cuba (dissolution defeated in 2010) had, at that time, the second-highest village tax rate in the county. Alfred (which underwent FRB review in 2014) had the fourth-highest average rate in the 2009–19 period. Wellsville (which rejected dissolution in 2006) had the highest average tax rate across the entire decade. In 2006, Wellsville studied reincorporating as a city among restructuring options—a step towards sharing in the distribution of county sales tax revenue. In Broome County, Johnson City had the second-highest village tax rate out of the county's seven villages (it rejected dissolution in 2009). The only other Broome County village with dissolution activity (a stalled petition in 2007), however, was below the county average.

In a handful of cases, a higher than average (for the county) village tax rate, or a sudden increase in the tax rate, explains why dissolution efforts were initiated. In Chautauqua County, for example, the successful dissolutions of Forestville (in 2015) and Cherry Creek (in 2017) followed a jump in the village tax rate of 195 percent and 104 percent, respectively (from 2009 to the year preceding the dissolution activity). Yet Forestville's full value tax rate was below the average for Chautauqua villages. Similarly in Wayne County, the two successful dissolutions reveal that Lyons (at an average of $19.02) was above the county average (of $11.08), while Macedon (at an average of $4.92) was well below. Moreover, there are several examples where a similar annual increase in the village full-value tax rate of 100 percent or more does not lead to observable dissolution activity.

Overall, higher village taxes relative to county peers does not appear to be a good explanation of dissolution activity. Nor does dissolution activity appear to be correlated with the village share of the taxes measured as a percentage of the all-in full-value tax rate (i.e., the combined cost of county, town, village, and school district taxes). Based on OSC data from 2009–12, the median of the four-year average of the villages' share of the total full-value assessment was 18.56 percent. Of the top one-hundred villages (in which the village share ranged from 29.25 percent to 48.71 percent of the total full-value assessment), only ten voted on dissolution and only one voted to dissolve. Another sixteen had dissolution activity at some point (not limited to the 2009–12 range of the tax share data). Thus, dissolution activity (broadly captured by including all years of activity from the 1990s to the present) is not correlated with village share of the all-in full-value tax burden as captured for the 2009–12 period.

Similarly, sorting villages by the differential between village and town taxes (village full value minus the town full value) from highest to lowest values does not reveal any correlation with dissolution activity (as measured across all years from the 1990s to the present). Of the one hundred villages with the highest average differentials between 2009 and 2012, thirteen voted on dissolution and only two voted to dissolve. Another thirteen had dissolution activity insufficient to make it onto the ballot (in all years). Thus, even casting the broadest net possible and relaxing any conditions of temporal ordering, the data do not hint at any statistical association between relative tax rates and dissolution activity.

Pandemic Pressures and Dissolution

If fiscal stress is causally linked to municipal reorganization, one might expect an uptick in dissolution activity as localities grappled with the fiscal realities of COVID. That is, a sudden economic downturn should theoretically lead more communities to consider reorganization as a possible solution to fiscal pressure. First, the quest to find efficiencies may lead localities in the direction of more intermunicipal cooperation or shared service agreements. Once such cooperation develops, it is an arguably shorter step toward a structural merger as the pathway to longer-term savings.[16] Second, in times of stress, we can anticipate more of what local government scholars refer to as "scalar dumping"—the downward shift of state fiscal pressures onto their local governments. Such pressure can potentially crowd out local efficiencies and growth, deter infrastructure investment, or result in deferred maintenance, all of which can add to long-term fiscal woes (Aldag and Warner 2018b; 2019). As stress cumulatively worsens, restructuring options may become increasingly more attractive or—in some cases—perhaps even inevitable.

Almost a quarter of villages between 2017 and 2019 had been running with two or three years of operational deficits, making them even more vulnerable to the external shock of the pandemic-related drop in revenues.[17] Indeed, New York was facing significant state-level fiscal woes even prior to becoming the epicenter of the COVID-19 crisis in the spring of 2020. The proposed budget (released in January 2020) had projected a $6.1 billion gap. By March, the executive order for a statewide shutdown resulted in a precipitous decline in municipal revenues.[18] As the April 1 budgeting deadline approached, the Division of the Budget (DOB) projected a $60.1 billion budget gap through FYE 2024.

The budget, as enacted, closed the anticipated shortfall through a multiplicity of approaches, including authorization of up to $8 billion in reductions to local aid—a step that had "no precedent in modern times" (FYE 2021 Enacted Budget 2020, 16). The budget provided that, if tax receipts came in lower than anticipated at specified periods, the state budget director could reduce local aid by "any amount needed to achieve a balanced budget" (FYE 2021 Enacted Budget 2020, 13).[19]

In March 2020, the federal government enacted several fiscal relief measures, the most significant of which was the Coronavirus Aid, Relief, and Economic Security Act (CARES Act) (P.L. 116–1360, March 27, 2020). The CARES Act provided direct funding to the states as well as to local governments with populations over 500,000.[20] Collectively, these early federal measures buffered states against the worst of the economic impacts, although New York's governor declared that the support simply was not enough.

The DOB began withholding 20 percent of AIM to localities and 20 percent of CETC payments to eligible governments in June 2020. Local government efficiency programs, including CREG study and implementation grants, were also suspended. The OLGS advised that if the funds eventually became available, the state would provide a look-back until April 1, allowing any consolidation or dissolution to be potentially covered, in part, by those grants. But Governor Cuomo warned that without additional federal assistance, those withholdings would be made permanent.

Additional federal action was delayed in Congress by the sticking point of state and local assistance. Congressional Republicans objected to a so-called "blue state" bailout, with the Senate majority leader suggesting that Congress should simply let the states "go bankrupt"—something that is not authorized by federal bankruptcy law. Cuomo, who gained national acclaim for his then-daily pandemic response briefings, sparred publicly with national Republicans, daring them to allow states to default on their debt in the middle of a national health crisis. For his critics at home, the governor was only postponing fiscal reckoning by betting on a federal bailout.

When the Coronavirus Response and Relief Supplemental Appropriations Act (CRRSA, P.L. 16-260, December 27, 2020) was finally passed, it was a slimmed-down compromise measure of $900 billion that did not include direct aid for states and localities, leaving the struggling states and municipalities perched on the edge of a fiscal cliff. New York's municipalities were encouraged by the OSC to engage in robust budget planning, but many local leaders felt abandoned by the state and resentful of the strategy of closing its budget gap through the reduction of local assistance.

The external shock of the pandemic thus set up something of a natural experiment: theoretically, the additional pressure brought on by the pandemic might inspire (or push) financially struggling communities to seriously consider dissolution or consolidation as a way out of the looming crisis. On the other hand, state-level woes also meant that there was even greater uncertainty with respect to the reliability of state-level incentives. Three New York villages held dissolution votes in this post-pandemic period, providing some insight into how fiscal pressure may (or may not) impact local government restructuring.

In the village of Spencer (Tioga County), a citizen petition was submitted in early 2020. An interim study, completed in April by the Laberge Group, concluded that residents would not see any savings *unless* 100 percent of the CETC were made available for property tax relief. If the CETC were not applied, then village taxes were projected *to increase* post-dissolution.[21] As COVID-19 infection rates trended alarmingly upward, Governor Cuomo had exercised his emergency power to postpone elections.[22] The referendum was thus rescheduled to September, after the state had begun withholding 20 percent of local government assistance. In advance of the vote, the Laberge Group reminded residents that CETC (always contingent on annual legislative appropriation and now reduced) was in no way guaranteed. It advised residents not to "count on the state being able to fulfill any incentive-payment promises" (Marx 2020b). Local media echoed that message, reminding voters that, because the state had suspended CREG grants, Spencer residents were already "on the hook for $25,000, Laberge's fee, paid upfront." (Marx 2020).

The voters rejected dissolution by an overwhelming margin of 198–21 (90.4 percent opposed). According to the mayor, many residents "were ready to vote 'yes' on principle because they believe in smaller, more efficient government or do not believe we need a village police department. However, when they listened to the Laberge Group's report and heard the tax increase projections, they changed their minds" (Marx 2020c). Between a possible tax increase, the cost of the dissolution study for which they might not be reimbursed, and doubts over the reliability of CETC funding, there simply was no fiscal incentive for residents to dissolve. That the citizen petition (filed prior to the onset of pandemic disruptions) had forced the question to a mandatory vote added to residents' seeming resentment of the process.

Dissolution talk had been ongoing for decades in Chaumont (Jefferson County), driven by growing fiscal concerns and resident apathy. In 1999, the village board sent a poll to residents to determine support for dissolving: 60 percent of residents were opposed.[23] A decade later, Chaumont applied for and received a $45,000 grant to study dissolution. That board-initiated dissolution study, contracted to CRG and completed in 2012, predicted a 49 percent decrease in village property taxes (Village of Chaumont Dissolution Study and Dissolution Plan, July 2012, 47). Although they had advanced the issue to a public vote, local officials expressed uncertainty about state incentives and the town's implementation of the plan. Residents voted it down with 61 percent opposition. The needle of public support had not moved.

In 2019, the Chaumont board passed another resolution to put dissolution up for a public vote. As the long-time mayor noted, "every year, we just don't have enough money, and we have too much to do, and it just got to the point where we feel this layer of government probably should go" (Chapman 2019). With the support of a $35,000 CREG grant (awarded in 2018), a DANC study conservatively reported that village residents would see their taxes cut by as much as 50 percent, with a small increase for TOV residents—a similar finding to CRG's 2012 report. On November 3, 2020, 53 percent of residents again voted against dissolving. Expressing surprise at the outcome, the mayor insisted that it was not a wasted effort: "What we will try to do is, we will take advantage of that dissolution study that we all went through and try to see if we can glean anything from that to possibly do some more shared services . . . [and identify] where we can save money for the village taxpayer" (Gault 2020).

The only village to approve dissolution amid the pandemic was South Nyack (Rockland County). While the effort was initially motivated by potential tax savings, arguably it was the sale of a former college site to an ultra-Orthodox developer that was the biggest factor driving many residents' votes. By dissolving, residents could "up-volve" any anticipated land-use controversies to the town of Orangetown, which many residents believed was better equipped and had more "financial muscle" to deal with the anticipated litigation (Traster 2021).

The first proposed consolidation of a preexisting village and town to be initiated under the Empowerment Act also took place in the shadow of the pandemic. Through a citizen petition, the proposed consolidation of the village and town of Pawling (Dutchess County) went to a public vote. Whereas only village residents vote on dissolution, the approval of both town and village residents is required for a consolidation. In a consolidation, one entity may absorb the other, or both entities may be terminated and a new consolidated entity created, operating either as a joint town-village entity, as a town, or as a town functioning primarily as a village. In a town-village consolidation, the law requires that the territory of the two be contiguous. Because a town cannot be dissolved and a village cannot exist outside the borders of a town, consultants to the village of Pawling (the Laberge Group) argued that continuing any newly consolidated entity as a village was not an option. Moreover, they cited a 2006 legal memorandum to conclude that a coterminous town-village would not meet the definition of consolidation under Article 17-A insofar as both would continue to exist as legal entities (New York Department of State 2006). State Finance Law (enacted in 2012), however, provided that if a town and village become coterminous after July 1, 2012, the town may seek CETC as the "surviving municipality" of the two (L. 2019, Ch. 435). "Upon signing this legislation, the Governor issued an approval message, memorializing the Legislature's commitment to enact a chapter amendment to require a new coterminous town-village to choose to operate principally *either as a town or village*, in order to ensure that the tax benefit would be available to actual consolidation and efficiency measures" (New York State Department of Taxation and Finance 2012, 4, emphasis added). Nevertheless, the consultants emphasized the legal uncertainty, warning that, if approved, lengthy and costly litigation was more than likely. They pointed out that there were no examples of successful Empowerment Act consolidations to follow and that the pandemic-related suspension of the CREG program (along with withholdings in AIM and CETC funding) left the state's support in doubt. The process would be "time consuming, complex and *expensive*" (Laberge Group 2020, 5, emphasis added). Indeed, the initial study and vote were estimated to cost between $50,000 and $80,000 (Codero 2020). Creation and implementation of a consolidation plan was estimated to be another $365,000 to $500,000. Without certainty of reimbursement by the state, it was characterized as a "huge risk."[24]

Pawling's consolidation proponents had patterned their efforts on successful village dissolution movements, focusing on a message of One Pawling, potential cost savings, and regional planning advantages. Their campaign was aggressively countered by village of Pawling officials who additionally warned that that village residents (who were roughly 40 percent of the total town population) would lose their political representation and suffer a diminution in their level of services as a result of consolidating (Village of Pawling 2020).

Voters rejected the consolidation. The higher level of town support (27.7 percent in favor versus only 13.4 percent support from village residents) was notable given that the preliminary study had emphasized a shift of the tax burden to TOV residents, who would see their taxes increase unless CETC were applied (Laberge 2020, 19). One interpretation was that more town voters saw an advantage in exploring shared services and efficiencies. For village residents, who stood to gain more financially, the loss of identity coupled with the uncertainties was just too great.

With the eased pathway for consolidation and dissolution of municipal units and mounting fiscal pressure stemming from the COVID-19 crisis, one might have expected an increase in public support for municipal consolidations and dissolution efforts. On the surface, the dissolution of South Nyack reflects an economically struggling community pushed to crisis by the additional fiscal pressures created by the pandemic. But it is not clear that savings alone would have been a sufficient catalyst without community concerns related to the sale of the local college and anticipated conflict over land-use and zoning issues.

Because sales revenues had come in stronger than expected, the governor announced in April 2021 that the state would pay back some of the withheld local aid payments as receipts allowed—but that still left a 5 percent reduction in AIM for New York's municipalities (Office of New York State Comptroller 2021). More worrisome for local governments was that the FYE 2022 executive budget proposal called for shifting the 137 remaining towns and villages from receiving direct AIM payment to AIM-related payments funded out of the counties' share of the sales tax, with a 20 percent overall reduction effective as of July 2021.[25] Under the proposed budget, cities would continue to receive AIM payments reduced overall by 5 percent, with cuts to individual cities ranging from 2.5 percent to 20 percent (depending on their AIM dependency, with less dependent communities subject to higher reductions). Other local aid programs would be subject to a 5 percent cut, and video lottery terminal (VLT) aid was slated to be eliminated for all localities aside from the city of Yonkers. Consolidation programs and initiatives, however, remained funded in the executive budget proposals albeit with a 5 percent reduction (assuming federal assistance did not fully materialize).

From the local government perspective, such cuts only add to the existing fiscal pressures on municipalities.[26] Counties particularly resented the diversion of state sales tax to fund state aid to localities. Legislative negotiations restored full AIM and AIM-related funding for towns and villages in the enacted budget (although it should be noted that the shift from direct AIM to AIM-related payments for most villages that was previously enacted in 2019 remained a permanent change).

The passage of the American Rescue Plan (ARP) in 2021 provided an additional $350 billion in state and local government assistance, alleviating New York's budgetary woes and averting cuts in local assistance. Indeed, some local governments found themselves suddenly awash in cash. The influx of federal stimulus funding, however, will expire in FYE 2024, and it is unclear whether state or local officials will adjust long-range choices to ease fiscal pressures on localities. In short, the pressure may have ratcheted down suddenly, but is likely to reemerge if long-term fiscal stability is not properly addressed at both the state and local levels.

The Tenuous Connection between Fiscal Stress and Municipal Reorganization

In New York State, the public's "understanding of local government fiscal stress has been dominated by the governor's narrative of too many inefficient units of local government" (Aldag and Warner 2017, 6). The state-level message has been that the way to save the taxpayers' money is fewer governmental entities making do with less. Dissolution is sometimes presented as a consequence of "economic decline and budgetary collapse" or else framed as a means of avoiding municipal bankruptcy, of ending it rather than fixing it (Anderson 2012, 138).[27] Even when touted as a progressive step, there is an underlying assumption that smaller units have inferior capacity. Dissolving, in other words, is a means of transferring or "up-vovling" policy control to a larger government that is capable of greater efficiency and economies of scale (Wachhaus 2014, 1121). A 1994 report by the Allegheny County, Pennsylvania, controller, for example, hailed voluntary disincorporation as a "new idea" for community renewal, a way of "reclaiming hope" when local governments have lost the capacity to provide services or function as a separate municipality (Lucchino 1994). Such messaging still implicitly links dissolution to fiscal stress or diminished capacity.

Zhang (2019) concludes that "dissolution is more likely to be considered and approved in a village where the economy struggles, the population declines, political trust undermines, and fiscal health deteriorates. In other words, the research suggests dissolution may not be as appealing or taking place in economically strong and politically dynamic areas" (941). Zhang's conceptual framework thus equates dissolution with municipal death: "Similar to how the death of a patient implies the end of a life, dissolution translates to the end of a village government's existence (Zhang 2019, 924). Utilizing survival analysis, he compares economic, demographic, and fiscal variables of voting and non-voting villages to find that the phenomenon is nonrandom.[28] Those villages that vote to dissolve tend to be economically struggling and homogenous (small)—conclusions also reached by Hattery (1998) and Boyd (2008). Zhang explains that "economic decline and depopulation" make a village susceptible to dissolution activity, whereas "a populous and wealthy village is likely to have a longer life span" (927). Neither conclusion is likely to be surprising to close observers of local government in New York State. Indeed, the barriers to any merger of services and units are higher in larger, more culturally diverse, or economically heterogenous communities (Creswell and Creswell 2015).

Given the low number of municipal reorganizations to study, assessing the predictive association between fiscal or environmental stress and reorganization is, however, difficult. While there is an extensive body of academic research on municipal fiscal stress, there is no universally agreed-on definition or uniform method of monitoring or intervening by state governments (Menifield 2017, 188). Poor fiscal health can result from a multitude of factors, some of which are unique to that municipality or else beyond local control.

Scholarship further suggests that local perceptions of stress may not necessarily match the reality of the objective indicators. Researchers, for example, have found "no statistical relationship between officials' perception of fiscal stress and empirical measures of fiscal stress" (Maher and Deller 2007, 1549). Perception, in other words, may be more important than reality. Moreover, stress may be differently regarded by the elected officials who manage municipal affairs than by the citizens who exercise restructuring approval at the ballot box. Residents are not likely to be familiar with their village's balance sheets but are sensitive to their own property tax assessments. And, as Aldag, Warner, and Kim (2017) note, "coalitions at the local level can help generate an alternative narrative about the true causes of local fiscal stress," effectively arguing for alternatives to dissolution as the solution to fiscal woes. Relatedly, the easiest targets for reorganization (villages) have lower rates of fiscal stress, particularly relative to cities and counties. This makes the case for assigning blame to other units easier and amplifies the argument that eliminating villages will not greatly ease the overall tax burden (because residents continue to pay town, county, school, and special district taxes).

Zhang's (2019) research relies on a survey of local officials (primarily mayors) to assess why villages dissolve. Zhang and Holzer (2020) similarly rely on a theory-driven survey instrument of village mayors (or to financial managers or clerks where mayors did not respond) to understand village perspectives on fiscal stress. Yet the qualitative case-study approach used here makes it clear that local elected officials tend to be resistant to dissolution as a policy solution. Local officials do not always have an objective view when it comes to the fiscal stability of their community. Indeed, when there are problems, local officials tend to blame the state rather than local capacity or structure and have a vested interest in defending the value of village government (as might be expected). The case studies reveal frequent blame-shifting as to who (or what) is responsible—the state blames the inefficiencies of excessive local fragmentation; localities blame state-level policy; towns point to villages; villages point to towns; both point to school districts as the drivers of the local tax burden. Dissolution, in other words, is steeped in the rivalries between municipal forms competing over the tax base and control of development, land use, zoning, and local law authority. Survey responses of village managers are likely to be affected by those same biases and intergovernmental tensions. Zhang additionally finds evidence that villages "more likely to dissolve are those where government officials do not trust their citizens very much" (2019, 926). Equally likely, it may be the case that where citizens have pushed dissolution through the petition process, local government officials have in turn developed a distrust of their constituents' judgment. Moreover, because the petition threshold was lowered, elected officials are increasingly likely to attribute dissolution efforts to the influence of disgruntled upstarts or even outsiders.

The Empowerment Act made it easier for citizens to compel their local elected officials to develop a dissolution or consolidation plan in response to public desire for less costly government services. Public discourse not only informs those choices but is a vital component of overcoming cultural resistance to change and ensuring there is adequate voter support at the referendum (Cresswell and Cresswell 2015). Village residents often express frustration with a perceived lack of information and agency in the dissolution process, in part because most dissolution studies and plans are conditioned on assumptions limited to estimated projections and ask residents to weigh a narrow set of monetized costs and benefits against broader intangible considerations or community values. Fiscal and environmental factors are not the only (or even primary) determinants of the residents' collective decision on dissolving their village government. Indeed, the next chapters focus on political and psychological factors, as well as the role of narrative policy persuasion, in framing and understanding the village dissolution debate.

Chapter 5

The Political Contexts of Dissolution

The politics behind village government dissolution are varied and complex. The in-depth analysis of cases in New York State reveals that support for (or opposition to) village dissolution is more pragmatic than partisan, driven by local economic and social dynamics, by local or micro politics—including personality conflicts within a community. Indeed, local municipal elections in most states are generally nonpartisan affairs. In New York, where nominations in village elections may be made either by a political party or an independent nominating petition, some (typically larger) village elections are partisan while others are not.[1] When dissolution is at issue, local parties, nominating committees, or citizen groups may endorse a candidate (or slate of candidates) in support or opposition to dissolving. But there is no clear or consistent pattern of a partisan cleavage on the issue.

Pro-dissolution movements can be either grassroots (generated by citizens) or grasstips (spearheaded by elites or community influencers). Pro-dissolution coalitions are typically comprised of a mix of home and business owners, property developers, and older individuals. Most dissolution supporters are worried about higher-than-necessary property taxes and long-term housing affordability. Others believe in economies of scale and that services can be more efficiently provided through a merger with the surrounding town(s). Only some identified as fiscal conservatives, members of the national Tea Party movement, or anti-statist libertarians who generally eschew governmental services and regulations.

Reorganization may also be championed by progressive reformers who want to promote regional or metro-governance or who believe the interests of the village and town are better served when regarded as one community. In a smaller subset of cases, distaste for the current village administration, disagreement over a specific policy outcome, or personal politics motivated the dissolution effort as a redistribution of political power. In particularly small jurisdictions, seemingly minor controversies (disputes over a zoning permit, code enforcement, or roadwork, for example) can create community discord sufficient to launch a dissolution effort.

What Baker (1991) identifies as a moral fabric of frugality shapes the political beliefs of many New Yorkers, uniting them in agreement that government services should be delivered as efficiently as possible. In this sense, the dissolution debate mirrors the schism that emerges in many incorporation battles between progressives (eager for development and growth) and conservatives (wishing to keep taxes and public expenditures low). Longtime residents are sometimes resentful of development that is driven by newcomers, those whom Lingerman (1980) calls "outlivers"— residents living outside the borders of an established municipality.

The "twin gods" of cost cutting and savings may drive some residents to resent growth when it leads to property tax increases (435). Anti-dissolution coalitions often include conservative voices who are resistant to that change, attributing dissolution efforts to newcomers, outsiders, or upstarts who are set on destroying the status quo and who are attacking their community, its values, and their preferred way of life. Business elites particularly can be sharply divided over dissolution, as either the champions of or opponents to change. For business owners, the outcome of a dissolution can be high stakes. There are potential savings (sometimes substantial) to be had from dissolving. But dissolving shifts taxing and zoning authority from the village to the town, so some business owners may fear losing influence over decision-making.

Dissolution and the National Context

Former Speaker of the US House of Representatives Tip O'Neill famously quipped that all politics is local. Yet national politics often gives context to local affairs. Indeed, the national economy, shifting intergovernmental relationships, federal mandates, and federal aid all impact state and local government, pushing fiscal and policy pressures downward. In periods of economic downturn, the pressure for local government reorganization may build.

The waves of dissolution that were observable in figure 2.1 fit within these broader national patterns. The surge in dissolutions in the 1930s, for example, reflected Great Depression–era realities, particularly for rural communities. The dissolutions of the 1970s were part of a nationwide wave of anti-taxation attitudes and taxpayer revolts. Support for dissolution is substantially related to local property taxes, the national public perception of which has grown increasingly negative (Brunori 2007). Not only does dissolution reflect contemporary interest in the impact of the Empowerment Act, it also encompasses some residual anti–big government, anti-tax sentiment of the Tea Party movement born of the Great Recession of 2009. For example, a citizen volunteer in one of the village dissolution efforts shared her dissatisfaction with the high salaries and benefits of public employees as motivating her involvement with the local downsizing and dissolution efforts. Yet when asked whether she identified with the national Tea Party movement, her startled response was "Gosh, no!" Dissolution opponents only rarely draw on the rhetoric of national-level politics. An online comment left by a self-identified libertarian, for example, invoked constitutional theory in support of retaining village government: "it is also obvious that if these lower levels of governance are removed then the people cannot be adequately represented, and tyranny will evolve. We should fear centralization as it robs us of our individual liberty and the necessary stages of truly representative government." But such explicit connections between dissolution and small-government philosophy are very infrequently voiced in person or in online commentary. Indeed, most of the representatives of the pro-dissolution groups with whom I spoke see their efforts as unrelated to their national politics or partisan identification. Repeatedly, they insisted their concerns were related to local property taxes or issues that were highly specific to their community. The conservative preference for smaller government, in other words, does not necessarily equate to support for the reduction in the total number of units, but rather reflects a desire for less intrusion from state and federal authority into everyday citizen affairs.

Pro-dissolution coalitions instead attract an ideological mix of supporters, the majority of whom see their support as largely disconnected from their partisan preferences. Those dissolution supporters who did identify as ideologically conservative saw no contradiction between distaste for a big federal government and wanting to eliminate village governments locally. Local control, they argued, was local control, and they saw no meaningful difference between village and town administration. Most do not see their support for dissolution as stemming from their anti-government attitudes generally. "We're not *anti-government*," one pro-dissolution coalition leader explained, "we're anti-*unnecessary government*. If I can get all the same services from the town, and lower my taxes, why wouldn't I support that, whatever my political persuasion might be?" To the extent that there was resentment against "big government," the villain for anti-dissolutionists seemed to be New York State for forcing reorganization on local residents. Some conservatives and rural voters who were anti-dissolution expressed frustrations with state-level policies or a dislike for Governor Cuomo.

Dissolution support may be tied to (or reinforced by) a bounded view of community and concern regarding to whom social obligation is owed (Wong 2010). Paying taxes is resented when one perceives there is no individual benefit to doing so, or that the expenditures support the welfare of others to whom there is no shared obligation or reciprocity. For example, TOV residents may resent "taking on" the village's burdens, or object to any increase in town taxes once the village is absorbed. Residents of both town and village and on both sides of the debate frequently argue that they are fed up with subsidizing services for the other or bearing a burden that they believe rightfully belongs to some other community. Village boundaries can demarcate an "us" from a "them"—a neighboring municipal, more urbanized area; or a racial, religious, or economic enclave. The demarcation of municipal boundaries, in other words, can reflect or create "empathy walls" (Hochschild 2016).

It is also important to note that, as public dissatisfaction with taxes has grown, so too have state tax-relief programs and state-imposed tax and expenditure limitations (TELs) on local government. While such measures alleviate the property tax burden for residents, they force localities to seek alternative revenue sources. Exemptions and property tax relief programs, along with a shrinking tax base, uneven home valuations, and assessment, further exacerbate perceptions of inequities and subsidization of selectively received services. Brunori (2007), for example, argues that the shift away from property tax funding toward state funding of education has severed the connection to the provision of this local service, making residents less supportive of educational needs (2007, 8). Similarly, fiscal federalism scholars have pointed out that the shift in federal funding to people *over* places has delinked localities from the provision of services in the voters' mind.

For suburban villages, angst over dissolution arises from their desire to maintain a separation from adjacent metropolitan areas. Having fled the cities in the 1960s, many "now find it impossible to sustain the socially and economically separate lives. . . . By cutting themselves off from the region's economic engine and primary tax base—the central city—and by continuously demanding top-quality services in isolated pockets rather than collectively, they have created for themselves a different set of equally complex problems from which there may be no ready escape" (Gardner 2010). Frustration over rising taxes may reflect anxiety about "maintaining their economic status," paradoxically inciting what Gardner likens to the vandalism of local institutions via the call for local government downsizing or dissolution. Yet suburbanites are also most likely to fear the redistributive aspects of regionalism, viewing their local government (and the "personalized representation" it provides) as the best barrier to protect their interests.

For regionalism advocates, such suburban self-interest is detrimental to the collective benefit of the larger area, inclusive of multiple municipalities. In their view, reimagining "the community" more broadly than one's own neighborhood shifts the focus of both problems and solutions, promotes cooperation, and, in the long run, provides greater benefit to all. Suburban residents of neighboring municipalities continue to rely on amenities, infrastructure, and services provided to cities without contributing to their tax base. Fragmentation "is regarded as the greatest single problem facing urban areas" because it is difficult to "coordinate planning and action over the whole urban complex when a multiplicity of units are each exercising varying powers of portions of the urban area" (Report of the Interim Urban Problems Committee 1959, 2–4). Overt prejudice, or desire to be separated from the problems of metropolitan areas, explains the defensive incorporation of municipalities along urban peripheries—by forming a village, residents avoid the threat of annexation and ensure that their taxes are directed toward their own local needs and services.

Such long-standing resentments between the central (or metropolitan) government and provincial (peripheral) governments date back to colonial times. Political schisms between urban, suburban, and rural places—and between upstate and downstate—remain readily apparent in New York State. Recession- and post-recession–related challenges have only exacerbated these perceptions, just as partisan polarization has reinforced a growing divide between citizens in urban versus rural places. The preference for local government reflects significant resentment of national and state politics, or the belief that state and federal leaders do not understand rural realities and problems, contributing to what`

Wurthnow (2018) calls "rural rage" and what Cramer (2016) identifies as the "politics of resentment."

Rural residents may particularly feel aggrieved by claims that village municipalities are increasingly unnecessary or obsolete. The same rural resentments identified by Wurthnow (2013, 2018) and Cramer (2016) as driving support for white national populism reinforces a comparatively more favorable attitude toward local governments. The anger and political resentment associated with dissolution efforts are similarly "grounded in loss" and the sense that certain places (and the people who live there) politically matter less (Cramer 2012; Wurthnow 2013, 2018). Dissolution, in other words, stirs up the same resentments for residents who feel left behind by national and state policies and who now feel that their local institutions are under attack. While Cramer's work does not address incorporation (or the importance of corporate status), she argues that there is a rural consciousness, or place-based lens, that is formed by a collective mistrust of centralized, urban authority (read the state capitol) and driven by feelings of rural alienation (Cramer 2012). Rural residents' views of politics and political objects are rooted, in Cramer's view, to this rural consciousness—"their sense of themselves as members of a rural community" (Cramer 2016, 51). This consciousness, she argues, is "about perceptions of power, or who makes decisions and who decides what to even discuss," and manifests with "respect to perceptions of values and lifestyles" and involves "perceptions "of resources or who gets what" (2016, 55).

While Cramer's research focuses on rural-urban divides between large metropolitan areas and peripheral or rural communities, shades of the same divide can be seen between more populated villages and surrounding rural townships. Similar resentments arise in both village incorporation and dissolution cases in disputes over who is subsiding whom and who receives services for the taxes paid. "Devolution since the late 1970s" also "means that local governments have been increasingly left to their own sources of revenue to provide services" (Cramer 2016, 97). She highlights the antipathy residents often express for the state and federal governments as rule makers that "parachute in and pronounce what is right and good and then leave without respecting local wisdom, wants, or needs" (37). The animosity that rural residents have for state-level policies stems from their "feeling overlooked, ignored, or disrespected" relative to urban areas (40).

Wurthnow (2018) similarly argues that the perception of an external threat only further tightens allegiance to one's immediate community: "rural communities' first line of response is the people they trust and look to for help when they need it" (8). Deep-rooted notions of local self-sufficiency are based on what Lingeman (1980) identified as the "old pioneer myths of neighborliness, equality, grass-roots democracy, self-sufficiency, and independence" (437). Katz and Nowak (2017) identify the growing perception of municipal governments as pragmatic problem solvers as a powerful counterpoint to the national populism. While this "new localism" is grounded in the same economic context and nostalgia for better days past, the authors view national populism as "political strategy to exploit those grievances" (6). New localism, on the other hand, is a problem-solving philosophy geared toward alleviating them," one that is non-ideological, pragmatic, and inclusive (Katz and Nowak 2017, 6). Recognizing that solutions are not forthcoming from the federal or state government, communities, in other words, are saving themselves. The adaptive partnerships between citizen groups and local businesses have played an important role in revitalizing struggling small towns, often with an inclusive, bipartisan approach that focuses on *community*, putting "aside tribal differences to do big hard things together in their collective interests" (Friedman 2018).

Public discourse on dissolution-related social media generally makes repeated reference to the notion of proximity, assuming that, as the general-purpose unit closest to the people, village government enjoys the most harmonious relationship with its residents. Comments about the value of knowing village officials personally, and the rapid or customized response of village employees, are common and reflect citizens' appreciation of the personal and familiar. Town government or officials are sometimes viewed as too far removed from village interests to respond to their unique concerns and needs. In some cases, long-standing tensions between the village and town governments (or officials) may have soured the relationship, resulting in distrust, resentment, or even hostility between those who identify with the village and those who identify with the town. In the anti-dissolution narratives, a rationale for prioritizing one's own community that is grounded in micro-politics frequently emerges. Village residents, they argue, have distinct concerns that cannot be entrusted to the town or will be diluted by merging into the larger community. For their part, town residents may be equally unwilling to assume responsibility for the problems they see as belonging to the village. Their resentment at having administration transferred to the town level is worsened by complaints that, as TOV residents, they have no vote on dissolution but are nevertheless "stuck" with the outcome.

Dissolution and Local Politics

The boundaries of a municipality are what "drives local politics" (Wong 2010, 11). Conversely, local politics also drives the formation of municipal boundaries—why they are drawn as they are, and how and when they are changed. The dissolution or consolidation of a village with the embracing town(s) reorganizes political power. Some former village employees may be hired by the town, but others, including the mayor and trustees, will see their positions eliminated. While residents of a former village were always part of a town, taking control of the property and administration of the former village may require town officials to recalibrate their governing focus. Town-elected officials may have new issues on which to run for office and may face potential election challenges from former village trustees or residents seeking election to the town board. Whatever former village problems existed are now exclusively town problems. Moreover, most dissolution studies project a decrease in property taxes for the former village residents frequently accompanied by an increase for TOV taxpayers. Thus, TOV residents worry about subsidizing (former) village services and paying more for services they personally do not use or need.

Municipal incorporation serves a boundary-defining function; the concept of an incorporation defines the parameters of the association to the exclusion of others (Cohen 1985). Boundaries "define the limits of particular arrangements of political power, particular kinds of service provision, certain characteristics of political participation and political accountability, and certain arrangements for funding the work of local government" (Burns 1994, 7). Villages have historically been marked by the "dichotomy of mutual devotion within and hostility without" (Lockridge 1970, 19–20). Whereas "the county faced outward; the village looked inward" (Teaford 1997, 27). The framework of their communal corporation is tribalism, and "the enteral desire to protect the ways of the community against the encroachment of change" (Lockridge 1970, 36). In 1885, an editorial in the *Penn Yan Democrat* wryly observed that among the many charms of local governments is the "amiable trait," of exhibiting "sovereign contempt" for "all the surrounding villages" (Tall 2016, 41).

Indeed, the venerated elements of village-style communities often include a sense of homogeneity, neighborliness, and timelessness. When residents speak of the value of village (or small-town) living, the homogeneity of the community is often implied (Teaford 1997, 5). But the prevailing myth of the type of enhanced democratic participation in villages must also be balanced by the "countervailing emphasis on peace, order, and consensual unity which were antithetical to 'democracy' in today's sense of equal individuals possessing both the freedom and power to dissent" (Lockridge 1970, 194). Preserving the "character" of a community can be a euphemism for the exclusion of others (Judd and Hinze 2015, 11). This resulting bifurcation of an "us" versus a "them" is the darker side of shared social capital (Keller 2003).

Moreover, despite municipal reforms that have led to the increased professionalization of municipal government, there is still a long-standing reputation for local governments, particularly small ones, to be driven by personalities, cliques, and internal feuds that are not always directly related to the administration of local affairs (Wurthnow 2013, 106). The elements of personal politics frequently come to the fore in village dissolutions or may even serve as the reason behind the dissolution push. At other times, the contentious nature of dissolution results in the debate becoming highly personalized. Local elected officials, including town supervisors and council members, frequently find themselves targets of personalized animosity for taking (or not taking) a stance on the issue, for failing to provide wanted information, and for lacking concrete answers or assurances as to the consequences for future service delivery.

Proponents of dissolution are frequently vilified as outsiders or upstarts who are threatening the shared community identity. They are sometimes characterized as being anti-police, anti-firefighter, or just anti-neighbor. Some variation of "if you don't like the village, leave!" is an all-too-frequent comment left by anti-dissolution residents on social media sites or shouted out at meetings. Those who rally around the village equate its preservation with saving the jobs of friends and neighbors or protecting an established "way of life." Dissolution fights can become highly contentious affairs that have a lasting impact on the community. Where one stands (or stood) on dissolution becomes an important factor in recruiting candidates to run for village office or in moving forward after the dissolution vote. Citizen participants in pro- or anti-dissolution campaigns are frequently former office holders or become motivated to run for office after having become involved in the dissolution fight.

The psychological attachment of residents to their village government is inextricably linked with the equation of the village governing structure with the community's overall identity and history. The benefits of village government are often framed in intangible terms: as essential to preserving a shared sense of community identity or place. As the mayor of Salem stated it, "If [authority] is still within the village, village people still have their own voice, not a combined voice. . . . There is something to be said for a small government" (Scanlon 2015). Incorporated status, village administration, and its physical manifestations (such as village facilities and equipment) are equated with the values of local autonomy, self-governance, and democracy. As the mayor of Keeseville noted, "I see people every single day. They stop me on the street. They come to the office. This direct access is democracy in its purest form" (McKinstry 2013). In a 2015 Sienna College poll, New York respondents rated local government as better at responding to their needs than the state by 70 percent to 20 percent.[2] Firefighters and police especially receive high marks—it is understandable then that when dissolution threatens existing police or emergency service arrangements, the opposition is often fierce. Indeed, the personalization of services and quality of representation is among the most-cited benefits of villages as the most "permeable and proximate" of general-purpose governments (Nabatchi and Amsler 2014, 63). As the Joint Legislative Committee on Villages put it, "In no other form of government in this state do voters participate to such a great extent in government as they do in villages" (Legislative Document No. 21 1965, 10).

Yet small places do not always offer the anonymity for a full-throated public debate. "If people fear alienating a neighbor or a friend, they will avoid the cauldron of politics and public life" (Keller 2003, 283). Local officials admit that their job often takes a personal toll, particularly where there are prolonged community disagreements. And when dysfunction or friction does arise, the resulting acrimony may be more personalized and harder to ignore in a smaller community (Wurthnow 2013, 308). The notion that small communities offer greater opportunity for participation is also belied by generally low turnout and participation, particularly in the development of community strategic planning, management, and budgeting decisions, which tend to be dominated by local elected leaders (Moulder and O'Neil 2009). When it comes to leadership, moreover, Wurthnow's extensive study of rural American communities found that residents "seldom mention" elected representatives but are more likely to identify "prominent members of their community who serve in a variety of formal and informal capabilities" (2013, 179).

The Everyday Politics of Place

To a significant degree, residential attitudes in village dissolution debates turn on the everyday politics of place and identity in a deeply ingrained psychological sense. Residents are often swayed as much by symbols and narratives as they are by discussions of taxes and services. The attachment of residents to a place varies, but a sense of identity that is "rooted in a known place" is a need that is "evident in almost all cultures (Tall 2016, 14). A "community is not simply an aggregate of persons living together as free agents. A community is a collectivity that has identities and purposes of its own" (Brown and Schafft 2011, 36). It provides a "sense of belonging, a 'we-ness' . . . commitment to a shared culture, including shared values, norms, and meaning" (Brown and Schafft 2011, 35).

Wachhaus (2014) calls the "relationship between people, place, and government that together constitutes municipal community" the *topos* (Greek for place) to convey a framework in which social meaning of all three is attached to, or embodied by, a specific locale (1110). His argument suggests that all three (people, place, and government) are required for a municipal community to "exist . . . in full" (1111). Indeed, he terms people and place, without a government, such as when "the framework of government has been removed through the phenomenon of municipal dissolution, as a "no-place" (2014, 1116). The loss of government, he argues, impacts not just the residents but also those who live in the surrounding communities. Because community is so closely tied to integration of place and government, Wachhaus believes that "when a municipality is formally dissolved, community is also destroyed" (1124). Local government, he argues, "provides structure around which a community can prosper"; thus dissolution "should not, in and of itself, be expected to restore either people or place" (Wachhaus 2014, 1125).

It is not, however, true that community identity cannot exist without a separate, general-purpose government. New York has hundreds of unincorporated hamlets that are recognizable from both within and without as a distinct community. Dissolved villages remain as hamlets or census-designated populated places and retain an identity and history separate from that of the township.[3] Even communities that have been long ago annexed by larger, more vibrant municipal units (like the village of Eastwood, annexed by the city of Syracuse in 1926) retain a distinctive sense of place. And even those long-"lost" communities like Ebenezer

(Erie County) have a lasting presence through place names and landmarks (Parshall 2012). The imprint may be fainter for some dissolved places, but "spatial signatures" remain in the form of place names, cemeteries, and landmarks (Keller 2003, 267). Contrary to the tendency to equate disincorporation with erasure from existence, the people who live there do not disappear simply because their village corporation has been formally dissolved. Nor is it true that once surrendered, incorporation can never be reclaimed.

As the former mayor of Edwards (St. Lawrence County) explained, "You can't ever lose [it] . . . history is history" (Ellen 2010). Civic institutions, like churches and community organizations, still exist. Basic services are still required and provided. Historical markers designate events and places of local interests. Thus, in both reality and in memory, communities typically outlast their incorporated existence. Residents can and do carve out and maintain a community identity irrespective of their past or current incorporation status. That the number of new village incorporations has dropped is another indicator that a separate government is not necessary for the provision of services or to establish a sense of place.

Nevertheless, incorporation tends to be equated with progress, while dissolution is seen as retrograde, a form of municipal death, euthanasia, or suicide. As one resident in the Keeseville case stated, "As long as the village lives, there is hope that she will recover. But once she's gone, you can't get her back." Such hyperbole goes beyond the feared loss of services to the perceived death of the community itself. Ironically, case studies suggest that the more dire the circumstances, the more desperately residents sometimes cling to incorporation as a last vestige of community well-being.

MUNICIPAL BUILDINGS, SIGNS, AND PUBLIC SPACES

There is no denying that the services, symbols, and iconography of the municipality subtly and powerfully imprint on the minds of voters. Drive through any community and take note of the manifestations of the community's identity in its signage, buildings, churches, fire stations, and schools. "Municipalities become the repository of symbols, whether in the forms of totems, football teams or war memorials . . . like the categories of a kinship system: they are symbolic markers of the community which distinguish it from other communities . . . they provide people with the means to make meaning" (Cohen 1985, 19).

When we "look inside" village government by visiting the places and spaces in which municipal services are delivered, we see the daily interaction of the community and direct provision of services that, while seemingly mundane, are essential to the social well-being of the residents. The public spaces of a village "offer meeting places for residents to interact and forge new connections. . . . Community anchor institutions, such as parks and recreation centers, can strengthen the fabric of civic, social, and political life" (Polimédio, Souris, and Russon-Gilman 2018, 11). Klineberg (2018, x) notes that "social infrastructure," or interpersonal networks, are the crucial "building blocks of all public life" and develop from "sustained, recurrent interaction." The decline of social capital, in Klinenberg's view, is integrally related to the decline of social infrastructure. The malaise felt by many rural places reinforces the narrative stories (addressed in chapter 6). Indeed, the physical place is the visible "setting" against which the village dissolution debate takes place. Pride of place can reinforce the desire to maintain the incorporation—as a visual testament (or rebuttal) to how well (or poorly) the local government is functioning. Places in which the infrastructure is aged or in ill repair reinforce the narrative of decline, providing evidence of a dying community, an incorporation that struggling residents can no longer sustain.

There is a wide range of physical spaces in which village government is located, from very modest and utilitarian buildings to grander structures that may also be of historical significance. The proximity of village offices to the downtown or central business district can be critical to the perception of overall responsiveness and personal attention to residents' concerns. In villages that are town population centers, the village, town, and county municipal buildings are often located in the village, sometimes adjacent to one another or even sharing the same building or space. In rural villages, town buildings and offices may be several miles away from the village center, creating the perception of reduced accessibility and therefore responsiveness. Yet town facilities, in many cases, are larger, better maintained, and more professional in their external appearance, creating a perception of superior service capacity.

In cases of fiscally or environmentally stressed villages, the physical appearance of municipal buildings sometimes reflects the economic hardships of the community. Even a modest, purely functional building can be symbolic of community health and longevity. These spaces serve a variety of community functions, as a central gathering place; as a location for municipally sponsored social, cultural, and historical events; and for an array of community or even private charitable activities. Water towers, parks, street signs, and municipal markers are equally iconographic of the community. They "symbolize the community's identity," whether it be a "grain elevator with the town's name emblazoned near the top . . . the water tower . . . [or] historic courthouse . . . the depot-turned museum, the renovated residence of the town's first mayor, [or] the community project that has 'beautified' the oldest buildings on Main Street" (Wurth-now 2018, 41). Abandoned or run-down village facilities, tattered signs, and dilapidated structures provide a powerful clue as to why residents fear dissolution. Empty places stripped of their signage become a tangible display signifying community decline and failure.

PROTECTING THE COMMUNITY: FIRE, POLICE, AND EMERGENCY SERVICES

Fire, police, and emergency services are also highly emblematic of the community: their presence and participation in a community's social traditions are part of the collective public identity. Firehalls particularly often serve as a venue of community activity; representing a collective enterprise of volunteerism and charitable giving in the service of one's neighbors, they are polling locations and places of refuge in natural disasters. Emergency services have a ceremonial role as well as a functional purpose and tend to be integral to civic activities and annual rituals. Speaking about the resistance to fire department consolidation, one fire official observed that "it's almost a local patriotic thing to have your own fire department—the first vehicle in the parade is the fire department, and folks are going to be emotional about holding onto the status quo" (Semuels 2021).

Police and fire protection are also, of course, an essential category of services. Not all villages maintain separate police, relying instead on the town, county, or state for policing. Especially in larger villages, or where there is a diverse or collegiate population, residents desire a dedicated police department, even if it is typically the largest expenditure for the village government. Similarly, fire protection is a point of deep contention, as dissolution of the village may require the consolidation of fire districts, or the legal incorporation of voluntary fire departments.

The flashpoints over police, fire, and emergency services in the dissolution debate are typically focused on three major concerns: 1) personnel issues, including job loss for displaced officers and firefighters, many of whom are village residents with social ties to the community and governing boards; 2) the potential diminution of services, including longer response times or less personalized attention to specific community concerns; and 3) the loss of volunteer or community-based services that embody the values of volunteerism and neighborliness that residents of smaller communities often seek and favor.

Moreover, there are legal barriers in the transfer or restructuring of police and fire services. New York law does not permit towns to create policing districts; instead, towns may only provide policing on a town-wide basis, funded by townwide taxes. When the town does not provide police services, transfer of that function will be to the county or else must contracted through an adjacent municipality. Because there currently is no way to provide police services on a districted (or non-townwide) basis, dissolving villages with police departments will continue to face resistance, particularly in cases where the village is more populous than the surrounding town.

The provision of fire services in New York is particularly complex. Under New York law, fire services cannot be provided townwide, but rather requires the creation of a fire or fire protection district, or else must be contracted through another municipality and funded by a tax on those properties serviced. "Cities and most villages have municipal fire departments, the structures of which can be complicated in themselves, especially in villages. Towns usually have independent fire districts, fire protection districts, or a combination of both. The organization and administration of these (not to mention the naming conventions) make the system as a whole difficult to understand at a glance" (Office of the New York State Comptroller 2017f, 2). Public employee contracts and protections under New York's Public Employees' Fair Employment Act (known as the Taylor Law) impose additional obstacles for the transfer or consolidation of public union-protected personnel.

INFRASTRUCTURE: PUBLIC AND PRIVATE PROPERTY

Local government has responsibility for maintaining a wide variety of public infrastructure. The cost and maintenance of roads, water systems, bridges, and sanitation are also frequent points of contention within communities, between municipal units, and between local and state government. As importantly, infrastructure maintenance is a major driver of property tax rates, directly impacting the quality of life within a community. Aging infrastructure is a common cause for concern and is physically symbolic of municipal decay. Deferred maintenance on infrastructure can be costly, creating a worsening cumulative effect when financially strapped localities are unable to fund necessary improvements.

The maintenance of private property is closely related to local zoning rules and code enforcement. The state of homes and businesses in the village visibly reflects the overall fiscal health of the community. In fiscally stressed places, the phenomenon of "aging in place" may be readily evident in the shabby conditions of the village—from unkempt parks and public spaces to unmaintained homes and closed business fronts. Conversely, some villages maintain an atmosphere of prosperity and commerce. Their public spaces and private properties are well maintained and there is a robust downtown or business district, the buildings and spaces of which communicate economic vibrancy. The visible manifestations of prosperity or blight play an indirect but important role in the debate over dissolution. Residents in places that are well maintained often point to their village government as integral to their preferred quality-of-living, while those in struggling communities may view blight as a sign of failed governance or cling to the incorporation as one of the last vestiges of community well-being.

Collective Identity and Pride: Festivals, Heritage, and Public Ritual

In many villages, municipally owned spaces, even if modest, offer residents pleasant places to congregate and socialize. Many of these places incorporate the historical heritage of the village into their design or serve as the location of public rituals, ranging from regular gatherings (like farmer's markets, concerts, and lecture series) to annual parades, community days, or centennials and jubilees that are critical to establishing a shared identity. In the dissolution debates, residents justify higher taxes as a worthwhile price to pay for the social amenities and lifestyle that are reflected in and reinforced by ritual celebrations. They fear that dissolving the village will result in a diminution of these manifestations of collective identity and civic pride.

Community rituals are a powerful form of boosterism, a means to encourage growth and investment by attracting resident and businesses (Wurthnow 2018). The celebration of the village's incorporation and the memorialization of its history in local museums, heritage centers, and community artwork or public murals explicitly connect the present to the past. Reclaiming the past is often part of intentional efforts at community revitalization and self-branding. Small communities particularly are often defined "as well by that which they are not—cities, unfamiliar places, and big government" (Wurthnow 2013, 3). The meanings and narrative that locals construct around their municipal existence reinforces their attachment to the place and to its governing institutions (Wurthnow 2013).

Schools and School Districts: Central to Community Identity

School districts and schools are also central to a community's identity, providing a source of common experience, intergenerational traditions, and community pride (Lyson 2002; Jakubowski and Kulka 2016). Schools are critical to communities, particularly small ones. When schools are closed, communities often suffer a corresponding loss of vitality. Thus, the belief that "viable villages generally contain schools; dying and dead ones either lack them or do not have them for long" makes them a "continuing indicator of a community's well-being" (Peshkin 1978, 161). School consolidation and closure "strips the town of a critical piece of its identity (Wurthnow 2013, 104). "As the population in rural places dwindles, the possibility of school consolidation increases and the identity of a town and its schools begins to decay" (Cramer 2016, 50).

In a study of rural New York villages (defined as those fewer than 500 in population), Lyson (2002) found that for the "smallest rural communities, the presence of a school is associated with many social and economic benefits" (136). For larger rural villages (those between 501 and 2,500), "on virtually every indicator of social and economic well-being, [those] that have schools ranked higher than communities without." (136). Because some residents view dissolution as a first step toward the eventual consolidation of area schools, they are reluctant to support elimination of their village government to merge with the town. As Bosman (2018) observes: "People worry about losing not just their schools but their town's future," that closing schools "will prompt the remaining residents and businesses to drift away and leave the place a ghost town." Because community identity and school districts "are closely intertwined," school consolidations, like village dissolutions, are resisted and, if anything, can be even more contentious (Cramer 2016, 51). Yet school district financing accounts for most of the local property tax burden: as much as 76 percent of residential tax bills goes toward funding schools. Village dissolution opponents point to this fact, arguing that the elimination of village government is therefore misguided. School districts, moreover, face the same challenges of a declining population and tax base and limits on their revenue-raising capacity. School district reorganizations are, however, expressly exempted from the provisions of the Empowerment Act.

Borders and Boundedness

Incorporation establishes jurisdictional boundaries around the community in line with deeply rooted conceptions of sovereignty and the American preference for territorial representation. Municipal boundaries separate the properties and residents falling within or beyond village authority and taxes, defining who may officially participate in village affairs. They create "a sense of boundedness that separates insiders from outsiders, stories and rituals that affirm the nature of this boundedness, and everyday practices that verbally and behaviorally reinforce common norms about a person's obligation to themselves, their neighbors, and the community" (Wurthnow 2018, 43). McCabe (2016) calls these the "bonds of reciprocity." Yet boundaries can also serve to enforce class biases, discourage dissent, and concentrate power in the hands of local elites.

Renewed scholarly attention to rural America helps to shed further light on the connection between place and identity. More than two-thirds of New York's villages are fewer than 3,000 in population. Wurthnow (2018) argues that the places in which rural residents live constitute a form of moral community—"a place to which and in which people feel an obligation to one another and to uphold the local of ways of being that govern their expectations about ordinary life and support their feelings of being at home and doing the right things" (4). Engaging in local life and politics cements one's identity with the community. "Although informal patterns of neighborliness may seem mundane, the interpersonal ties created through regular social interaction are often critical to vibrant communities" (McCabe 2016, 89). It is then through everyday politics that "people interact with one another and form loyalties to one another and to the places in which their interaction takes place. These enduring interactions and the obligations and identities they entail constitute the community as a home" (Wurthnow 2018, 4). Civic pride is tied to the place and "their communities' achievements, if only something as locally significant as a new fire truck or a winning basketball team" (Wurthnow 2018, 7).

Place identity is thus interwoven with perceptions of power. Incorporation does not exempt communities from state or federal policies, but it gives them greater control over their own local affairs. Those who feel powerless to influence the town or statehouse want a dedicated government that is directly responsive to their unique demands. Village government provides both a leadership structure and an institutional framework for responding to localized needs and concerns. Geographic distance to the seat of the embracing town(s) may also contribute to one's support for dissolving. Having to travel, even a few miles, to the town administrative buildings is an inconvenience. For elderly or poor residents, the barrier can be significant. Such concerns may be mitigated when a village is the seat of town (or county government). When dissolution negatively impacts the residents' "perception of their communities' standing relative to other places," the loss of corporate status and the feeling of ceding power to another entity may seem greater (Cramer 2012, 530).

The boundedness created by incorporation embodies what Keller (2003) argues are the building blocks of a transcendent "spirit" of the community. When we cross municipal jurisdictions, we are greeted by welcoming placards and signage that typically proclaim the founding or incorporation date. Dissolution erases jurisdictional boundaries and authority, melding the village with the surrounding town(s). To TOV residents, or residents living in unincorporated places (hamlets or towns), fears over dissolving may seem superfluous or even silly. Residents of otherwise unincorporated territory within a town often comment that they feel no less a community and perceive no deficiencies in services despite their lack of a dedicated village government. For anti-dissolution residents, however, the incorporation may be inextricably tied to what "they consider to be right and good. It matters greatly, therefore, if people perceive—correctly or incorrectly—that the communities upholding their way of life are in danger" (Wurthnow 2018, 43).

Wurthnow's focus on rural America does not distinguish between types of municipalities or incorporated or unincorporated places, but he concludes that social capital is what matters, that the *social* networks are what give meaning to the place (Wurthnow 2013, 2–3). "It's long been understood that social cohesion develops through repeated human interaction and joint participation in shared projects, not merely from a principled commitment to abstract values and belief. Alexis de Tocqueville admired the laws that formally established America's democratic order, but he argued that voluntary organizations were the real source of the nation's robust civic life. John Dewey claimed that social connection is predicated on 'the vitality and depth of close and direct intercourse and attachment. 'Democracy must begin at home,' he famously wrote, 'and its home is the neighborly community'" (Klinenberg 2018, 12).

Social networks can exist independently and irrespective of municipal boundaries. Much of what constitutes a community is imagined—a social or mental construct, demarcating to whom we perceive a shared association and bonds of obligation (Wong 2010). The variability in the states' local government structures and laws also creates misunderstandings as to the effects of dissolving. For example, Anderson (2012) assumes that village dissolution always reverts to administration by the county. Wachauus (2014) similarly assumes that without a dedicated city or village government, communities are "no places." In New York, even when incorporated, villages remain part of the town, their residents pay town taxes, vote in town elections, and receive representation and some level of service from the town.

Dissolution as Regionalism

The debate over village dissolution reveals competing conceptualizations of the function of municipal incorporation. For some residents, municipalities exist primarily as service providers, as an artificial legal entity that can not only be separated from the underlying community but also can be oppressive upon it when the cost can no longer be sustained. For others, incorporation as a legal entity is indispensable to their community identity. The sense that small towns and communities are dying exacerbates these underlying tensions and heightens resentments against efforts to eliminate smaller units of government as duplicative or obsolete.

Localism, and its commitment to the autonomy of smaller municipal units, is arguably an impediment to regional cooperation and planning.[4] The "stickiness" of an outmoded municipal structure and the proliferation of units, the boundaries of which are fixed, arguably impede agglomerative efficiency and create multiple veto points to regional policy efforts (Schliecher 2017). As one elected official put it, "we are trying to address modern day problems that overlap municipal units through a local government structure that was designed for the 19th Century." By contrast, regionalism is the view that interjurisdictional problems require interjurisdictional solutions and governance. Regionalism thus presumes that "the economically, socially, and ecologically relevant local area is often the region" and would "shift some authority from local governments, restrict local autonomy, or, at the very least, constrain the ability of local governments to pursue local interests" (Briffault 2000, 1). Municipal reorganization thus not only is linked to efforts to alleviate heavy property tax burdens, but also has the broader purposes of reducing the political fragmentation[5] and local autonomy that impede regional progress.[6]

The 1990s witnessed a national resurgence of interest in regionalism marked by "concern about [urban] sprawl, a recognition of the concentration of poverty within metropolitan areas, and a belief that regions will be hampered in their ability to engage in economic competition unless they address their internal economic and social inequalities" (Briffault 2000, 2). There is a redistributive component to regionalism as well, as the fragmentation of units in suburban or metro adjacent areas reinforces social inequities. As Schragger (2003) writes:

> The rhetoric of local autonomy has become synonymous with local ownership—the ownership of the collective property within the boundaries of the jurisdiction, and ownership of the jurisdictional boundaries themselves. . . . This attention to local boundaries is a product of the political economy of privatized local government. If one believes that one has "paid" for a particular service by buying entry into a jurisdiction, then any distribution across jurisdictional lines raises the specter that one is not getting what one has paid for. (Schragger 2003, 1848)

As "shareholders in municipal corporations," homeowners are "more likely to vote for or against proposed public goods perceived to increase (or decrease) residential property values" (Dehring, Depken, and Ward 2008, 156). In local politics, homeowners dominate on issues of land use, school finance, and the choice of local government institutions (Fischel 2001). Their primary motivation in local civic participation is to support policies that maximize property values. "The central idea of the homevoter hypothesis then, is that property values and local government tax and spending decisions are fused." The thesis, built on Tiebout's theories, does not account for "regional or interlocal spillover effects" that may impact property values beyond any single municipality's control (Schragger 2003, 1831).

Homeownership is generally correlated with higher rate of civic participation. Yet economic self-interest means that "this participation contributes to patterns of segregation and social exclusion in their neighborhoods, raising doubts about the benefits to communities that come from active, engaged citizenship" (McCabe 2016, 5). The negative consequence of their enhanced participation is exclusionary policies and a tendency toward NIMBYism (not-in-my-backyard) wherein property owners view their narrow economic concerns as more important than larger community or social goals. Racial and social exclusion becomes "hardened into a political and constitutional entitlement, successfully defended through the rhetoric of local autonomy and freedom of choice" (Schragger 2003, 1852).

Residential voters may be willing to forego some services (usually those that are more broadly dispersed to the community) to reduce their individual property tax burden. The desire to restrict tax benefits (services) to those who are funding the lion's share of the cost may lead some residents to favor incorporation as a separation of their community from their neighbors. Municipal reorganization thus is a fight over the tax base and the concentration of benefits derived from the property taxed. Whether one supports dissolution (or not) depends on the context of the situation and whichever stance is believed most advantageous to one's self-interest.

While "contemporary efforts to encourage homeownership often center on the importance of owning a home for economic mobility, political leaders continue to lean on these historic arguments to claim that homeownership anchors citizens in their neighborhoods, generates shared interests in those places, and fortifies the social bonds that are central to safe, vibrant communities" (McCabe 2016, 8). Local leaders seek to preserve municipal longevity by incentivizing residential stability. "Residential stability in a community helps citizens deepen the social networks and strengthen the interpersonal relationships that are central to active, engaged, citizenship. . . . It may also strengthen the sense of place that Americans feel in their communities, deepening the loyalties in a neighborhood and generating a stronger sense of community pride" (McCabe 2016, 74).

But Schleicher (2017) argues that residential stability aided by local municipal policies impedes residential mobility by creating both entry and exit barriers. Zoning and land use regulations (the desired control over which often drives municipal incorporation) can also be a driver of escalating property values and taxes and can limit who may enter a neighborhood. Social ties, limits on public pension portability, reliance on public benefits (based on differing eligibility standards of states and localities), and housing prices all place restrictions on residents wishing to exit. Thus, whereas public choice models see the local provision of services as a desirable mechanism for home ownership and residential choice, Schleicher argues that the notion of residents selecting based on preferred service levels is problematic, as "this fit comes at a cost; it undermines agglomerative efficiency because it forces people to choose their locations based on packages of services rather than solely on economic calculus" (2017, 123). Moreover, municipalities lack the ability and policies to adjust to decline, as they are unable to shrink their boundaries or downsize government in the face of a dwindling tax base or excessively growing service needs. Municipal bankruptcy is an extreme option that offers few solutions in terms of needed structural reform, as the federal statutes preclude judicial interference with political and governing authority, municipal properties, or revenues. Schleicher views the "noble instinct" to protect dying communities, or to preserve "historic modes of living," through state or federal subsidies as misplaced. There is a cost to local control and the quest for residential stability and municipal longevity that, from a federal policy perspective, makes little or no sense (Schleicher 2017). Porter (2018) similarly questions whether continued place-based state assistance is an effective means of revitalization for areas that are in "relentless economic decline" (Porter 2018).

Regional approaches, by contrast, often call for investing in cities and reinforcing their linkage to the fate of surrounding suburban and rural areas (Arnosti and Liu 2019). Indeed, for regionalism advocates, the fragmentation of units in suburban or semi-urban areas is particularly problematic, and the best targets of village dissolution may not be just the small rural villages, but also those at the periphery of adjacent cities.

Bucki (2008) argues that, to varying degrees, regionalism proponents pushed intermunicipal consolidation as a "silver-bullet solution" without the initial buy-in of area residents.[7] By failing to develop consensus from within, the effort was doomed from the outset. The general demise of regionalism, according to Bucki (2008), was also the consequence of reformers having focused too narrowly on structural reform and city-county consolidation as a panacea. The consolidation approach had "resulted not from reflective debate among a broad range of community leaders, but rather from promotion by a small group of influential powerbrokers" (Bucki 2008, 120).

He warned that "unless such a plan arises from a comprehensive effort to solicit genuine feedback" and local buy-in, "the cause of regionalism will continue to suffer" (Bucki 2008, 157).

While consolidation reform has met with a lack of success, the philosophy of "new regionalism" has gained some traction. This variation argues that regional governance is best achieved not through the reorganization of the existing governments but through the flexible and voluntary cooperation of public and private sector coalitions acting according to shared, strategic, regional interests (Wallis 1994).[8] These rival visions of regionalism and its growing ranks of proponents have shaped reform efforts, lessening receptivity for structural solutions. Indeed, the debate between new and old regional approaches focuses on the benefits and costs of interjurisdictional competition, with new regionalism placing a shifting emphasis on the impact of competition on economic development and growth (Levine 2001, 183). Public choice theories, which provide the foundation for new regionalism, "posit that competitive behavior increases with the number of jurisdictions in a region" (Basalo 2003, 453). New regionalist approaches, in other words, suggest that economic competition and self-interest in both the public and private sectors may be harnessed to foster cooperative strategies for regional governance and growth.

THE 2010 DISSOLUTION EFFORT IN WESTERN NEW YORK

In the late 1990s, a local civic activist and Buffalo-based attorney named Kevin Gaughan received public acclaim for having organized a conference on regionalism at the renowned Chautauqua Institute. The conference was focused on a proposed consolidation between the city of Buffalo (the second-largest municipality in New York State) and Erie County. Despite the heightened attention the conference gave to the idea of regionalism, there was resistance from Erie County's smaller municipal governments and limited public support outside the urban core.[9] When a budgetary crisis put the city of Buffalo under the authority of a hard fiscal control board in 2003, the already weak public appetite for city-county consolidation dissipated entirely.

In 2008, Gaughan turned his attention to reforming the local government structure as an alternative pathway to regionalism. Using a relatively obscure provision of Town Law, he led a public campaign to downsize or reduce membership of town boards through the process of public petition (Finch 2008; O'Brien 2008b). His downsizing tour, which he presented

in each of Erie County's twenty-five towns, ended with a call to simultaneously abolish *all* sixteen of Erie County's villages (Chipp 2008). Rather
than elites foisting regionalism on a resistant public, Gaughan cast local
politicians as the roadblock to meaningful municipal reform and argued
that reducing their number would facilitate greater regional cooperation.

Assisted by the passage of the Empowerment Act in 2009, he spearheaded a citizen-led initiative to dissolve all of Erie County's villages.[10] The
campaign provoked an immediate, negative reaction from local elected
officials, a response from NYCOM, and preemptive efforts on the part
of villages to head off the effort (Williams 2008).[11] Given the pushback,
Gaughan settled on a more limited push, strategically selecting three
villages: a tiny rural village (Farnham), an economically challenged community (Sloan), and a prosperous suburban community (Williamsville)
(Parshall 2011). The differing characteristics of the three communities set
up a natural experiment of sorts, in which the ensuing debate and the
countering strategies of village elected officials were subtly tailored to the
circumstances of each place.

In Williamsville, the village board had debated what action to take
even before a petition was filed. Several trustees favored a proactive stand
to arm the voters against potential "misinformation" (Jackson 2009). Others thought such an approach was premature and dangerous, preferring
instead to adopt a stance of official neutrality lest they give oxygen to
the effort (Jackson 2009). Several village officials candidly expressed their
personal opposition to the idea. As one stated, "I'm sickened by this process, that fewer people than voted me into office can dissolve the village
we've worked so hard for and that an outside individual can come in for
his own personal gain. I will fight to my last dying breath to prevent it"
(Mockler 2010).

The public stance of the village board, however, was one of deliberate
detachment that left private citizens to carry the pro-village, anti-dissolution banner. The Williamsville Citizen's Study Group (a coalition of
residents formed in December 2009) took upon itself the task of amassing
the data necessary for residents to make an informed choice (Andriatch
2009; Spina 2010).[12] A second citizens group, the Friends of the Village
of Williamsville, dedicated itself to highlighting the social benefits and
amenities of the village. From the beginning, public support was weak. An
uncommissioned poll (voluntarily undertaken by a village resident who
owned a polling organization) found overwhelming opposition, with fewer
than 10 percent of residents in support of dissolving (*Buffalo News* 2010).[13]

When the petition was officially filed, the board held a special meeting to discuss a referendum date. The petitioners wanted the referendum to coincide with local primaries, promising up to ten community meetings prior to the vote (Mockler 2010b). The board unanimously scheduled it as early in the sixty- to ninety-day window as possible, thereby truncating the opportunity for pro-dissolution campaigning and debate (Mockler 2010b).

In the following weeks, the opposing pro- and anti-dissolution citizen coalitions presented dueling "studies" on the potential impact of dissolving. The conflicting studies, along with the interjection of yet a third set of figures by the *Buffalo News*, frustrated the voters. No one, it seemed, could agree what village residents paid in additional taxes (relative to TOV residents) or whether dissolution would decrease or increase their tax liability. Village and town officials, presumably best in the know, refused to provide the information. They refused invitations to participate in a debate, opting instead to arrange a presentation by NYCOM.

On the eve of the vote, village officials were reportedly "a little jittery" (*Buffalo News* 2010b). The *Buffalo News* ran a last-minute story that framed the question as a choice between paying extra taxes to guarantee a "quality of life in the face of an *uncertain* level of services if the village . . . were dissolved" (Tan 2010). The *Amherst Bee* likewise focused on uncertainty, emphasizing the short time frame (180 days) that the village board would have to "manage the numerous legal, financial and political questions that would arise from a knee-jerk decision" to dissolve (Amherst Bee 2010). Throughout election day, the Friends of Williamsville, assisted by members of the local fire department, handed out flyers urging fellow citizens to vote "no."

On August 17, Williamsville voters rejected dissolution by a margin of five to one. As residents celebrated the outcome, village officials downplayed the victory even as they accepted congratulations from voters. One trustee remarked, "it's been challenging at times to remain in a neutral position" (Specht 2010).

The dissolution effort in Sloan followed essentially the same timeline as Williamsville, with petitions submitted on the very same day (Krueger 2010). The mayor announced that Sloan would follow Williamsville's example in scheduling the referendum for the same early date of August 17: "Let's get this over with" (*Buffalo News* 2010). He asserted that the two villages were not collaborating to fight dissolution together but admitted that "the mayor [of Williamsville] did call me and say we should try to stick together" (Krueger 2010c). But whereas Williamsville's elected officials stayed in the background, Sloan officials were at the forefront of the fight. The board "mailed several pamphlets," doing "their best to educate the residents, so that if the issue does come to a vote, they will be well informed" (Krueger 2010b). Village leaders also arranged public forums, inviting both NYCOM (which gave a lengthy presentation on the shortcomings of the Empowerment Act) and town officials, who offered very few assurances. The Cheektowaga town supervisor would say only that "this is a village decision that needs to be made by the village itself. I don't know what the consequences would be" (Krueger 2010d). Sloan's leaders refused to engage with the pro-dissolution leader, denying him the use of community venues (Krueger 2010e). As in Williamsville, a week ahead of the vote, the *Cheektowaga Bee* printed an editorial opposing dissolution as a diminution of the residents' political power.

Nearly 58 percent of eligible Sloan residents turned out to defeat dissolution by a vote of 1,031 to 236 (81 percent opposed) (Krueger 2010f). Village officials were unabashedly celebratory, toasting the outcome with champagne (D'Agostino 2010). Decrying the "ugliness" and "venom" that had occasionally accompanied the debate, the *Cheektowaga Bee* declared the champagne celebration a "well-deserved" demonstration of village "pride" (*Cheektowaga Bee* 2010).

In contrast, officials in the tiny rural village of Farnham (population 322) adopted a slower, seemingly more measured approach. Upon receipt of the petition (also submitted June 2, 2010), officials opted for a stand-alone election on September 28 (*Buffalo News* 2010b). Political observers were second-guessing the strategy of having Williamsville vote first, given its relative affluence, asking whether a first effort in Farnham would have been the wiser course (Andriatch 2010). Of course, the petitioners had no control over the scheduling, or sequence, of the referenda dates. But after the resounding rejection in Williamsville and Sloan, the referendum in Farnham was largely ignored, perhaps as a foregone conclusion or because it was too small to signify. Like his counterparts, Farnham's mayor refused an offer for a public debate on the merits of dissolving (Myer 2010). Pressured by anti-dissolution residents to take a firmer public stand, he went door-to-door in the village to meet with residents and denounce the effort (Knotts 2010). The proposed dissolution of Farnham did receive the backing of one local news outlet, the *Hamburg Sun News*, whose editorial board assured residents that neither services nor quality of life would be diminished if Farnham were to rejoin the town of Brant (Myer 2010b).

When referendum day at last arrived, Erie County's smallest village delivered a big message: with 73 percent turnout, dissolution was defeated by a vote of 130–37 (78 percent opposed). On the same night as the Farnham vote, in neighboring Allegany County, the village of Cuba also voted against dissolution (402–43). Although the effort there was entirely independent of the Erie County campaign, the simultaneous defeats were interpreted as a repudiation of the reform effort. "People live in villages for a specific reason," Farnham's mayor explained. In the end, they vote "on emotion not information" (Caber 2010).

In all three communities, officials rejected the need for reorganization, using the typical techniques of agenda denial (Anderson 2011). Sloan's mayor put it succinctly: "The village is 114 years old. If it's not broke, don't fix it" (Krueger 2010b). The real problem, they argued, lay elsewhere: "Our greatest frustrations come from problems we have no control over—not only the economic and historical trends, but the actions of the layers of government far removed from our streets" (Krebs 2009). It was a point echoed by the *Buffalo News:* "You can get rid of all your villages, but you still won't get rid of the lion in the room, taxes paid to school districts and counties" (*Buffalo News* 2010b).[14]

Even some who believed that New York has too many governments questioned whether targeting villages was the most productive course of action. "Why pick a fight with the people who seem to be the most satisfied?" (Duvall 2010). Satisfaction with the status quo was most apparent in Williamsville, where residents were well positioned to deny village government was obsolete or broken. Sloan, with its lower property values, blighted streets, history of official malfeasance, and the highest property taxes in the county, had a harder time claiming all was functioning smoothly. Indeed, many dissolution proponents at the Sloan forum pointed to the incompetence and neglect of village administrators as reason enough to dissolve.[15] At a dissolution meeting, the mayor's rallying cry to "keep Sloan the way it is" was met with heckling by one of the residents: "But it's a $#!*-hole!" The situation in Farnham (described as having one dirt road and no businesses) was arguably even more bleak. Throughout the campaign, the pro-dissolution coalition had deliberately avoided personalizing the debate or attacking village officials personally. Although sobering data on declining population and rising costs were presented, care was taken not to alienate or insult residents by focusing on the negative. Instead, they too appealed to residential pride, praising the unique aspects of each place and promising no diminution of services upon rejoining the town(s).

To the extent that Sloan or Farnham's woes were a focal point, their anti-dissolution coalitions successfully transmogrified those points into a defense of the status quo: however bad things may be, without a village government, the situation would be far worse. To surrender the incorporation was portrayed as defeatist, as an admission that the community itself was moribund. Keeping the village incorporation thus became a reaffirmation of community pride.

In all three cases, the anti-dissolution coalition attacked the legitimacy of the proposal and the integrity of its proponents. Critics disputed the level of grassroots citizen support, reducing the movement to "a one-man traveling slide show," suggesting that dissolution supporters were dupes, anti-government cranks, or victims of the local political pied piper (Taczkowski 2007). The attacks were often personal and pointed. "Get out Gaughan" and "Gaughan be Gone" signs were a staple of the anti-dissolution message, as were verbal accusations at his public events that he was untrustworthy and an outsider. By tacit agreement, elected officials in all three villages refused to debate him or would not allow him (as a non-resident) to speak at publicly sponsored meetings. Citizens groups followed suit, refusing the invitation to host joint forums and (in the Williamsville and Sloan cases) pressuring businesses in the village to deny him a public venue for his presentations.

Perhaps most powerfully, in all three cases, the anti-dissolution coalition relied on narratives of uncertainty and fear over the loss of services, particularly fire protection—a service that is not likely to be eliminated, regardless of incorporated status, for the very reason that it is critical. Yet claims were made with increasing frequency that the reconfiguration of fire districts, or relocation of a fire house, would lead to slower response times and higher home insurance costs.

Presentations by NYCOM reinforced the uncertainty narrative by emphasizing that the process required residents to vote *before* a formal study had been undertaken or a plan was in place. The same study process that NYCOM had long discouraged as a costly waste of time (when required by Article 19) was now argued to be indispensable. "I'm not necessarily opposed to dissolution, but I just think we need more study" was a common sentiment expressed by residents. The Empowerment Act does not preclude local officials from undertaking an informal study or gathering and sharing information. But in the Erie County cases, local elected officials (both village and town) refused to supply the necessary information, leaving that responsibility to citizen groups on both sides of the issue.

The Erie County cases in 2010 were unique in that dissolution was explicitly tied to the larger goal of regionalism. A study by Nathan and Benjamin (2001) had concluded that governmental efficiency or cost savings were the surest means of winning public support for regionalism as most compatible with community values (Nathan and Benjamin 2001, 257). But while regional benefits may have resonated with some voters, arguing its merits also seemed to entrench local self-interest only further. Antipathy toward the redistributive aspects of dissolving was most acute in Williamsville. As one agitated resident asked, why should Williamsville residents give up their local government to help solve Buffalo's problems? "I feel like you're wrongly blaming us." Regional problems, they reasoned, were too extensive to be much affected by the elimination of one or two villages. Directly challenging such views by explaining how suburban fragmentation contributes to the plight of cities would arguably only exacerbate the perception of an external threat, leading to an even tighter circling of the wagons. As Nathan and Benjamin (2001) explain, because residents equate local government with the social network of their friends and family, reform efforts are often seen as "attacks on the community" (Nathan and Benjamin 2001, 164). The hostile reception given to the regional goals of the dissolution campaign was perhaps most evident in the "outsider" narrative that attributed the dissolution effort to the political ambitions of an "interloper with no understanding of villages and no respect for the things those who live in them value" (Cervantes 2010; 2010b).

The *Buffalo News* advocated alternative reforms, including metropolitan consolidation or the dissolution of towns, even while acknowledging that it was not possible without changes in state law, or without the command of a state mandate (Sherman 2010). The argument had come full circle, urging alternate strategies that had already failed (city-county consolidation), were politically impractical (state-mandated reform) or legally unsupported (dissolution of towns). In the end, the dissolution route to regionalism was branded a failed experiment for the same reason that doomed city-county consolidation efforts: suburban resistance (Vogel 2005). Dissolution proponents had sought to break the back of political fragmentation by loosening the psychological bond to the local governments thought to be closest to their interests and values—towns and villages. In that sense, the village dissolution campaign was the most direct, but most daunting, of all the possible approaches to regionalism.

Chapter 6

Narrative Policy Persuasion
in the Dissolution Debate

The Empowerment Act has made the process of *initiating* village dissolution easier. To prevent election officials (who are charged with formulating the plan) from stalling or derailing the process, the Empowerment Act restored elements of the earlier model of direct control that allowed voters to *compel* officials to draft a feasible plan. While the law has increased the pace and number of dissolutions, the Empowerment Act has in some ways complicated reorganization efforts by requiring residents to vote *before* a dissolution plan is formulated in citizen-initiated proceedings and by establishing a shorter timeline for study. The public resistance to dissolution can be explained by a single word: "uncertainty." It is difficult to convince voters of the wisdom of transferring administration from the often long-standing familiarity of the village to uncertain administration by the town. The Empowerment Act thus provided dissolution opponents with a powerful narrative point: *voters are asked to vote on the dissolution of their village before any study or plan is required* (Parshall 2011a). Dissolution opponents have strategically amplified this perceived deficiency to reinforce uncertainty, arguing that voting *before* there is a dissolution plan is like "voting on an absolute pig in a poke" (Johnson 2010).

Dissolution plans have never offered guaranteed certainty, even when required under Article 19, because their implementation has always been contingent on implementation by the town(s). Still, residents are observably reluctant to relinquish village government or its services "without fully understanding the alternative" (Baynes 2010). Representatives of NYCOM, elected officials, and even some consulting firms amplify this point in their public presentations, reminding residents that in citizen-initiated dissolution efforts, the vote precedes creation of a final plan and that all plans are based on assumptions and estimated projections. Rarely are residents educated on the rationale underlying the changes made by the Empowerment Act—that the study process mandated under the old procedures had allowed local officials the opportunity to delay or obstruct citizen-led efforts to dissolve. NYCOM has succeeded in having it all ways—the very study process that it denounced as meaningless and expensive when Article 19 procedures were in effect is now claimed an indispensable element, the absence of which renders the Empowerment Act fundamentally flawed.

Of course, the Empowerment Act does not prevent local officials from undertaking an informal study in advance of an anticipated citizen-initiated petition or once a referendum has been scheduled. Indeed, some villages take advantage of state funding grants to commission a preliminary study even if not required to do so. When basic information on the merits and likely impact is lacking, fault often lies with local officials (both village and town) who refuse to supply information that voters need to feel well informed. Village officials and personnel are rarely disinterested in the outcome, deriving both employment benefits and social status from their positions. Most develop legitimate psychological attachments to the community that they serve. For them, dissolution *is* deeply personal, and they struggle to separate their personal views from "what the voters have mandated that they do." As one trustee described it, "it is a dilemma of "divided loyalties" (Clodgo 2013). In multiple cases, local officials actively discourage residents throughout the process, signaling their opposition to the idea of dissolving.

For their part, most town officials typically adopt a deliberate hands-off approach. Because only village residents may vote on the proposed dissolution, town officials may be reluctant to engage in the process until the outcome of the referendum is certain. Recall too, that village residents are part of the town and vote in town elections, so electoral self-interest in navigating the often contentious debate undoubtedly plays a role. When villages dissolve, the number of local elected positions decreases, and former village officials may enter town elections. Moreover, any outstanding problems of the village will be inherited by the town if dissolution is approved. When, however, town officials *are* involved from the outset, providing both information and reassurance to voters, the fear of uncertainty appears to be greatly reduced.

Whether dissolution is citizen or board-initiated, the policy narratives used in the ensuing debate matter. Elected officials and citizens in the pro- and anti-dissolutions alike simultaneously understand the debate and try to influence the outcome through dueling narrative frames and perspectives. They offer competing stories of who (or what) is to blame and why dissolution is (or is not) a legitimate policy solution. State-level policies, by contrast, regard dissolution as a simple choice of service delivery in which the key question for residents is whether dissolution will produce cost savings. The evidence of potential savings is usually presented in probabilistic and technical terms (i.e., if we assume this service delivery change, we project this net change in costs) and is typically reduced to the post-dissolution net change in taxes per $1,000 of assessed home value. Although most dissolution studies project some anticipated savings, residents often reject the outcome based on the intangible benefits, such as preserving a sense of community, identity, or shared history. The case-study evidence suggests, in other words, that the narrative persuasion strategies used in the dissolution debate are as important as (or more important than) the cost-to-benefit assessment provided by a dissolution study or report (Parshall 2011; 2012; 2019b).

Competing Narrative Frames

Conceptualizations of community have long been separated into formalistic (focusing on legal, institutional criteria) versus humanistic (emphasizing attachment and belonging) approaches (Keller 2003, 235). The view that dissolution will benefit village residents, in most cases, is driven by a pragmatic desire to reduce property taxes, eliminate duplicative services, and promote more efficient governance. Indeed, the cost of retaining village amenities may not be sustainable or affordable for all. Rising property tax burdens make it difficult for older residents to keep their homes, for their adult children to stay in the area, and for the less economically advantaged to keep pace with property tax increases. Dissolution can also be a way to be rid of dysfunctional, inept, or corrupt local management. Alternatively, the effort to dissolve may reflect a progressive desire for a unified community, one that can more effectively address regional policy problems. For scholars like Glaeser (2011), policies that prioritize preservation of the locale over the changing needs of the residents are misguided.

Restoring or clinging to the past impedes progress that might be made. Administration by the town or county can be more efficient, professional, and even-handed (i.e., less susceptible to highly personalized or localized politics). Dissolution, in other words, can be presented as a solution to an existing problem (or problems)—as a positive change, remedy, or advantage that will result in improved circumstances for residents.

Anti-dissolution advocates, by contrast, argue for maintaining the status quo, either by denying that a problem exists or arguing that dissolution may result in residents being worse off for having surrendered their village government. If high taxes are the problem, the argument goes, the real culprit is not village government but school districts, state policies and mandates, or town governments. In other words, look elsewhere for the problem. Potential tax savings, moreover, are regarded as secondary to the relative benefits of living in a village. Dissolution opponents tend to emphasize identity and the sense of belonging that the village incorporation safeguards (i.e., save your village; protect our village). Their preference for local representation is reflected in their frequent references to the virtues of small government and by raising fears that village residents will not receive the same level of support or attention from the town. Efforts to dissolve the village as a legal corporation are typically framed as violating the norms of being a "good neighbor"—a virtue that is highly valued in small communities (Wurthnow 2013).

The slogans of an anti-dissolution group in the tiny village of Cuba (Allegany County) well illustrate these general framing techniques. Although rudimentary in design (consisting mostly of clip art), the messaging was simple and direct:

1. "Dissolution is not the Solution. Support your Village. Vote No on Dissolution"

2. "Join us to improve the Village. Don't dissolve it!"

3. "Keep Your Government small. Vote No on Dissolution."

4. "Stand up for your Village. Keep your services. Vote No on Dissolution!"

5. "Dissolving our Village won't save money, but it will dilute services."

6. "Want to be uncertain who to call? Just dissolve the Village"

7. Why fix something that isn't broken?

8. Don't take out your frustration with big government on our small efficient government.

Fighting dissolution becomes part of a push-back for those who resent the implied irrelevance of small-town communities. "Save our village" as a slogan thus is tantamount to a plea to "preserve our way of life."

Wurthnow (2013) views the narrative that small-town America is a thing of the past as a fiction but recognizes that many small-town residents live with the "gnawing fear that never seems to quite go away—that the community itself is on the verge of collapse" (Wurthnow 2013, 79). That the celebrations that take place after a failed dissolution vote are often exuberant reinforces this notion—they are a victory party celebrating the vindication of community.

A related anti-dissolution narrative is to emphasize the virtue of continuity over change. Wurthow's study of rural America identified a preference for the "familiarity of changeless places" as value that many residents associate with small-town living. "They like the fact that things stay the same" (2013, 55). That familiarity—or sense of being "rooted" in place—fosters "a sense of personal security" (2013, 57). Continuity keeps the connection between the individual and a shared, collective past. "Myths, images, sagas, and legends are symbolic modes of solidifying communities" (Keller 2003, 267). For many residents, then, the "illusion of changeless-ness" is intrinsically valued (Keller 2003, 267). It becomes important to them that the incorporation lives on, long after those who formed it are gone. "Spirit inheres in common memories and mutual understanding, a kind of tacit consensus as well as repertoire of shared values that may at times involve something akin to worship or a sense of sacredness about the collectivity of which all are members" (Wurthnow 2013, 52).

While change is inevitable, it stands to reason that gradual change is less traumatic than abrupt disruption. Residents certainly lament declining populations or the loss of businesses, but such changes often happen incrementally, sometimes over a prolonged period such that nostalgic affection for a romanticized, more prosperous past may warp the accuracy of those memories—things are often remembered as far better (or worse) than they actually were. Dissolution, even when it has been long debated or previously attempted, culminates into a single decision point, a referendum in which residents must make an immediate decision. That they often must do so without assurances of the outcome of that choice only exacerbates anxiety. If approved, a dissolution date marks a clear point of termination after which the village government ceases to operate. The mistaken belief that dissolution is irrevocable—that, once dissolved, the community is "gone forever"—only raises the stakes of the decision. Reestablishing an incorporation can be done; both Nyack and Ovid dissolved and then reincorporated. Practically speaking, however, dissolving and reincorporating would be a wasted expenditure of resources. Thus, the argument that "we can always go back," while true, likely would have limited appeal as a pro-dissolution talking point.

The desire for continuity and the fear of change create a substantial challenge for those who look to dissolution (or consolidation) as a pathway toward community renewal. Even change that has positive economic impacts may be lamented by locals. Long-time residents may resent the urbanization undertaken to attract new, often younger, more affluent residents, or efforts to promote tourism. Such economic development or change may be viewed as destructive to the former community and its existing social and economic relationships. Growth and development can create new problems even while solving old ones. As communities rejuvenate, the corresponding rise in property values and taxes will sometimes price out former residents or attract newcomers who may change the character of the existing community.

Applying Narrative Policy Framing Theory to the Dissolution Debate

Narrative policy framing (NPF) theory helps to explain why village dissolutions are so often unsuccessful. The durability of village government derives, in part, from the symbolic importance of the village as an ideograph, from the powerful narratives used by the anti-dissolution coalitions, and from the special role that village officials and employees have in framing and influencing the debate. Narratives "influence the public's perceptions of a policy" and thus impact public support (Pierce 2014, 32). For evidence-based policy scholars, understanding the role of narrative framing and how voters' perceptions of the facts are filtered through narratives is important. To what degree do narrative strategies impact the community-level decision to dissolve? Are policy narratives equally persuasive or more persuasive than the presentation of fiscal data in the decision-making process?

The focus here is at the macro and meso levels, the existence of meta-narratives and the use of narrative policy strategies in the dissolution debate (as opposed to studying the influence of narratives on individual voters). Meta-narratives are what Hochschild (2016) calls the "deep-story," or metaphors through which individuals understand the world.

There are four points in the citizen-led dissolution process at which the persuasive power of competing narratives may be inferred by the outcome:

1. The initiation/mobilization phase as measured by the success or failure to collect the requisite number of signatures to trigger a mandatory public referendum.

2. The debate and referendum phase as measured by the success (approval) or failure (rejection) of the proposed dissolution in a public referendum.

3. The reconsideration and permissive petition phase as measured by the success or failure to collect the requisite number of votes to trigger a permissive (second) referendum.

4. The debate and permissive referendum phase as measured by the success (approval) or failure (rejection) of the final dissolution in a permissive referendum.

The onus in the first two stages is on the pro-dissolution coalition to mobilize sufficient support for the petition (requiring signatures of 10 percent of the number of electors with no time limit for their collection) and to convince a majority of residents to support dissolution at the polls (even if there has not yet been a study or plan). After dissolution is approved in referendum, the burden shifts to the anti-dissolution coalition to mobilize sufficient interest to force a revote. Recall that to successfully do so requires filing a petition containing signatures of 25 percent of qualified voters, which must be collected within a forty-five-day window (a higher burden). The data and evidence available for voter consideration may be different in this reconsideration phase because the Empowerment Act imposes an obligation on the village board to prepare and finalize a dissolution plan within 210 days of the initial vote to dissolve. Thus, in the permissive-referendum stage, voters likely have more detailed information in the form of a "final" plan (although it should be recognized that even final plans are subject to implementation by the town).

In board-initiated proceedings, there are two stages or points at which the success of narrative policy persuasion can be inferred from the outcome:

1. The mobilization/initiation phase as measured by the success or failure of a village board to a) initiate a dissolution study and b) pass a resolution to put the dissolution to a public vote.

2. The dissolution debate and decision stage as measured by the success (approval) or failure (rejection) of the proposed dissolution in a public referendum.

In the first phase, the merits of studying dissolution are debated, and pro- and anti-dissolution coalitions try to influence the decisions of the board. In the second phase of board-initiated proceedings, the merits of the proposed dissolution plan are publicly debated, and the pro- and anti-dissolution groups campaign to influence the outcome of the vote. There is no reconsideration phase in the board-initiated process, so the burden remains on pro-dissolution supporters throughout.

Because the process is initiated and advanced by a resolution of the village board, the scope of the conflict may appear to be smaller, or internally contained, in board-initiated proceedings. Yet external pressure may be placed on board members in the pro- and anti-dissolution coalitions, and the threat of a citizen-led petition effort may be used to try to compel boards to initiate the process. In board-initiated proceedings, the timing of the resolution (which then triggers the time frame for finalization of a plan under the Empowerment Act) is under the control of the board, as are decisions to apply for state study grants, to hire an outside (third-party) organization to assist in the study, and/or to appoint a study commission that may or may not include citizens or town government representatives. Once the final dissolution plan is created, it is up to the village board to adopt it and set a date for the referendum.

In both citizen-initiated and board-initiated proceeding, once the issue advances to referendum, citizen coalitions also act as intermediary organizations, hosting public meetings, advocating in favor of or against dissolution, and engaging in strategic social media or voter mobilization efforts. Because elected officials are legally barred from using public resources to advocate on ballot measures, the competing citizen coalitions take the forefront in the direct campaigning to residents (Stern v. Kramarsky 1975; Office of the New York State Comptroller, Opinion No. 80-762, 1980).[1]

Those village residents who are qualified to vote have the opportunity for direct input on the decision by casting a ballot in the public referendum. TOV residents, although directly impacted by the dissolution, have no direct role in the process (aside perhaps from representatives serving on dissolution committees) but may join citizen coalitions in trying to influence the vote. If approved at referendum, the implementation of the dissolution plan and administration of village services falls to the town. Other actors, including NYCOM, consulting organizations, and the Office of Local Government Services, play an indirect role by providing expertise or guidance with respect to the process. Although typically presented as neutral, as voices of authority, these actors are pivotal in providing cues and information to the voters. Their presentations, the facts and information they emphasize, and the tone in which they communicate can intentionally or unintentionally signal bias to village residents or may serve to amplify or diminish fears of uncertainty. In some cases, study data will dictate a recommendation by the consulting organizations—that dissolution may or may not be in the community's best interest based on the projections of cost or legal constraints on service delivery options.

NPF theory argues that "narrative stories are the principle means for defining and contesting policy problems" (Stone 2012, 158). That is, problem definition and advocacy for (or against) a specific policy solution are communicated using "rhetorical narratives strategies (character driven plots, melodramatic narratives, stories of decline, metaphors)" (Shanahan et al. 2018, 192; Shanahan et al. 2013). Research suggests that narratives "to a greater degree are more likely to prevail in policy debates than those using technical or scientific communication" (Shanahan et al. 2018, 192). Narrative strategies are associated with policy outcomes, serving as an "artifact that can (1) either reflect the beliefs and actions of policy stakeholders . . . or (2) be viewed as important influences within policy processes" (Crow and Berggren 2014, 134). Narratives, in other words, can be used to manipulate public opinion and to infuse facts with values (or to filter facts through the lens of values). Thus the "role of narratives is critical to understanding the policy process, on various terrains and at multiple junctures" (Jones et al. 2014, 173).

Pro- and anti-dissolution coalitions "construct and disseminate narratives" about the meaning and value of a village government. That is, the competing coalitions engage in deliberate messaging designed to influence the outcome of the dissolution vote. For citizens, in whose hands the dissolution choice lies, much of the debate takes place in the public venue (i.e., at village board meetings and public information meetings hosted by pro-/anti-dissolution groups or third-party consultants and outside experts; and through websites, letters to the editor, and media reporting on the debate). An individual's (micro-level) choice is influenced by information that is shaped or filtered through the competing policy narratives put forward by the pro- and anti-dissolution coalitions. The competing coalitions selectively draw upon and present information to craft and fit their preferred narratives. It is not that information does not matter, but that information may be selectively deployed and its meaningfulness (or utility) magnified or diminished through its presentation within a broader, narrative structure. Those facts that are emphasized, and their importance or meaning, are influenced by the dominant narrative frame through which they are viewed.

The policy environment (external contextual factors), including the fiscal health of the community, population demographics, and state-level support and incentives, provide the setting and context for the debate. External actors, including state-level actors, municipal organizations, consultants, and town officials, serve not just as informational sources, but also as important characters in these competing narratives, or stories. What may seem a relatively straightforward choice (whether residents will be economically better off for a governmental reorganization) is a complicated calculus requiring voters to weigh monetized costs and benefits against intangible ones weighted by psychological attachments and personal loyalties. The individual choices of the voters translate into the ballot outcome, as depicted in figure 6.1.

Although each village dissolution is arguably unique in its fine details, common themes are echoed by the competing coalitions across time and place. Applying the NPF framework to the dissolution debate illuminates these themes as *a deliberate form of strategic narrative persuasion*. NPF research has identified four core elements of any policy narrative: 1) the setting, 2) the characters, 3) the plot, and 4) the moral of the story. The competing coalitions deploy these narrative elements to tap into existing policy beliefs and strategically craft a policy narrative (or story) that persuades the audience (in this case, the village voters) to their point of view. Differences in how pro- and anti-dissolution coalitions deploy these narrative elements are summarized in table 6.1.

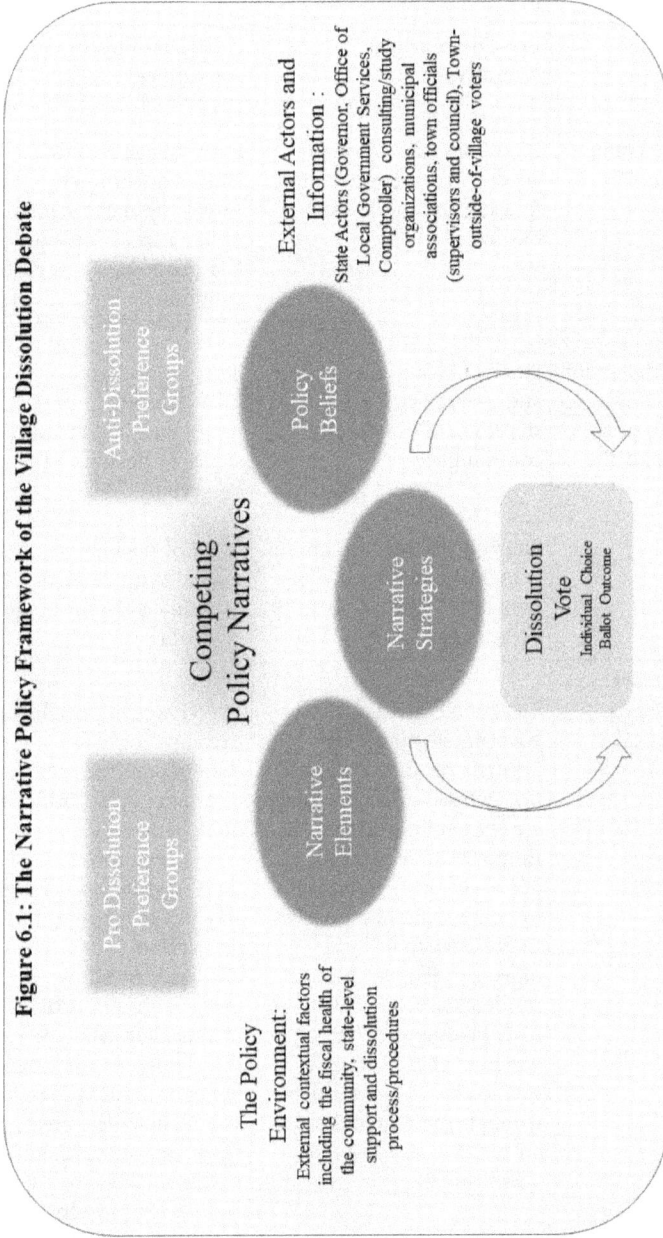

Figure 6.1. The Narrative Policy Framework of the Village Dissolution Debate.

Figure 6.1: The Narrative Policy Framework of the Village Dissolution Debate

Pro Dissolution Preference Groups

Anti-Dissolution Preference Groups

Competing Policy Narratives

Policy Beliefs

Narrative Strategies

Narrative Elements

Dissolution Vote
Individual Choice
Ballot Outcome

External Actors and Information :
State Actors (Governor, Office of Local Government Services, Comptroller) consulting/study organizations, municipal associations, town officials (supervisors and council), Town-outside-of-village voters

The Policy Environment:
External contextual factors including the fiscal health of the community, state-level support and dissolution process/procedures

Source: Author created graphic.

Table 6.1. The use of narrative elements by pro- and anti-dissolution coalitions

NPF Narrative Elements	Pro-Dissolution Narratives	Anti-Dissolution Narratives
The Setting The specific context and place of the narrative	New York has too many governments, contributing to a high property tax burden.	Each village is unique, and its government serves the narrow interests of its citizens: dissolution is a break with the past/ continuity.
The Plot The arc of the action where events interact with actions of the characters and the setting	Story of rising: dissolution and merge are a positive step toward building one community Story of decline: dissolution is logical consequence of population loss—a form of rightsizing	Story of rising: incorporation is part of progressive arc/growth, signal of health and longevity Story of decline: dissolution is a form of municipal retrograde or death
The Characters Victims, villains, and heroes	The problem (excessive government) imposes burdens on the taxpayers (as victims) and prescribed a policy solution (the Empowerment Act) to allow citizens (as heroes) to compel dissolution over the resistance of local officials (villains). Village residents are the victims of high taxes and declining services who can free themselves of the burden through the elimination of an unnecessary level of government.	The village, its employees, and loyal residents (heroes) are the victims of a disgruntled minority of citizens (villains) who are attacking their identity and chosen way of life. Pro-dissolution supporters are often portrayed as upstarts, recent arrivals, or outsiders who are threatening to dismantle the community's identity and history. The creation of an "us-versus-them" narrative plays to emotions of loyalty and tribalism, calling on shared collective identity to fend off the perceived threat to the community.

The Setting

NPF scholars remind us that "specific policy problems are situated within specific policy contexts" (Shanahan et al. 2018, 176). In New York, the broader context for the village dissolution debate is the assertion that New York has "too much government." This view, championed by Cuomo as both attorney general and governor, argues that the excessive layers of government contribute to the untenable tax burden on state residents. This view is not new, nor is the problem unique to New York. But the combination of environmental factors (declining populations, fiscal stress, high property tax burdens) means that many of New York's villages are experiencing challenges that can be fitted within the broader context of deindustrialization.

While communities may draw from a common reservoir of narratives, each place will have its own micropolitics and characteristics. Each village, within the surrounding town (or towns), is the precise setting of the debate. Its conditions (namely relative affluence, population, economic development and opportunities, existing village-town relations, tax burden, property tax base/values, and fiscal stressors) will vary. The unique history and circumstances of the place play an important role in the framing and the saliency of the narratives, all of which make *the village itself* (or the voter's perception of it) a major character in the drama. These are not hypothetical debates over service-delivery structures but are a referendum on the continued incorporation of a specific community with which its residents have direct experiences and connections. Residents tend to see the municipal corporation, as synonymous with the community. Some speak of the village in anthropomorphic terms—sometimes as a patient who needs to be either saved or allowed to fade away.

The Plot

The plot "situates the characters and their relationship in time and space"; it "provides the arc of the action where events interact with actions of the characters and the setting, sometimes arranged in a beginning, middle, and end sequence" (Shanahan et al. 2018, 176). The plot thus defines the problem, assigns blame or causality, and proposes specific solutions (Kear and Wells 104, 171; Stone 2012). Dissolution proponents, in other words, frame narratives that mobilize voters to dissolve, presenting dissolution as a policy solution to an identified problem (like high property tax burdens, dysfunction, or economic decline). The anti-dissolution coalition will craft counternarratives that favor maintaining the municipal corporation, whether by denying the existence or severity of any problems, rejecting village government as a causal reason for those problems, discrediting the benefits of dissolving, or highlighting the costs or uncertainty of the proposed dissolution. These competing narratives thus offer alternative explanations of who (or what) is to blame and whether dissolution is a viable policy solution.

In so doing, the competing coalitions draw on powerful metaphors or "deep stories," including the "story of decline" and its mirror image, "the story of rising," as identified by narrative framing scholars (Stone 2012, 158). Indeed, village dissolution takes place against a larger, often unspoken meta-narrative in which continuity (or longevity) and growth are viewed as a progressive, positive development. Incorporation, in this view, is indicative of community prosperity and growth, analogous in a life-span cycle to the community's birth. Population and economic growth are similarly and frequently believed to be indicative of healthy development, moving a community toward a progressive evolution—reincorporation as a city, for example—or toward stable, healthy maturation. Incorporation thus is firmly embedded within the narrative arc that Stone (2012) identifies as the story of "rising and progress" (Stone 2012, 159).

Some dissolution efforts are framed through this narrative of rising: dissolution is presented as a positive, progressive step toward a community's renewal or revitalization. Villages have sometimes dissolved to allow the community to take advantage of revenue opportunities, to benefit from state or private project funding, or to share in revenue streams from adjacent landfills, damns, or waterwork projects. The concept of disincorporation as a *progressive* development is a less common script, but it is one that pro-dissolution groups have sometimes successfully leveraged—and it is a narrative strategy that holds potential in facilitating further village-town mergers.

Disincorporation, on the other hand, is commonly associated with the story of decline, of population and economic deterioration or mis-management. Dissolution is frequently equated with retrograde or even municipal death. "What gives the decline story dramatic tension is the assumption, sometimes stated and sometimes implicit, that things were once better than they are now and that change for the worse causes or will soon cause suffering" (Stone 2012, 160). Many New York villages readily fit what Stone refers to as the story of "stymied progress" (2012, 159)—of once booming places now gone bust, impacted by the loss of key industries, by the rerouting of commerce in the industrial era, and by post–World War II forces of suburbanization and deindustrialization. Anti-dissolution coalitions draw on nostalgic remembrance of a once illustrious past juxtaposed against contemporary calls to terminate the village's existence to rally residents to preserve or save the village. To dissolve is to give into the story of decline and is something to be actively fought.

Pro-dissolution arguments may also employ the story of decline, presenting dissolution as the inevitable outcome of a downward trajectory in its health or circumstances. In this narrative frame, the village is dying (or dead), and dissolution is the inescapable or even natural conclusion. Framing dissolution within the familiar metaphor of the life span offers psychological permission to residents to "let go," to accept that decay and decline are natural, and that all things have a terminus. Dissolving thus can be framed as a way of preserving the underlying community through a logical downsizing. It also may be framed as an opportunity for metamorphosis or renewal, through rejoining the body politic of the town. But while portraying the village as moribund may convince some residents to surrender its incorporated status, it may arouse others to resist.

THE CHARACTERS

"As with any good story, there may be victims who are harmed, villains who do the harm, and heroes who provide or promise to provide relief from the harm and presume to solve the policy problem" (Shanahan et al. 2018, 176). In the dissolution debates, there are several common storylines in which the competing coalitions readily assign the roles of heroes, victims, and villains to the various actors. Indeed, the adoption of the Empowerment Act was framed in such terms: Cuomo (the hero) identified the alleged problem (excessive government) imposing burdens on the taxpayers (as victims) and prescribed a policy solution (the Empowerment Act) to allow citizens (as heroes) to compel dissolution over the resistance of local officials (villains). Many of the citizen-initiated dissolution efforts adhere to this story line, portraying village residents as the victims of high taxes and declining services who can free themselves of the burden through the elimination of an unnecessary level of government.

Of course, anti-dissolution groups have competing perceptions and story lines as to who are the villains, victims, and heroes. In their view, the village, its employees, and its loyal residents (heroes) are often viewed as the victims of a disgruntled minority of citizens (villains) who are attacking their identity and chosen way of life. Pro-dissolution supporters are often portrayed as upstarts, recent arrivals, or outsiders whose anti-neighborliness is a direct threat to the community. The crafting of an "us-versus-them" narrative plays to emotions of loyalty and tribalism to fend off a common threat.

Local officials, who play a prominent role in the dissolution process, can be cast in either the victim or villain role—as hard-working public servants (who are often part-time employees or volunteers) or as entrenched interests (protecting their unnecessary salaries and benefits at the public's expense). As "political actors [they too rely on symbols and stories] strategically to define problems in a way that will persuade doubters and attract supporters for their own side in a conflict" (Stone 2012, 160). NPF literature finds that "individuals are more receptive of policy stories that come from sources they trust"—that narrator trust enhances the persuasive power of the narrative (Jones 2014, 14; Jones and McBeth 2010). Village representatives and personnel, in other words, enjoy a status that lends special authority to their voice. When police and fire personnel become involved, they wield an additional level of gravitas, respect, and authority. Not only are residents fearful of a diminution of these critical services, but support for dissolving is also often framed as a direct insult to police and firefighters as local, self-sacrificing heroes.

Of course, village officials and employees have a professional and personal stake in the outcome, raising interesting ethical questions regarding their obligation under state dissolution procedures and law. Village clerks bear responsibility for verification of the petitions, while mayors and trustees have a duty to provide accurate information (facts and data) that have bearing on the public's decision. The Empowerment Act places elected officials in the position of neutral experts (to effectuate the wishes of the community, serve as a source of information in the process, and develop a dissolution plan). Whether (and how efficiently) information is shared affects the level of confidence that residents feel in making an informed choice. As power elites, village personnel are well positioned to sway the outcome both through their control of factual data/information and through their own narrative tactics. While some village representatives are candid concerning their own biases, others engage in "stake inoculation," an obfuscation or denial of their own self-interest in the outcome (Potter 1996; LeCouteur, Rapley, and Auguoustinos 2001).

The characterization of insiders and outsiders serves as another powerful part of the narrative element of heroes versus villains. Dissolution often leads to the division of "us" versus "them"—not just between the pro- and anti-dissolution coalitions, but also between those who reside in the village (in whose hands the decision of whether to dissolve lies) and the TOV voters (who have no direct input in the decision to incorporate or dissolve). Under the Empowerment Act, town officials have no formal role in the dissolution process, yet they are charged with its ultimate implementation and administration of village services post-dissolution. While TOV residents cannot vote on dissolution, they stand to see their taxes and services impacted by the town's absorption of the village. Thus, town-village relationships, whether cooperative or contentious, become part of the story. The village versus the TOV can be drawn into the narrative strategy of defining outsiders and insiders and may manifest in disputes over who is shouldering the tax burden in the framing strategy.

THE MORAL OF THE STORY

The moral or lesson "gives purpose to the character' actions and motives" and is often equated with the policy solution (Shanahan et al. 2018, 176). In the dissolution debate, the outcome is the collective choice of action (remaining as an incorporated entity or merging with the town). Various actors may attempt to draw lessons from other communities' experiences (often interpreted or selectively presented according to one's own narrative frame). There are, however, relatively few successful dissolutions from which to draw. Moreover, evidence-based evaluations of long-term *post-dissolution* impact are lacking. Often, the moral of the story is drawn from anecdotal evidence that a prior dissolution was successful (or not), filtered through existing biases. That is, pro-dissolution supporters may point to a dissolution example as a success story, while dissolution opponents will point to the same case as an abject failure—an example of Wilson's law of policy evaluation that holds that policy outcome will be evaluated as a success by supporters of the policy intervention and as a failure by its opponents (Wilson 1973).

Narrative Policy Persuasion in Select Case Studies

The voter-rejected dissolutions from Erie County in 2010 (addressed in chapter 5) revealed commonalities and contrasts in the narrative strategies employed between three differently situated villages (Parshall 2018). Recall that those efforts were spearheaded by a local activist whose goal was to encourage regionalism through the dissolution of all sixteen Erie County villages. While both the Williamsville and Sloan village boards adopted the same strategy on scheduling, their anti-dissolution coalitions diverged sharply in their messaging strategies. In Williamsville, emphasis was on the overall good health of the community and preservation of its high level of services. There was no need to dissolve, as nothing in the village was "broken." In Sloan, where conditions overall were grimmer, dissolving was framed as defeatist—as surrendering. Retaining the village was seen as a vestige of community well-being. In both cases, dissolution was soundly defeated and celebrated as a vindication of village pride.

Parshall (2019) moved a step closer toward empirical verification of deliberate messaging strategies by shifting the focus to the web and Facebook pages of pro- and anti-dissolution coalitions, testing theories developed in prior research against "specific observations from within a single case" (or set of cases) (Mahoney 2012, 570). The webpages and associated Facebook pages of the pro- and anti-dissolution groups in Lyons in Wayne County (2014) and Brockport in Monroe County (2016) cases were analyzed, for content and message, to answer the following questions:

1. What are the dominant narrative themes they utilized?

2. Does the persuasive strategy rely more heavily upon the presentation of data (facts and figures) or on narrative framing and storytelling?

3. Are the anticipated narrative elements present in the text or in the visuals?

   a. Is the setting (place) emphasized as part of a narrative strategy?

   b. Does the narrative strategy include metaphors or stories of rising/decline?

   c. Does the narrative strategy identify heroes and villains?

   d. Does the narrative strategy associate the policy outcome of dissolution to a moral of the story?[2]

Pro-Dissolution Narratives in Brockport (Monroe County) and Lyons (Wayne County)

The primary coalition supporting the 2016 petition for dissolution was an organization called NY Villagers for Efficient Government, the now-defunct site of which was accessed through an online digital archive. The text-heavy content of the website concentrated on three central themes:

1. Taxes and Fiscal Considerations

2. Village Elected Officials

3. Better Off Together/One Community

The central argument of the group was that residents were paying too much for too little. The website offered statistical comparisons of relative tax burdens, along with links to news items about taxes and efficiencies to be gained by transferring villages services to the town of Sweden. The few photos that punctuated the textual elements focused on financial issues: a stock photo of a man pulling out an empty pocket and a stack of one-hundred-dollar bills. The group logo was Lady Liberty, signifying freedom from excessive taxation. The moral of the story was straightforward: if residents want to save money, they should support dissolution. A second theme discredited village officials for keeping residents "in the dark," using original artwork to argue that village officials were thwarting public will. One hand-drawn cartoon was of a man in a top hat holding a lit match to sheet of paper as a bejeweled woman, in a dress from a bygone era, watches. The paper being lit on fire reads: "CGR Pre-Vote Study." The same drawing was shared to the group's Facebook page, asking, "Why is the Village Board keeping you in the dark? What are they afraid of? Is the Village Board using ignorance as a tool to instill fear of change, control our vote, and keep the status quo?" A second drawing shows the same couple in a rowboat, the "SS Brockport." A sign on the prow reads, "Property of the Village of Brockport." On the stern, another sign reads, "Sweet ride." The boat is passing the shoreline, where an elaborately ornate façade is identified by a sign as the "New Boat Launch." To the right, the skyline includes an outline of a church steeple, buildings, and hills; those on one side are grand, while those on the other appear to be in disrepair. The boat is heading into an eddy labeled "highest village taxes." In the vortex of the whirlpool are the words "village poor people." The caption reads: "Drowning in Taxes? Have they focused so long on the canal that they no longer can see the decline of the village's assets and no longer see YOU, the taxpayer?" The context, not evident from the drawing alone, was dissatisfaction with monies spent to restore the historic canal district. The moral of the story was dichotomized realities: that the less-affluent residents are funding public amenities benefiting an elite few. Both cartoons played on Brockport's self-promotion as a "Victorian Village on the Canal." The couple representing the trustees are affluent villains with the mindset of an earlier era, acting against the interest of low-income residents for whom the group argues even modest projected savings could provide substantial relief.

Of the three discernable themes, the one-community message was less well developed, but the website argued that the town of Sweden was more than capable of assuming essential services. There was an image of two human figures cooperatively fitting together two pieces of a jigsaw puzzle labeled town and village. The webpage did not include direct reference to more contentious aspects of the debate that played out prominently in local media (including alleged abuse by local police and code enforcement officers or verbal clashes between public officials and pro-dissolution coalition leaders). These omissions reveal a strategic use of narratives—certain negative, ugly aspects of the debate were downplayed or ignored to generate a more attractive pro-dissolution message. Links to the pro-dissolution groups in the villages of Lyons and Macedon confirm that there were interaction, communication, and policy learning between the different community groups.

Overall, the messaging of NY Villagers for Efficient Government was aimed at pocketbook considerations, crafting its message around lowering taxes, maintaining services, and overcoming the self-interest of entrenched village officials who were concealing the potential benefits of dissolving from the taxpayers. Dissolution was presented as a relatively straightforward policy solution to the problem of ever rising property taxes.

OneLyons, the pro-dissolution group at the forefront of the effort to dissolve the village of Lyons, deliberately focused its messaging strategy predominantly on the theme of "one community," as reflected in their organization's name, with a secondary focus on savings. The dominant themes of its website were:

1. One Community

2. Taxes and Fiscal Considerations

Its primary message was that unification would be a progressive step toward better, shared governance. There were multiple visual reinforcements, including full-color photographs of Lyons depicting a vibrant and picturesque community. Rather than invoking themes of decline or dysfunction (a story of decline), the photos focused on the positive image of a united, healthier community under a reduced tax burden (the story of rising). The moral of the story was "Together, we can unite under one government and work to solve our issues."

Such framing allowed citizens supporting this vision to perceive themselves as heroes—nothing was being destroyed; a stronger community was being created. The one-community theme included a preemptive response to an outsider narrative. Members of the coalition identified themselves in a group photo, providing personal biographies that emphasized their long-standing and deep community ties. They provided fact-heavy information (data on past dissolution/consolidation studies, the current, relative tax burden in comparable communities, and the projected savings of merging village and town services, along with various state-level audits and reports of the village and its water-system). Their messaging countered fears of lost heritage and history by framing the reorganization as an opportunity to solve problems and to enhance the shared interests of the village and town. The appeal to voters thus was both practical (focusing on property taxes, savings, service efficiency) and emotive (drawing on community pride and connection).

ANTI-DISSOLUTION/PRO-VILLAGE NARRATIVES IN BROCKPORT (MONROE COUNTY) AND LYONS (WAYNE COUNTY)

The pro-Brockport coalition's webpages were extraordinarily heavy on narrative persuasion, employing professional-looking, ad-like messaging that combined both text and images, concentrating on four dominant themes:

1. Loss of Services, With an Emphasis on Police, Fire, and Emergency Services

2. Us v. Them

3. Loss of History and Community Identity

4. Uncertainty

The loss of services message focused predominantly on emergency services. The moral of the story was stark: dissolution would literally cost some residents their lives. Police, ambulance, and fire personnel were depicted as heroes whose livelihoods were being threatened. Real people would lose their jobs, with real consequences for those who depended on their services in moments of crisis.

Dissolution was framed as an effort by wealthy, distant landlords seeking to lower their taxes and escape residential code enforcement. These forces were depicted as fat-cat capitalists, using a figure resembling the Mr. Pennybags character from the board game Monopoly. The message was: If "They" win, "You" lose. One ad reads, "landlords are trying to destroy our 187-year-old Village, just to eliminate police and code enforcement." Such caricatures, or cartoon villains, serve as a condensation symbol—an emblem that distills complex arguments into "simple, manageable, or memorable forms" (Achter 2004, 315).

Closely connected was an emphasis on the threat to and loss of community identity, history, and heritage. In their narrative framing, pro-dissolution supporters were the villains, synonymized with wealthy landlords; the victims were the village and its loyal residents. One appeal warned that "outsiders" are attempting to interfere with local self-governance in a way that threatens "village landmarks' and "village identity." In another ad, the Mr. Pennybags character dances gleefully on a grave while the headstone reads, "Brockport 1829–2016." Pro-Brockport thus visually equated dissolution with municipal death and the eradication of the community. The loss of incorporated status, they warned, would be the end of Brockport and of its familiar way of life.

The uncertainty message was less prominent but was equally clear: "Don't jump into the great unknown. With dissolution there is no plan." A tagline running throughout many of the ads reads, "dissolution is not unification, it's elimination!" Rather than a viable solution to real issues, dissolution was presented as an uncertain path to an unknown, but likely dire, result.

By contrast, the anti-dissolution group in Lyons, Save the Village of Lyons, relied almost exclusively on "uncertainty" as its dominant message, likely because the webpage was created *after* dissolution had been approved by the voters. As such, its messaging was exclusively targeted around forcing a permissive referendum, or re-vote. Their two variations on the same theme were:

1. Uncertainty
2. It's Not Too Late to Reconsider

A stock image (clip art) of a horse following a cart was a clear reference to a defect in the Empowerment Act: the vote to dissolve had taken place prior to the development of a dissolution plan, a backward process that put the proverbial cart before the horse. A photo of a pair of dice communicated a similar message: voting to dissolve was a game a chance, a roll of the dice. While proponents were betting that things would improve, the Save Lyons group warned that residents might very well lose everything on this gamble. On the day of the permissive referendum, they posted a colorful photo of the village of Lyons welcome sign as "The Peppermint Village" along with a message imploring residents that it was not too late to reverse course.

In both cases, and on both sides, there was strong evidence of intentionality and purpose in the crafting of narratives. The messaging was narrower, and much more *targeted* around specific themes than those covered by local media, suggesting a deliberate strategy in appealing to voters. In both cases, the place (setting), history, and character of the village were central to the messaging (plot and moral). The stories of decline and rising, however, were implied rather than overt, fitting with the idea of an unspoken meta-narrative, or deep story. For example, Brockport's pro-dissolution coalition portrayed the village government as antiquated, suited for a past prosperity that no longer existed. Dissolution was a logical (and equitable) solution—a way forward. The Pro-Brockport group contested the story of decline, and instead equated dissolving with municipal death, a solution that was not warranted given the overall positive quality of life. The narrative of rising was most overtly used by OneLyons, which framed dissolution as a progressive development, allowing both communities to flourish together. The anti-dissolution group conversely portrayed it as a final, negative step, a backward path in a literally backward process (i.e., placing the cart before the horse).

The use of narrative framing (i.e., storytelling) through visuals, condensation symbols, heroes and villains, and emotional appeal was most prevalent for the anti-dissolution coalition in the Brockport case, which made extensive use of well-designed ads that were professional in appearance. The pro-Brockport group was far better organized than its Lyons counterpart (likely a result of policy learning from Brockport's 2010 dissolution attempt). The narrower focus of the pro-village group, Save Lyons, was attributable as well to its creation *after* the vote had taken place. At that point, the onus was on them to force a permissive referendum by emphasizing uncertainty and through emotive appeal.

It is important to note that the webpages in both cases were more heavily focused on service provision and cost savings than had been predicted. The competing coalitions engaged in evidence-based arguments about the projected savings. Interestingly, the benefits (in the form of property tax savings) were often presented as more diffuse (generalized savings), while the framing of the costs (loss of services) was more particularized and personalized, especially as to the impact of emergency services. Whereas the status quo is known, until dissolution is implemented, actual savings cannot be guaranteed. Between the competing narratives, then, anti-dissolution (pro-village) coalitions arguably have an easier narrative task.

In both cases, the coalition with the more developed narrative strategy prevailed to different outcomes. Yet it would be far too simple to conclude that Lyons dissolved because the pro-dissolution group there told a better story or that Brockport did not dissolve because the pro-Brockport coalition had graphically superior messages. Indeed, the imagery and messaging in these two cases are relatively typical and reflect arguments that are familiar across place and time. However well-worn they may be, such narrative frames are powerful tools that have the capacity to sway voters even when the studies predict a property tax savings. A central principle of NPF theory is that people "are *homo narrans*: they are more likely to respond to narratives than to expert-based information" (Veselkova 2017, 171). When the narratives are unmasked, voters may be more self-aware of what is influencing their decision (logic or emotion). By understanding the power of narrative framing techniques, the pro- and anti-dissolution coalitions can learn to craft more effective messaging best adapted to the circumstances of each case.

Most importantly, NPF theory provides a richer understanding of the dissolution debate, helping to explain why village dissolution efforts are not more successful and why, despite state incentives, potential cost savings, and a declining need for new villages, dissolution more often than not is defeated at the ballot box. In short, dissolution proponents are losing the narrative.

Chapter 7

Explaining Municipal Reorganization
Success and Failure

The existing literature on municipal reorganization is limited in terms of both the number of studies and the number of cases in each study. Moreover, it has primarily focused on city-county consolidation efforts in the progressive (good government) or new-regionalism mold. Consolidations, particularly those in metropolitan areas, on which most of the theories are based, are relatively rare (Leland and Johnson 2000; Leland and Johnson 2004, 25). As importantly, there are open questions as to whether consolidations produce the anticipated benefits (Feiock 2004). While consolidation mirrors the village dissolution debate (i.e., reducing fragmentation, duplication, producing economies of scale, promoting regional thinking, and responses to shared problems), there are significant differences in process and context. While dissolution is functionally akin to consolidation, the primary difference in the procedure is that in dissolutions, *only* village residents may vote. Consolidations, moreover, create a new legal entity, generally requiring the adoption of a new charter. In dissolutions, the embracing town(s) assume control over the property and administration of the former village.

An Advisory Committee on Intergovernmental Relations (ACIR) study of consolidation in metro areas identified the factors affecting reorganization efforts (Advisory Committee on Intergovernmental Relations 1962). Among the favorable factors were:

1. the sympathetic support of state-level actors

2. the use of local knowledge in development of study/recommendations

3. extensive public hearings

4. attention to implementation issues and problems for various constituencies

Among those factors determined to be unfavorable to consolidation were:

1. the absence of a crisis or widespread consensus of a problem

2. vague or underspecified reorganization proposals

3. active or covert opposition of political figures

4. weak or disorganized effort

5. local distrust of media support for reorganization

6. uncertainty/fears of effect on proposed reorganization on local taxes

7. failure to communicate reorganization to unsophisticated voters

8. failure to anticipate organized opposition (7–8).

Given the hurdles, the ACIR recommended that reorganization efforts "should not be undertaken lightly but with full recognition of the obstacles to their success" (1962, 8).

Building on these ACIR findings, subsequent academic theories on consolidation have concluded, that for reorganization to gain the necessary political support, there must be some disequilibrium or disruption (Rosenbaum and Henderson 1972; 1973). In other words, there must be dysfunction or a crisis that is sufficient to overcome the tendency toward inertia and incrementalism. Critical situations may be ignited by the presence of an accelerating event such as scandal, an emergency, the attention of outside evaluators, or even the incapacitation or death of local leaders (Rosenbaum and Henderson 1972, 454).

The Rosenbaum and Kammerer model (1974) posited that there were three necessary stages for a successful consolidation to occur: First, a crisis climate must emerge. Second, an inadequate or failed governmental response triggers a power deflation—an intense or decreasing confidence in the existing governmental structure. In the power deflation stage, the opinions of elites or "community influentials" fuels the demand for change. Third, there needs to be an accelerating event to act as catalyst or kindling for public support. In this theory, a successful consolidation will only materialize *if* the existing units of government fail to adequately respond, thereby eroding confidence in the current system. An adequate response or the ability of the existing governmental structure to handle the crisis will dissipate demand and popular support for change. In this model, crisis or dysfunction rather than the search for operational efficiency is a critical element. So too is support of community elites and elected officials, many of whom have vested interest in the status quo or who otherwise might well "bleed on the altar of reform" (Rosenbaum and Henderson 1973, 255). Along with what they found to be an overall lack of resonance of economic efficiency arguments, Rosenbaum and Henderson also found evidence that even among elites, broad slogans mattered more than the details of the consolidation plan. Indeed, they questioned whether residents were typically familiar with plan details (Rosenbaum and Henderson 1973, 257–58).

The R&K model, as it is come to be known, was the dominant explanatory theory of municipal reorganization for more than three decades. Applications of the model emphasized the influence of professionalized campaigns for and against the consolidation effort (Messinger 1989; Johnson and Feiock 1999). Johnson and Feiock (1999), for example, recognized the importance of consolidation entrepreneurs, noting that "political, civic, and academic leadership can provide the stimulus to introduce consolidation as an alternative in the reform effort in a period of power deflation. Their support can provide a sustaining catalyst through the acceleration and the driving force in a campaign" (47). Feiock and Carr further broke the process into the agenda-setting phase (the focus of the R&K model) and the referenda stage, in which elites present competing pro- and anti-reorganization campaigns to the voting public (Feiock and Carr 2000).

The R&K model represents a "heroic" view of reform as radical, a form of "creative destruction" (Shepsle 2003) or "revolutionary change" (Carr 2004). But for the model's critics, reorganization is a regular "part of an ongoing struggle in communities, whereby different interests seek to institutionalize their preferences into the structure of local government" (Carr 2004, 15). Echoing Burns (1994), who found that economic self-interest is the motivator for municipal formation, Carr (2004) argued that those who support restructuring are more likely "motivated by the pursuit of these selective benefits" than of collective or regionally based ones more typically associated with radical reform (16).

Johnson (2004) identified additional problems with the R&K model, including its emphasis on a failed government response and power deflation. Her work broadened the scope of influentials in the process to include policy entrepreneurs as champions of change, as well as defenders of the status quo with a vested interest in maintaining the current governing structure. Business associations and the media, as major influencers of public sentiment, might be included in either the change or status quo camps, depending on the case. Moreover, she reframed the R&K model to account for the constitutional setting and legal rules, such as provisions for conducting and forcing the referendum, for determining who may participate in the vote, and for regulating how authority may be allocated post-consolidation. Focused on city-county consolidation, Johnson's model presumes that a study commission and development of a charter (or binding plan) is a required step prior to referendum, as the stage where power deflation must occur and where support coalesces or erodes.

Leland and Thurmaier (2005) found that the efficiency argument is a loser in most consolidation efforts, but that focusing on the economic development potential of the new, consolidated entity is critical. In their view, "the essential element of a successful consolidation is a group of civic elites who define the economic development vision for the community, determine that the existing political structure is incapable of supporting and implementing that vision, and convince the voters that city–county consolidation is the key to economic development that will benefit the whole community, not just the elites" (2005, 475).

Leland and Thurmaier (2004, 2014) proposed an enhanced R&K model, which they dubbed the C^3 model, that identified thirteen categories (or sets) of variables drawn from their own and existing research. To test the influence of these variable sets, they conducted intensive, comparative case studies of twelve city-county consolidations. Their analysis led to the conclusion that "consolidations are not about crisis" (2004, 481). They found no support that an accelerating event was necessary. Similarly, creation of a "successfully crafted consolidation charter" was a necessary but insufficient condition for consolidation success. What their research determined, however, was that the referenda messaging matters. In particular, the support of elected officials as part of the pro-consolidation campaign was essential to success. In terms of messaging, they further concluded that equity arguments (regionalism and socioracial distribution of benefits) were largely unpersuasive but that an economic development message would prevail if there was strong elite support (and a weak anti-consolidation coalition). Contrary to R&K's thesis, a climate crisis or power deflation was not required. Rather, "the essential elements of a successful consolidation, then, are civic elites who are able to define the economic development vision for the community, determine that the existing political structure is inadequate to support and implement that vision, and then successfully convince the average voter that consolidation *is the solution to the economic development problem* that will benefit the whole community, not just the elites" (2004, 487, emphasis added).

Subsequent scholars agreed that "efforts to reorganize local governments are not fought in terms of the likely costs and benefits," but rather are contested through competing narratives in which *framing* and heresthetical strategies are more important than substance: "The claims they make often have little to do with the actual effects of the proposed reorganization, but this is largely irrelevant. . . . Instead, we see the outcome as a result of strategic efforts to frame the issue and control the decision-making process" (Feiock, Carr, and Johnson 2006, 276–77). They concur that "city–county consolidation is not about efficiency, racial division, or even economic development. It is fundamentally about political losers trying to be winners and the current winners trying to prevent this turn of events" (Feiock, Carr, and Johnson 2006, 276–77). Yet, aside from identifying heresthetical strategies and the mobilization of "latent attitudes," the existing models offer few insights as to which messaging contributes to winning strategy (Carr 2004; Feiock, Carr, and Johnson 2006, 276–77).

Bringing the Study of Village Dissolution in New York into Existing Theory

The within and cross-case study analysis of village dissolution efforts in New York State offers lessons that both reinforce and challenge the existing theories of municipal consolidation:

1) THE SUPPORT OF LOCAL ELECTED OFFICIALS AND CIVIC ELITES IS CRITICAL TO SUCCESSFUL DISSOLUTION ATTEMPTS

New York's village dissolution debate affirms that local elected officials and civic elites are critical to any successful reorganization attempt. As a form of municipal reorganization, village dissolution realigns the existing structure of political power. Not surprisingly then, village elected officials are often highly resistant to dissolution efforts and threatened by the "perceived loss of political power and control" (Leland and Thurmaier 2014, 304). Even in the period of "Direct Command" (1847–1972), when the voters were given authority to directly compel dissolution at the ballot box, local officials often discouraged those efforts by raising legal objections to a petition, refusing to schedule the referendum, or otherwise delaying or impeding the implementation of an approved dissolution. In 1972, at the urging of municipal organizations, Article 19 procedures shifted the locus of control to local elected officials by requiring a study and formulation of a dissolution plan prior to a public vote. The Empowerment Act, in turn, sought to re-empower the voters by allowing them to direct elected officials to develop a plan through the power of referendum (bypassing the study process that was often used to delay action). The state further incentivized citizen interest through study and implementation grants, efficiency competitions, and tax credits. Yet village officials frequently take an active stance against dissolving, exerting elite influence in the debate.

Although the case studies suggest that the engaged and reassuring involvement of town officials can be pivotal to the outcome, town officials often remain silent, having no formal or required role under the Empowerment Act and little incentive to become involved before dissolution is fully approved by the voters.

2) The Legal Context and Institutional Setting Matter

Contrary to the findings in the consolidation research, village dissolution in New York demonstrates that the legal context, institutional rules, and legal mechanism under which reorganization takes place absolutely matter to the rate of success. By lowering the petition requirements, the Empowerment Act increased both the number of annual dissolution votes and the number of actual dissolutions—even though the rate of success (as measured by percentage of votes in which dissolution is approved) has decreased relative to Article 19. Changes to the state's dissolution provisions, enacted in 1972 and revised via the Empowerment Act, explain why dissolution efforts have accelerated statewide since 2010. The legal processes or mechanism under which a dissolution may legally proceed matter more than existing theories acknowledge. Research that fails to account for changes in or ease of the legal process is missing an important part of the municipal reorganization story.

The Empowerment Act's absence of a mandated study process prior to the public vote in citizen-initiated dissolutions has been successfully messaged as a deficiency in the law. At the petitioning stage, voters are often confused as to whether they are merely endorsing a study or calling the question to vote. Similarly, residents often mistakenly believe that a permissive referendum will automatically take place. The fear of moving forward without a finalized plan has been fueled by local elected officials, NYCOM representatives, and even some consultants who emphasize the element of uncertainty in public presentations. While residents are routinely made aware of this alleged deficiency in the Empowerment Act, they are rarely educated on the reason for its revisions—that it was meant to prevent local officials from using the study process to indefinitely delay or dissuade support for dissolution. Nor are residents informed that study and plan requirements prior to a vote (such as those formerly required under Article 19) never provided voters with definitive answers or binding guarantees. Rather, the implementation of any "final" plan is always contingent on the town(s). Indeed, there is regular evidence that elected officials continue to use the guise of a pre-vote study as a method of dissuasion: they may reinforce the idea that a vote is invalid without a prior study; they may overemphasize the costs of a study; they may refrain from providing, or may only selectively share, data and information; they may stress the aspects of uncertainty and possible service diminutions; or they may use their position of authority to dissuade the effort. Lost in the process is the central idea of citizen empowerment—that by voting to dissolve, citizens are essentially given power to command their elected officials to develop a *feasible and savings-producing plan and then* move that plan forward.

The role of elected officials is admittedly complex. Their task is to develop and implement a plan as *expressed by the will of the voters who voted to dissolve*, but many of them are personally predisposed against dissolution and resist it as a viable policy solution. Yet under the Empowerment Act, they are tasked with providing neutral information to guide the voters as to service options and efficiency opportunities and to craft a dissolution plan that comports with the voters' desire to retain an acceptable level of services via a more efficient service delivery arrangement. In this task, they are not allowed (per legally binding precedent) to use public expenditures to advocate one way or the other on dissolution (Stern v. Kramarsky 1975; Office of the New York State Comptroller 1980).

In multiple cases, however, one can observe the fuzzy line that sometimes exists between information provision and advocacy. Even while maintaining an official stance of neutrality, mayors and trustees frequently signal their own views using their public platform and resources to dissuade voters. Thus far, there have been few (and no successful) legal challenges to the use of public resources or the display of anti-dissolution bias by official actors. Town officials are in a similar bind, as they cannot lawfully spend money to influence the outcome of the vote and have no formal role in the study or planning process. Some town supervisors offer reassurances that can assuage residents' concerns over pending uncertainties, but most remain quiet. Public employees, including public safety and fire personnel, often openly enter the fray in support of retaining the village incorporation. Like elected officials, they are important community influencers, and their voice carries special gravitas in the debate over critical services.

Although there is no requirement that a study be conducted prior to the vote in citizen-initiated proceedings, it could be argued it has been informally reinstituted as village officials often apply for CREG study grants or prepare a preliminary report in advance of the vote. In so doing, they may emphasize its partial and preliminary nature or else publicly lament that there was insufficient time for a fuller study to be conducted.

3) Fiscal or Government Stress may be a Contributing Factor but Is Not a Sufficient or Necessary Condition for a Successful Dissolution

Most of the villages to dissolve in New York (before and since the Empowerment Act) have been small, rural, and economically struggling (Boyd 2008, 15). Historically, several became defunct by ceasing to exercise corporate powers or by functionally abandoning their charter. In the contemporary context, smaller municipalities may have more limited fiscal toolboxes of budgetary responses, requiring them to take the more drastic step of dissolution. That is, they may not have excess employees or spending to trim, may have a minimal fund balance, or are already pared down to essential services, leaving them with less flexibility and fewer options to find efficiencies. In a handful of cases, diminished capacity and mismanagement serve as a catalyst for village dissolution. When residents become apathetic or disaffected by poor village administration, dissolution can be a means of terminating an unsustainable situation. As revenues and services decline, residents may be more likely to have grievances with the administration of services, find fault with elected officials, or question the value of incorporation. Stress, in other words, may facilitate the political will (or remove political resistance to dissolution). Poor fiscal health may also impact the relative power of municipal governments to respond to challenges or leverage economic opportunities (a form of power deflation), thus encouraging pro-dissolution coalitions that are motivated by dissatisfaction with the status quo (Specter 2010).

Fiscal stress then can be a motivator to consider dissolution as one of several policy solutions. Aldag and Warner (2018b) liken the demographic, economic, and state-level policy pressures to a tightening vice that may eventually compel local governments to "leap" toward shared service or reorganizational reform. But they also compare the pressures to the proverbial boiling of the frog—that the pressures mount so gradually that some municipalities may be slow to respond (refusing to leap before it is too late). Scholarship on municipal responses to fiscal stress, moreover, suggests that municipalities will resort to less drastic budgetary solutions (such as reduction of services, shared service agreements, borrowing, or layoffs) before considering functional or structural reorganization.

The evidence from village dissolutions in New York State reveals no meaningful correlation between fiscal stress indicators, as measured by the OSC, and dissolution activity. This finding echoes a national study of 133 municipal dissolutions in which Beck and Stone (2017) identified six non–mutually exclusive factors to explain why municipalities dissolve. Contrary to their expectations, only 10 percent of municipal dissolutions (thirteen cases) were primarily attributed to fiscal distress (47). By contrast, the search for efficiencies and tax savings was cited in more than half of the cases. Other factors included citizen apathy (33 percent of cases), population exodus (14 percent of cases), county or state mandates (4 percent), or unique events (17 percent of cases) (Beck and Stone 2017).

Applying Beck and Stone's (2017) approach and analytical framework to the eighteen successful village dissolutions under the Empowerment Act (as detailed in chapter 3) produces similar results to their national study. As summarized in table 7.1, the search for operational efficiency was a dominant factor in 60 percent (eleven of the successful cases). Population exodus was a factor in 28 percent (five cases), while citizen apathy was a main driver in 11 percent (three cases). Fiscal distress was an issue in 22 percent (four cases), with Forestville being the most obvious example. There were two cases in which unique circumstances contributed to the search for operational efficiency. Dysfunction was present in several cases (most notably Mastic Beach, Macedon, and Altmar, although the latter was not uncovered until after the fact). As noted, the

Table 7.1. Primary drivers in successful dissolutions under the Empowerment Act

Village	Operational Efficiency	Citizen Apathy	Population Exodus	Fiscal Distress	Unique Circumstances	State or County Mandate
Altmar		X				
Lyons	X					
Keeseville			X			
Bridgewater		X		X		
Salem	X					
Prospect				X		
Macedon	X					
Hermon	X					
Port Henry	X					
Forestville				X		
Harrisville		X	X			
Mastic Beach	X				X	
Cherry Creek	X		X			
Barneveld	X		X			
Van Etten						
Morristown	X			X		
Harrisville	X					
South Nyack	X				X	

drivers as identified by Beck and Stone (2017) are not mutually exclusive, and there is an element of evaluator subjectivity in attributing a primary cause to any one category. However, this study of village dissolution in New York affirms their finding that fiscal stress alone is insufficient to understanding why some communities choose to dissolve.[1]

Beck and Stone's (2017) explanation for the low explanatory power of fiscal stress as a driver of municipal dissolution is that in most juris-dictions (and under precedence of the United States Supreme Court), dissolving does not free residents of the debt obligations incurred by their municipality. "Hence, dissolution is not an attractive option for munic-ipalities hoping to avoid debt payments" (47). Nevertheless, the authors recommend enhanced fiscal monitoring and the revision of state laws to make it "easier for local governments to improve operating efficiency by merging, consolidating, or entering into shared service agreements (49).

While it is true that fiscal and governmental stress are part of the village dissolution story (and may certainly contribute to the consider-ation and approval of municipal reorganization), neither is a necessary or sufficient condition for a successful village dissolution. Rather, the factors contributing to the decision to dissolve are complex. Because many of New York's villages face similar combinations of variables in terms of antecedent conditions, a case study approach and process tracing may provide a better analytical understanding than either fiscal indicators or surveys of local leaders.[2] There is also a temptation to infer acute fiscal problems from dissolution success. For example, Leland and Thurmaier (2004) found that civic problems (like depopulation, revenue decline, or service cuts) were discernible in most cases but concluded that such problems had reached a "crisis level" or were sufficiently present only in those cases of consolidation success (479). But their C^3 model does not clearly define what constitutes a crisis level, nor does it differentiate between long-term (chronic) or short-term shock (acute) stressors. The literature on fiscal stress, moreover, reflects disagreement as to whether perception matters more than objective fiscal indicators. Swanson (2004), for example, argued that crisis as identified by the R&K model was the artifact of elite perception and persuasion rather than being objectively present (as measured by fiscal stress metrics).

Leland and Thurmaier (2004) also suggest differentiating between economic decline and economic *growing pains* (479). This acknowledges that expansion, economic development, or rapid population or demographic changes may also trigger (or deter) municipal reorganization as a means of gaining power or retaining control over land use and development decisions. Boundary changes (incorporation, dissolution, annexation) may be necessary to meet new service needs, to block or control zoning and development authority, or to (re)define community membership. New growth places new stresses on existing infrastructure, results in new fiscal demands on the existing government, and creates potential flash points as local governments respond to the opportunities and threats. In this way, stress is not exclusive to struggling communities but may exist for high-development and rapid growth places as well.

How local governments respond to economic opportunities or threats may certainly lead to power deflation and therefore to reorganization efforts. Dysfunction, corruption, or crisis may be precipitating events sparking citizen-led campaigns to dissolve. But while there are village dissolution cases that lend credence to the R&K model, an acute crisis or accelerating event is not always necessary to spark dissolution efforts or success. In some cases, the slippage is gradual. There are also examples of successful dissolutions that were undertaken to promote a unified community vision or to otherwise leverage an economic opportunity or new revenue potentials that do not necessarily reflect power deflation so much as reimagined configuration to spur community growth and renewal.

4) Local Government Formation and Dissolution Is Increasingly about Zoning, Land Use, and Development

Consistent with Burns's (1994) thesis, the formation and disincorporation of local governments is largely driven by the economic self-interest of coalitions that mobilize citizen support. Indeed, New York's village dissolution debate illustrates how the incorporation, dissolution, or consolidation of these governing entities is integrally tied to the economic and social interest of residents, business and political elites, and community influentials who coalesce around the campaign to incorporate or dissolve. In the voters' calculus, the impact on their own property tax burden is a major factor of consideration. The ability to control or tailor zoning and land use regulations to community desires is another—and may offset the burden of higher property taxes. The power to exclude is connected both to the protection of private property (home values) as well as to the definition of community character. The impetus to incorporate or dissolve must be sparked by a coalition of like-minded individuals to initiate and steer the petition through the necessary requirements and legal challenges. In the ensuing effort, other community influentials, business, or elected officials may join (or oppose) the movement, attempting to sway and persuade their neighbors to support or oppose the proposal.[3]

Disputes between the pro- and anti-dissolution coalitions, between denser population centers and less dense areas in the suburban or rural areas of the embracing town (or towns), along with concerns over encroaching development or racial/religious tensions, play into both incorporation and dissolution efforts. The desire to protect existing property values, to retain amenities, or to preserve the lower-density or rural character of the community can exclude or price out minorities, restrict development, or turn affluent communities into enclaves of self-governing privilege (Mangin 2014).

5) Efficiency and Taxes Drives the Majority of Dissolution Attempts

Most of New York's dissolution efforts have been led by citizen coalitions seeking to reduce their property tax burden, with the debate centered largely on the potential benefits (or risks) as measured in resulting changes in tax rates. The economic focus fits with the state-level linkage of the property tax burden to New York's excessive number of local governments and the mounting fiscal pressures they face. Yet while most dissolved villages have been small and financially struggling, there is no correlation between indicators of fiscal stress and dissolution activity or success. The decision at the ballot box, in other words, appears to be driven by more than dollars and cents. Indeed, most dissolution studies demonstrate the potential for some savings for village residents, yet 60 percent of dissolution efforts are still rejected at the polls. Even the promise of a substantial savings is not enough to ensure that residents will support dissolution.

6) Policy Narratives Matter

The study of village dissolution in New York State adds substantial weight to the argument that policy narratives are instrumental to placing dissolution on the agenda and to its ultimate success or failure. Municipal reorganization "disrupts the citizen's established orientations toward his local government institutions and symbols" (Rosenbaum and Henderson 1972, 435). Residents must weigh potential savings against amenities and other intangible benefits. Dissolution campaigns that embrace a progressive agenda of unified community, or as the pathway to economic opportunity, have a greater chance at success—but articulation of that vision is tricky. Promoting dissolution as a policy solution in affluent or vibrant villages is difficult and countered by the argument that "if it ain't broke, don't fix it." At the same time, in struggling communities, disincorporation is portrayed in the anti-dissolution rhetoric and narrative framing as capitulation to decline or even as community death—something to be actively resisted. In other words, when residents enter the voting booth, their perception of the underlying problems (or even whether problems exist) and whether they see dissolution as a viable solution will be heavily influenced by meta-narratives that equate incorporation with progress and growth and dissolution with retrograde and decline. Their choice is influenced, moreover, by the strategic narrative framing and persuasion of the anti-dissolution coalition, which arguably has the easier narrative task of raising the specter of uncertainty and stoking the fear of change.

State-level policies that rely exclusively on fiscal incentives and pressures, or appeal primarily to efficiencies and savings, are likely to remain ineffective. In focusing on future reforms, more space needs to be given to facilitating community conversations that are guided by a better understanding of how narrative tactics impact voter choice (and therefore reorganizational success or failure). One element of the Empowerment Act's initial proposal that has not been fully realized is the creation of a "Local Reorganization Knowledge Network"—a consortium of experts and institutions to support citizen-initiated efforts and assist in messaging (Cuomo 2010, 19). While the intent to *empower* residents is reflected in the name (the *Empowerment* Act), most residents do not understand the rationale of its provisions—that the revised process was designed to allow citizens to force reluctant elected officials to develop a viable plan that will retain an acceptable level of service at reduced costs. Governor Cuomo (as chief advocate) instead frequently placed blame on the inefficiencies of local government, rallying loyal residents to defend rather than critically examine existing local service arrangements. Understanding how certain arguments resonate with residents might also warrant legislative responses or changes in town law, such as allowing policing to be provided by towns on a districted basis or authorizing towns to provide fire services, for example. The elimination of such legal barriers was initially proposed as a related step to the Empowerment Act, yet restrictions on the delivery of these critical services remain major sticking points discouraging dissolution support.

The lessons of narrative policy understanding, however, will continue to play out primarily in the public discourse and debate. Success stories suggest that progressive arguments, such as village-town unification and one-community themes, are more likely to gain traction. Narratives focused on stories of rising (or moving toward something better) appear more successful than those focusing on community despair. Indeed, even in cases of obvious decline, residents openly resent dissolution, rhetorically equating it with failure.

In the crafting of a new community vision, community leaders, like businesses and historical, religious, and cultural organizations, can play an important role not just in assuaging fear of loss, but also in fostering deliberate and creative placemaking, community rituals, and social interactions that can exist separate and apart from municipal sponsorship. Indeed, the robust support of community and placemaking often exists *within* municipalities at the neighborhood level (think of theater, business, or art districts) and in unincorporated places. There are social networking functions that can be facilitated by town (or county) governments as well as by voluntary citizen or cultural organizations. Tapping into these resources as part of a pro-dissolution campaign, building on the creative entrepreneurialism of cultural organizations and influencers, or demonstrating how such community-facilitating activities will continue to exist (or can be created) in the absence of a village government might also be more powerfully employed by pro-dissolution coalitions in future public debates. Insofar as dissolution proponents have the harder narrative task, understanding the psychological attachment of residents to their local governments (and the everyday politics through which such attachments form) is essential to crafting a successful pro-dissolution campaign.

7) Regionalism and Equity Messages Have Limited Effect in Encouraging Dissolution

Maintaining more than 550 village governments, the majority of which are small, may not make sense from a statewide perspective, but when residents vote on dissolution, they are evaluating their choice from a decidedly local point of view. Local communities have reason to be exclusionary and few incentives to think regionally (Kazis 2020). Leland and Thurmaier (2004) found that, in metro-consolidations, equity arguments tend to fall on deaf ears. The same is true in the village dissolution effort. The Erie County cases in 2010 were a coordinated (and unusual) effort to promote dissolution

as a pathway to regionalism and countywide benefits—an argument that
was soundly rejected at the polls. Residents of affluent communities are
typically willing to shoulder higher taxes in return for what they perceive
as greater quality of services. Residents of struggling communities resist
dissolution as conceding to decline or irrelevancy. In either case, their
scope of concern tends to be narrowly restricted to the direct impact on
their own taxes, services, and daily quality of life. County or statewide
benefits appear to rank far lower in the residents' calculus.

TOV residents have no vote on village dissolution—a reality that
fosters resentment and leads to claims and counterclaims over who is
subsidizing whom. That same desire to pay only for services of direct
benefit, or to create augmented services that are superior, has also led to
wealthier enclaves seeking to withdraw from the surrounding community
by forming their own government. As a form of boundary change, village
dissolution reshapes the definition of the community and the boundaries
of shared obligation. Such competing self-interests are perhaps most dramatically demonstrated in the Hudson Valley cases, where tensions created
by growing ultra-Orthodox communities have led to the creation and
dissolution of villages to either protect or dilute that community's political power and influence over matters of zoning and local law authority.

8) There Is Policy Learning Between Communities and Between Dissolution Attempts

The evidence of policy learning between villages and over time confirms
findings of previous consolidation research. Interviews with pro- and
anti-dissolution coalition leaders confirms that they use other community
examples to inform their own efforts, borrowing techniques and messaging
from other groups. Moreover, the effort to dissolve can be repeated in
unsuccessful cases once the moratorium has expired. Subsequent dissolution
attempts reveal differences in approach based on the lessons of the prior
effort. Community debate over the relative advantages and disadvantages
of incorporation is not a static, onetime discussion. Contemporary debates
over dissolution follow old and familiar themes—a rehash of the same
arguments that were used in cases from the 1880s or that attended the
original debate over incorporation. Then, as now, pro- and anti-dissolution
supporters feuded over the anticipated tax savings, the potential loss of
services, the fear of losing their community or historical identity, and
the need to retain dedicated representatives. A better understanding of

past dissolutions and the evolution of dissolution procedures may help alleviate modern fears.

While every community feels that it is unique, it grapples with most of the same concerns and arguments as its peers—present and past. What has changed is a marked decline in the number of new village incorporations—an apparent byproduct of the expansion of town and suburban town powers and the ability to provide services through the creation of special town districts. A village government may not be as necessary to providing local services as it was in the past, but once created and in existence for many years, there is a disinclination for residents to surrender their village government.

9) Significant Impediments to Dissolution Efforts Remain

Evolutionary models of reorganization, such as that offered by Hughes and Lee (1999), suggest that mergers represent a "natural progression from the cooperation of local governments in fiscal and service delivery needs to a complete structural consolidation" (Johnson 2004, 156). As such, the sharing of services or the consolidation of functions is often viewed as a stepping-stone toward structural reform. The argument is that, rather than pushing for dissolution of villages, the state ought to promote shared services and functional collaboration to reduce costs and create a more natural, evolutionary pathway toward village-town consolidations.

Gradual mergers eased by the largely amiable cooperation between village and town officials are in some ways, the best-case scenario. At the same time, such developments reinforce the view of dissolution as the inevitable outcome of decline. Maintaining the current level of services and the same number of service-providing units, however, reduces the net savings and may produce what Savitch and Adhikari (2017) term "fragmented regionalism" wherein the push-pull of centripetal and centrifugal forces leaves local autonomy intact even as regional authorities with selective powers emerge. Such "back-door" regionalism, they argue, contributes to (rather than reduces) municipal fragmentation in metropolitan areas (396–97).

Moreover, greater shared services may also serve as an obstacle to reorganizing insofar as it presents an *alternative* that maintains the status quo. That is, rather than eliminating entire units, the argument is for greater service sharing or functional consolidation. For particularly sticky services—like fire and police protection—options that maintain the status quo are likely to generate increased support but at the cost of potential savings. Pro-reorganization advocates often point out that shared-service options represent "low-hanging fruit"—an option in which the easiest efficiencies are recognized first, are quickly maximized, or dissipate with time, meaning they have limited overall effect. Indeed, fiscal management scholars have found that "governments start with the easiest and least disruptive tools for adapting to fiscal threats and then move toward harder and more disruptive options as the threat increases or continues or if they have used up tools at a lower level" (Hendrick 2011, 249). Writing in the aftermath of the Great Recession, Hendrick agrees that sustained fiscal stress can force governments to move beyond budgetary controls into functional or structural reorganization. But she also notes that the pressures may be different in suburban metro areas than in rural places, where the transaction costs are higher and the collaborative benefits are lower (254–55). The distribution of pressures to dissolve or consolidate is not random, but the explanatory power is not simplistically related to fiscal stress.

The Future of Local Government Reform in New York State

Most of the legislative proposals to revise the Empowerment Act thus far have been procedural or technical revisions designed to remedy deficiencies either by adding a timeline for the collection of signatures, by reinstituting a formal pre-vote study process, by increasing the petition requirement threshold, or by extending the period for formulating a final plan.[4] Other legislative proposals would preempt citizen-initiated petitions where there is already a board resolution in place or would require that any citizen-initiated dissolutions be twice approved at the ballot box (once upon the filing of the petition and again following the finalization of a formal dissolution plan). Other proposals would exempt villages entirely from the Empowerment Act's provisions on the grounds that they are critical service providers[5] or would allow towns to create a hamlet district to continue the services of the former village.[6] Other bills have called for a moratorium on all incorporations and dissolutions while the legislature studies the issue.[7] These latter measures have been influenced by the Rockland and Orange County cases where incorporation and dissolution efforts around expanding ultra-Orthodox communities are particularly politically fraught.

County reorganization authority, revitalized by the Empowerment Act, remains an unused provision within the law. Rather than leaving local government dissolution (or consolidation) up to the officials and voters of individual villages, there may need to be greater emphasis on the mechanism wherein county residents may vote to reorganize sub-county government structures or to simultaneously dissolve all villages within the county. The present exemption of town government from citizen-initiated dissolution and consolidation procedures might also be reconsidered. The more drastic of these approaches would recognize that any problems resulting from an outmoded and inefficient local government structure (including the costs of maintaining multiple, overlapping units of government) exceed the territorial reach of a single village entity. That is, that the locus of decision-making authority must be removed from local hands.

There is a dearth of scholarly research and information on municipal dissolution (or disincorporation) to guide future reform. Studying village dissolution in New York State, Zhang (2022) finds that dissolution impacts revenue source composition but does not reduce overall revenue or spending (as service provision costs are transferred to the town and efficiencies already maximized), nor does it impact housing sale prices. There must be more research as to the practical consequences through the examination of the effects of dissolution five, ten, or twenty years out—a question that the state has, thus far, neither funded nor studied. The state might play an even greater role in educating the voters on the dissolution process, opportunities, and pitfalls, and the statewide costs of maintaining multiple general-purpose governments. Instead, New York has taken an evolutionary approach to dissolution, one that is largely reactive, and has been consistently deferential to local control (redefined to give primacy to elected officials over the will of the citizens).

Moreover, even as the state has dedicated substantial resources to encouraging consolidation and dissolution, New York retains an outmoded incorporation process—one that similarly cedes authority to local desire, subject to only statutorily prescribed minimal population and territorial limitations, without any process for a substantive review that considers the merits of incorporating in terms of fiscal viability or the overall public interest. A more revolutionary approach then may be in order—one in which the state mandates municipal reclassification or reorganization or brings all border change (incorporation, dissolution, annexation) under the auspices of state review, either through a legislative committee or state boundary commission. A relatively elemental but powerful step would be a reclassification of municipal forms and powers based on relative population size—one that legislatively reclassifies small cities as villages and larger villages as cities, simultaneously providing for an automatic dissolution vote, or even the forced dissolution, of the state's smallest villages. A legislative reclassification of municipal entities might also account for the differences in service delivery needs based on a cluster analysis of municipal characteristics, such as that suggested by the Office of the State Comptroller in 2008. Under such a system, the assignment to a class (and the corresponding powers and formulas for state local government aid) would account for the size, rural-to-urban characteristics, adjacency to or overlap with other municipal entities, and corresponding differences in service needs, making localities within each class more homogenous in character (Office of New York State Comptroller 2008).

As the champion of consolidation, Andrew Cuomo successfully seized on the long-standing claim that New York's local government structure was outmoded and unnecessarily duplicative. The Empowerment Act was partially predicated on the findings of the Lundine Commission (2008) but did not embrace all of its recommendations.[8] Cuomo's executive budgets regularly dedicated substantial resources to incentivizing reorganization efforts, including state grants, tax credits, and enhanced efficiency program funding. At the same time, his policies pressured local governments through the enactment of a property tax cap and the replacement of direct AIM funding to most towns and villages with AIM-related payments that are subtracted from the counties' share of state internet sales taxes. The centerpieces of these reorganization efforts—the Empowerment Act and the Citizen Empowerment Tax Credit—have always been contingent on annual budgetary appropriations.

Whether legislative commitment to continuing such payments indefinitely remains to be seen and will be contingent on the policy preferences of future executives. Current Governor Kathy Hochul (who became governor upon Cuomo's resignation in 2021) has more extensive local government experience than any previous governor.[9] Thus far, she has not taken a stance on local government consolidation efforts, but her first executive budget proposal included increases for CETC and efficiency programs as well as a restoration of direct AIM payments to all municipalities (New York State Executive Budget Briefing Book 2022). A bolder move would be for the executive to reappoint a study commission, encourage legislative study initiatives, or advocate for the creation of a

New York State boundary commission to review the substantive impact of *all proposed municipal boundary changes.*

Scavo and Washington (2012) report that thirty-one states have had some form of local government streamlining or efficiency study commission. Among the most notable of these, Indiana and Michigan have taken governor-led, top-down approaches. In Indiana, with the support of the state and local chambers of commerce, the 2006 Government Modernization Act (IC Title 36, Ch. 1.5, Art. 4) provided a process for municipal consolidation, resulting in seven consolidation attempts between 2008 and 2012 (two city-county, one city-town, and four town-township, of which two town-township consolidations were successful) before municipal and public backlash killed the effort (Morse and Stenberg 2018).[10]

In 2011, Michigan authorized the appointment of emergency managers for fiscally stressed municipalities, a measure that was controversial and politically unpopular even before the Flint emergency manager's decision to draw the city's water supply directly from the Flint River resulted in one of the nation's worst public health disasters.

Other states, like Ohio and Pennsylvania, have authorized study commissions or (as in Pennsylvania) have legislatively eased pathways for the consolidation and merger of municipal entities. Ohio provides for involuntary municipal dissolution in cases of prolonged fiscal emergency (ORC §118.31) as well as for small villages (those fewer than 150 in population and 2.5 square miles) that meet at least two of six statutory criteria as determined by the auditor of the state (ORC §703.201). But while Ohio authorizes forced dissolution, this authority is rarely invoked. Instead, the eleven small Ohio villages that have dissolved since 2010 have been voluntary, citizen-initiated efforts (under ORC §703.20) and are largely driven by residential concerns about fiscal woes and rising taxes (Parshall (2022).

New Jersey (a state in which villages exist in name only) has been the closest to New York in its combined approach of state policy pressures and incentives. New Jersey launched a Local Unit Alignment Consolidation and Reorganization Commission (LUACRC) to study and make legislative recommendations, required efficiency review and shared services accompanied by reductions in state aid, and made it easier for voters to initiate and approve mergers. The results were mixed (Morse and Stenberg 2018). Overall, Morse and Stenberg (2018) conclude that local government distrust and pushback against state-level reforms have stymied state restructuring efforts. They recommend partnership and incentivized (bottom-up) approaches over mandated (top-down) reform, and advocate for capitalizing on the areas that are most ripe for reform first (such as shared-service initiatives).

Mandated reform has always been dismissed as politically impractical, although the authority of the state over its subdivisions is well established. Deference to local control (particularly where the locus of that control and access to necessary information rests not with taxpayers but with the elected representatives of the local governing entity) has proven equally unpragmatic. The intent behind the Empowerment Act was to better enable local citizens to reimagine local government structure, making it easier to consolidate and merge services. Yet there is a certain impetus behind the creation of a village and a certain amount of inertia underlying its continued existence. The major stumbling block of municipal consolidation continues to be local control over the decision. New York State continues to incentivize consolidation and dissolution, leaving it to local choice and ceding control to those least motivated to pursue the option: local elected officials. It also may be time for the state to overhaul its approach to home rule (including the 1963 constitutional revisions that granted equal constitutional status to counties, cities, towns, and villages alike). The class of powers granted to each municipal form might also be redefined as a means of forcing local governments to adopt the form most suitable to their population and residential character.

Village dissolutions are often regarded as discrete, insular events, but should be viewed both historically and within the context of local government development. Contemporary dissolution debates still narrowly focus on the anticipated post-dissolution property tax savings for village and TOV residents. To effect meaningful change, New York State policy makers may need to reconsider whether the solution to a structural, statewide problem with spillover effects for adjacent municipalities is truly best left in local hands.

Appendixes

Appendix A: Pre-1900 Dissolutions

Disincorporated by Legislative Repeal		
Village (County)	**Incorporated**	**Repealed**
Columbiaville (Columbia)	1812	1833 (L. 1833, Ch. 186)
Douglas (Delaware and Sullivan)	1867	1878 (L. 1878, Ch. 242)
Gaines (Orleans)	1832	1857 (L. 1857, Ch. 393)
Montezuma (Cayuga)	1866	1889 (L. 1889, Ch. 340)
Ovid (Seneca)	1816	1849 (L. 1849, Ch. 387) (Reincorporated 1852)
Port Ontario (Oswego)	1837	1844 (L. 1844, Ch. 323)
Ceased to Exercise Corporate Rights		
		Lapsed/Abandoned
Brewerton (Onondaga)	1872	1878
Clintonville (Clinton)	1825	1890s
Constantia (Clinton)	1836	1870s
Ebenezer (Erie)	1846	1860s
Unresolved Cases*		
Auroraville (Erie)	1836 (L. 1836, Ch. 454)	
Durhamville (Oneida and Madison)	1849 (L. 1860, Ch 133)	
Knowlesville (Orleans)	1836 (Incorporated L. 1836, Ch. 535, Charter Renewed L. 1840, Ch. 114)	

continued on next page

Appendix A *(continued)*

Unresolved Cases*		
Sullivan (Madison)	1823 (L. 1823, Ch. 196)	
Dissolved Under General Village Law		
Nyack (Rockland)	1872	1877 (Reincorporated 1883)
St. Regis Falls (Franklin)	1887	1888 (Legislatively affirmed L. 1913, Ch. 184)**

*The mechanism and circumstances under which the incorporated village became disincorporated is not clear, but their charters were likely abandoned, and they were never reincorporated under General Village Law. Only Durhamville (originally incorporated in 1849; charter amended 1869) is a potential candidate for dissolution under the general law provisions. The Verona town historian had no documentation of the circumstances under which Durhamville lost its incorporated status (telephone interview, August 20, 2011).

Appendix B: Village Dissolutions 1900–2009

Village (County)	Incorporated	Dissolved
Roxbury (Delaware)	1883	1900
Prattsville (Greene)	1888	1900
Rifton (Ulster)	1883	1919
Belfast† (Allegany)	1905	1920
Union** (Broome)	1871	1921
La Fargerville (Jefferson)	1922	1922
Brookfield (Madison)	1887	1923
Oramel (Allegany)	1856	1925
Marlboro** (Ulster)	1906	1923
Eastwood** (Onadaga)	1894	1926
Newfield (Tompkins)	1895	1926
Pleasant Valley (Dutchess)	1903	1926
Sound Avenue** (Suffolk)	1921	1927
Marlborough** (Ulster)	1788	1923
Belleville (Jefferson)	1860	1930
Northville (Suffolk)	1921	1930
Jamaica Square** (Nassau)	1925	1931
Henderson (Jefferson)	1886	1933

Old Forge (Herkimer)	1906	1933
North Bangor (Franklin)	1914	1939
Forestport (Oneida)	1903	1940
Village of Landing (Suffolk)	1927	1940
Downsville (Delaware)	1921	1950
Amchir (Orange)	1964	1968
Prattsburg (Stueben)	1877	1972
Fort Covington (Franklin)	1889	1975
Friendship (Allegany)	1898	1977
Rosendale (Ulster)	1890	1977
Savannah (Wayne)	1867	1979
Elizabethtown (Essex)	1875	1980
Bloomindale (Essex)	1905	1985
Pine Hill (Ulster)	1895	1986
Woodhull (Steuben)	1899	1986
Pine Valley (Suffolk)	1988	1991
Westport (Essex)	1907	1992
Ticonderoga (Essex)	1889	1993
Filmore (Allegany)	1924	1994
Schenevus (Otsego)	1870	1994
Mooers (Clinton)	1899	1995
Andes (Delaware)	1863	2003
Pike (Wyoming)	1848	2008
Limestone (Cattaraugus)	1877	2009

Data for 1900–2006 were taken from the New York Department of State's website and cross-checked by the author's research at the New York State Archives where incorporation files of villages are maintained. Appendix B does not include the consolidation of the villages of Pelham and North Pelham (Westchester County) in 1975 and the consolidation of the villages of East Bloomfield and Holocomb (Ontario County) in 1990, which are typically reported as dissolutions in the state sources.

**Notes of caution: The reported dissolution of Jamaica Square (Nassau County) appears to be an error. The village was renamed South Floral Park in 1931 and remains in existence. Three of the dissolutions reported by the state were annexations: the village of Union merged into the village of Endicott in 1921; the village of Eastwood was annexed to the city of Syracuse in 1926, and the village of Amchir was annexed by the city of Middletown in 1968. The village of Sound Avenue (Suffolk County) was renamed Northville in 1927 and officially dissolved in 1930. Thus, it was reported twice by state sources. The villages of Marlboro and Marlborough (Ulster County) appear to be the same community alternatively spelled.

†Note: The village of Belfast (Allegany County) was not included by state sources but was dissolved by L. 1920, Ch. 292, which transferred real property of the "dissolved village of Belfast" to the water district of the town of Belfast.

Appendix C: Village Dissolution Votes 2010–21

Village	Town	County	Outcome	Village Law Provision	Initiated by:	Referendum Date(s)	Votes In Favor	Votes Against	% Support
Randolph	Randolph	Cattaraugus	Approved	Article 19	Board	March 16, 2010	125	13	91%
East Randolph	Randolph	Cattaraugus	Approved	Article 19	Board	March 16, 2010	57	13	81%
Perrysburg	Randolph	Cattaraugus	Approved	Article 19	Board	March 16, 2010	60	9	87%
Seneca Falls	Seneca Falls	Seneca	Approved	Article 19	Board	March 16, 2010	1198	1112	52%
Port Henry	Moriah	Essex	Rejected	Article 19	Board	March 16, 2010	146	186	44%
Empowerment Act Effective March 21, 2010									
Brockport	Sweden	Monroe	Rejected	Empowerment Act	Citizen	June 15, 2010	652	959	40%
Williamsville	Amherst	Erie	Rejected	Empowerment Act	Citizen	August 17, 2010	309	1546	17%
Sloan	Cheektowaga	Erie	Rejected	Empowerment Act	Citizen	August 17, 2010	236	1331	15%
Lakewood	Busti	Chautauqua	Rejected	Empowerment Act	Citizen	August 25, 2010	353	848	29%
Farnham	Brant	Erie	Rejected	Empowerment Act	Citizen	September 28, 2010	37	130	22%
Cuba	Cuba	Allegany	Rejected	Empowerment Act	Citizen	September 28, 2010	43	402	10%
Macedon	Macedon	Wayne	Rejected	Empowerment Act	Citizen	October 12, 2010	199	295	40%

Altmar	Albion	Oswego	Approved	Empowerment Act	Citizen	November 10, 2010	80	74	52%
Altmar**	Albion	Oswego	Approved			December 6, 2011	54	50	52%
Odessa	Catharine	Schuyler	Rejected	Empowerment Act	Citizen	December 7, 2010	74	154	32%
Whitesboro	Whitestown	Oneida	Rejected	Empowerment Act	Citizen	January 4, 2011	366	709	34%
Edwards	Edwards	St. Lawrence	Approved	Article 19	Board	March 11, 2011	55	9	86%
Candor	Candor	Tioga	Rejected	Article 19	Citizen	March 15, 2011	70	165	30%
Schuylerville	Saratoga	Saratoga	Rejected	Article 19	Citizen	March, 2011	73	321	19%
Potsdam	Potsdam	St. Lawrence	Rejected	Article 19	Board	November 8, 2011	334	687	33%
Camillus	Camillus	Onadaga	Rejected	Empowerment Act	Citizen	November 8, 2011	158	229	41%
Leicester	Leicester	Livingston	Rejected	Empowerment Act	Citizen	December 20, 2011	48	135	26%
Corinth	Corinth	Saratoga	Rejected	Article 19	Citizen	January 17, 2012	209	338	38%
Lyons	Lyons	Wayne	Approved	Empowerment Act	Citizen	November 6, 2012	569	524	52%
Lyons**	Lyons	Wayne	Approved			March 18, 2014	519	353	60%
Malone	Malone	Franklin	Rejected	Empowerment Act	Board	November 6, 2012	562	1117	33%

continued on next page

Appendix C (*continued*)

Village	Town	County	Outcome	Village Law Provision	Initiated by:	Referendum Date(s)	Votes In Favor	Votes Against	% Support
Chaumont	Lyme	Jefferson	Rejected	Article 19	Board	November 6, 2012	102	145	41%
Victory (Victory Mills)	Saratoga	Saratoga	Rejected	Article 19	Citizen	March 19, 2013	82	143	36%
Keeseville	Ausable/ Chesterfield	Clinton/ Essex	Approved	Empowerment Act	Citizen	January 22, 2013	268	176	60%
Keeseville**	Ausable/ Chesterfield	Clinton/ Essex	Approved		Citizen	October 22, 2013	288	200	59%
Painted Post	Erwin	Stueben	Rejected	Empowerment Act	Citizen	January 24, 2013	291	376	44%
Middleburgh	Middleburgh	Schoarie	Rejected	Empowerment Act	Citizen	February 19, 2013	71	344	17%
Champlain	Champlain	Clinton	Rejected	Empowerment Act	Citizen	March 19, 2013	59	199	23%
Mannsville	Ellisburg	Jefferson	Rejected	Empowerment Act	Board	March 19, 2013	17	106	14%
Bridgewater	Bridgewater	Oneida	Approved	Empowerment Act	Board	March 18, 2013	40	8	83%
Richfield Springs	Richfield	Otsego	Rejected	Empowerment Act	Citizen	October 15, 2013	48	288	14%

Greenwich	Greenwich/ Easton	Washington	Rejected	Empowerment Act	Citizen	June 24, 2014	203	281	42%
Salem	Salem	Washington	Approved	Empowerment Act	Citizen	August 5, 2014	192	49	80%
Wilson	Wilson	Niagara	Rejected	Empowerment Act	Citizen	August 26, 2014	209	222	48%
Bloomingburg	Makating	Sullivan	Rejected	Empowerment Act	Citizen	September 30, 2014	85	107	44%
Medina	Ridgeway/ Shelby	Orleans	Rejected	Article 19	Citizen	January 20, 2015	527	949	36%
Prospect	Trenton	Oneida	Approved	Empowerment Act	Board	July 21, 2015	91	7	93%
Macedon	Macedon	Wayne	Approved	Empowerment Act	Citizen	June 10, 2015	300	246	55%
Macedon**	Macedon	Wayne	Approved		Citizen	March 16, 2016	324	181	64%
Hermon	Hermon	St. Lawrence	Approved	Empowerment Act	Board	October 26, 2015	95	15	86%
Port Henry	Moriah	Essex	Approved	Empowerment Act	Citizen	October 27, 2015	190	71	73%
Port Henry**	Moriah	Essex	Approved		Citizen		208	188	53%
Forrestville	Hanover	Chautauqua	Approved	Empowerment Act	Citizen	November 3, 2015	137	97	59%

continued on next page

Appendix C (continued)

Village	Town	County	Outcome	Village Law Provision	Initiated by:	Referendum Date(s)	Votes In Favor	Votes Against	% Support
Forrestville**	Hanover	Chautauqua	Approved		Citizen	November 9, 2016	195	125	61%
Herrings	Wilna	Jefferson	Approved	Empowerment Act	Citizen	November 3, 2015	19	9	68%
Brockport	Sweden	Monroe	Rejected	Empowerment Act	Citizen	May 24, 2016	632	817	44%
Sherman	Sherman	Chautauqua	Rejected	Empowerment Act	Citizen	December 20, 2016	115	117	50%
Mastic Beach	Brookhaven	Suffolk	Approved	Empowerment Act	Citizen	November 16, 2016	1922	1215	61%
Depew	Lancaster/ Cheektowaga	Erie	Rejected	Empowerment Act	Citizen	January 17, 2017	1165	3006	28%
Rushville	Potter/ Gorham	Yates/ Ontario	Rejected	Empowerment Act	Citizen	June 27, 2017	96	179	35%
Cherry Creek	Cherry Creek	Chautauqua	Approved	Empowerment Act	Citizen	February 3, 2017	70	32	69%
Barneveld	Trenton	Oneida	Approved	Empowerment Act	Citizen	June 6, 2017	54	12	82%
Van Etten	Van Etten	Chemung	Approved	Empowerment Act	Citizen	December 11, 2017	103	76	58%

Morristown	Morristown	St. Lawrence	Approved	Empowerment Act	Board	June 26, 2018	130	47	73%
Harrisville	Diana/Ogdensburg	Lewis	Approved	Empowerment Act	Board	May 15, 2019	112	70	62%
Sinclairville	Charlotte/Gerry	Chautauqua	Rejected	Empowerment Act	Citizen	August 13, 2019	94	128	42%
Fleischmanns	Middletown	Delaware	Rejected	Empowerment Act	Citizen	December 20, 2019	46	70	40%
Spencer	Spencer	Tioga	Rejected	Empowerment Act	Board	September 15, 2020	21	198	10%
Chaumont	Lyme	Jefferson	Rejected	Empowerment Act	Board	November 3, 2020	119	136	47%
South Nyack	Orangetown	Rockland	Approved	Empowerment Act	Citizen	December 17, 2020	508	292	64%
Highland Falls	Highlands	Orange	Rejected	Empowerment Act	Citizen	November 8, 2022	450	779	37%
Consolidation Votes									
Tuxedo	Tuxedo		Consolidation Approved	Empowerment Act	Citizen				
Pawling	Pawling		Consolidation Defeated	Empowerment Act	Citizen	November 30, 2020	84	843	9%

**Permissive referendum.

Notes

Introduction

1. In New York, cities and villages are voluntary incorporations, created by local request or action (i.e., request for special, charter legislation) or incorporated via local petition under applicable state law. They may be incorporated within an otherwise unincorporated territory of the town (i.e, from territory that is not already part of an incorporated city or village). Towns and counties are incorporated by the state and thus are generally considered involuntary incorporations (although Town Law authorizes the alternation of boundaries under Article 5-A, §§73–79 and the dissolution and consolidation of towns under Article 5-A, §79-A). Technically then, New York does not have unincorporated territory; when villages are incorporated, they remain part of the town; when villages are dissolved, the administration and government and property of the former village reverts back to the town, becoming an otherwise unincorporated place. The merger of a village and town may be effectively accomplished through the legal process of consolidation (the merger of two or more governing entities into a surviving governmental entity) or dissolution (the unilateral disincorporation of a governing entity) that typically transfers its functions or authority to the embracing jurisdiction(s).

2. "The constitutional and statutory foundation for local government in New York State provides that counties, cities, towns and villages are 'general-purpose' units of local government. They are granted broad home rule powers to regulate the quality of life in communities and to provide direct services to the people. In doing so, local governments must operate within powers accorded them by statute and the New York and United States Constitutions" (New York Department of State 2018b, 1). Special-purpose districts include fire and school districts as well as public authorities (a corporate instrumentality of the state created only by the legislature or through legislative enabling legislation). These special districts "normally provide a single service or type of service, such as water and sewer services, airport management, or industrial development, rather than

the gamut of government services provided by the general-purpose municipality"
(91). Special districts are administrative units of the town used to accommodate
the need for services that cannot (or need not) be provided on a townwide basis.
"Most special districts are established under general provisions of Articles 12 and
12-A of the Town Law. Those which cannot, must be created by act of the State
Legislature" (2018b, 78).

3. The incorporation files housed at the New Yok State Archives span
1866–1988, Collection N-AR 13243, and are parenthetically referenced by collection, box, and folder number or name as applicable (New York State Archives
1886–1988). New York legislation impacting village incorporation, dissolution, and
annexation provisions were identified using the Hein Online Database, Session
Laws of New York State 1691–, William S. Hein: Buffalo, New York. The year and
chapter number of the relevant act are parenthetically referenced.

4. Frank C. Moore served as the executive secretary of the State Association
of Towns (1933–1940), as the New York State comptroller (1942–1950), as New
York State lieutenant governor (1951–1953), and as the chair of the Government
Affairs Foundation (1953–1968). He participated in the Constitutional Conventions
of 1938, 1959 and 1967 and was recognized as one of the foremost authorities on
local government in New York State. The collection includes materials spanning
much of his career in state and local politics. Materials from this collection are
referenced by item in the bibliographical references.

5. The role of narrative policy framing is understudied in cases of direct
democracy despite the clear connection between "voting outcomes and narrative
components and strategies (Kear and Wells 2014, 160–61).

Chapter 1

1. Hamlet is not a legal municipal classification in New York but is
commonly used to denote a Census Designated Place or identified community
within a town that is not otherwise incorporated as a village. Villages that dissolve
sometimes change their designation to a hamlet.

2. About a dozen villages have not reincorporated under the general laws
but continue to operate under legislative charter. They are subject to the general village laws to the extent that their application does not conflict with their
charter (New York Department of State 2018, 82). These include the villages of
Alexander (Genesee County), Carthage (Jefferson), Catskill (Greene), Cooper-
stown (Otsego), Deposit (Broome and Delaware), Fredonia (Chautauqua), Ilion
(Herkimer), Mohawk (Herkimer), Ossining (Westchester), Owego (Tioga), Port
Chester (Westchester), and Waterford (Saratoga).

3. L. 1913, Ch. 658 validated and legalized all such incorporations heretofore
undertaken in compliance with the provisions of L. 1910, Ch. 258.

4. In 1954, the legislature granted town governments in Nassau County the authority to determine whether such annexation of territory was "in the public interest" (L. 1954, Ch. 818).

5. For details on the historical tensions between towns and villages with respect to overlapping highway services, see Legislative Document No. 25 (1956, 22–23).

6. As previously discussed, the classification of villages was first enacted with L. 1897, Ch. 414, §40. In 1906, the law was repealed and amended (L. 1906, Ch. 602). Villages containing a population of more than 5,000 were now designated as first-class, those with populations between 3,000 and 5,000 as second-class, those with between 1,000 and 3,000 as third-class, and those with fewer than 1,000 in population as villages of the fourth-class. L. 1906, Ch. 34, further amended L. 1897, Ch. 414 to add a new article XIII-A to the general village laws with provisions applicable to villages of more than 14,000. Provisions changing the classification based on population changes were added by L. 1910, Ch. 64 and amended by L. 1927, Ch. 650, §40(a). In 1964, as part of a piecemeal recodification, Chapter 740 repealed Village Law, Article 3, §§40–69 and replaced it with a renumbered Article 4, which retained a classification scheme in which villages of fewer than 1,000 were deemed fourth-class. The classification of villages based on population would be eliminated entirely in the 1972 recodification of the General Village Law.

7. NYCOM unsuccessfully advocated for the creation of "urban villages" that would exempt village residents from that portion of the town budget funding services in unincorporated areas (New York Conference of Mayors 1965, 9).

8. In the late 1960s, the courts invalidated village and education law that restricted the voice of non-property owners (Pierce v. Village of Ossining 1968; *New York Times* 1968; 1969).

9. The case involved a local law adopted by the town of Ramapo (Rockland County) that required that any new village incorporation be in the "over-all public interest" of the town (1967 NY Local Law 1919–10, No. 3). In rejecting the town's bid, the state's highest court embraced the view that the judicial role in hearing challenges to a new village incorporation is strictly limited to reviewing whether the town supervisor's determination of the sufficiency of the petition was warranted (Marcus v. Baron 1982). Thus, under village law, the reviewing court(s) are limited in their review to determining *whether the town supervisor's ruling was "illegal, based on insufficient evidence, or contrary to the weight of the evidence"* (N.Y. Village Law, § 2–210[1], emphasis added).

10. General Village Law, Article II, §254 was modified to include reference to the new Article 17-A of the General Municipal Law (or the Empowerment Act) to provide that villages incorporated prior to April 1, 1965, may abolish districts with which they are coterminous by local law.

11. Home rule proponents pushed for expanded authority for cities at the 1915 Constitutional Convention to limited effect.

12. Richland (1954) attributed the failures in home rule expansion in the 1950s to opposition from rural areas concerned about losing power to the cities, to the timidity of home rule advocates in the face of the state concern doctrine, and to restrictive interpretations of home rule authority by the courts.

13. The Temporary Commission on Town and Village Laws was established in 1954 (L. 1954, Ch. 533). The work was continued by the New York State Joint Legislative Committee to Study, Codify, Revise and Make Uniform Existing Laws Relating to Town and Village Governments and Other Matters Related Thereto and to Continue the Work of the Temporary State Commission, which issued several reports that informed the constitutional amendments of 1963.

14. See N.Y. Const. Art. IX, §2(b)(1), which provides that "Subject to the bill of rights of local governments and other applicable provisions of this constitution, the legislature: . . . Shall enact, and may from time to time amend, a statute of local governments granting to local governments powers including but not limited to those of local legislation and administration in addition to the powers vested in them by this article." The ten areas of local lawmaking authority granted by Article IX, §2 include setting the number, qualifications, selection, powers, duties, and removal of municipal officers and employees; legislative membership and composition; conduct of municipal affairs, incurring of debt, legal obligations, and claims against the municipality; construction, repair, and management of highways, roads, streets, and property; acquisition, ownership, and operation of transit facilities; assessment and collection of local taxes; wages, salaries, and protection of contracted workers; and governance, protection, good order, conduct, safety, health, and welfare of municipal residents and property (N.Y. Const. Art. IX, §2[C][ii][1–10]).

15. In testifying before the Committee on Villages, NYCOM's director declined to say that smaller villages were satisfied with their existing home rule powers yet acknowledged "there has been no demand for it," so "it would be better to proceed carefully and slowly" (Frank C. Moore Papers, Hearing of the Village Committee, N.D. Box 9, Folder 4). At the same time, there was no opposition to extending home rule to first-class villages on the part of smaller villages or cities. Instead, debate was whether it should be accomplished as an independent proposal or by amendment to city home rule law (Frank C. Moore Papers, Hearing of the Village Committee, N.D. Box 9, Folders 4 and 5).

16. As Benjamin explains, the extension of constitutional home rule protections to all municipal classes (counties, cities, towns, and villages), regardless of population size, was accompanied by the removal of "constitutional references to the possible elimination of local government" (Benjamin 2017b, 27).

17. While municipal home rule empowers reorganization and experimentation in service delivery, it also includes the right to reject municipal reform. More pithily expressed, home rule includes a "right to be misgoverned by your

friends" (Frank C. Moore, Letter to Editor of the *Rochester Times Union*, February 6, 1964. Frank C. Moore Papers, Box 16, File 1).

18. The Feeney Commission (1975) divided municipal development trends into four main periods: the Colonial Period (1609–1776), the Early Statehood Period (1777–1865), the Period of Consolidation (1865–1945), and the Modern Period (1945–75). Village formation for purposes of service provision was most prevalent prior to adoption of a General District Law in 1926. It was in the 1865–1945 period of Consolidation, influenced by industrialization and population growth, that village and incorporations proliferated. Perceived deficiencies in existing forms, particularly towns, led to the recodification and adoption of general municipal laws (including comprehensive town law, county law, village law, general city law, general municipal law, and general district law).

19. Pratt sought incorporation of a separate county, one with Prattsville as the county seat. Neither his influence as a member of the United States House of Representatives nor his promise to pay for a county building was sufficient for legislative approval in 1841 or 1846.

20. The city of Buffalo absorbed the village of Black Rock (1854); Rochester annexed Brighton (1905) and Charlotte (1915); Albany annexed Colonie (1815); Rensselaer annexed Greenbush (1897); Niagara Falls annexed La Salle (1927); Troy annexed Lansingburgh (1900); and Amsterdam annexed Rockton (1901). Eighteen village governments were annexed when these communities became part of New York City in 1898. In 1857, Seneca Village, was dissolved by legislative action to create Central Park (Burrows and Wallace 1994; Barker 2019). This vibrant community was composed mostly of African Americans, who had established eligibility to vote through property ownership. In 1853, the state legislature authorized the taking of properties, displacing, or evicting inhabitants for the construction of Central Park. There are no records of the incorporation of Seneca Village in either the New York State Archives or in State Session Laws.

21. City incorporation requires a State Legislative Act. See La Guardia v. Smith, 288 NY 1, 41 N.E. 2nd 153, appeal denied 262 Appellate Division 726, 28 N.Y. 2d 705 (1942).

22. The city of Sherrill's City Charter (1916) specifically provides that it is to be treated as a village.

23. Miscellaneous news items from unidentified sources reported the villages of Mamaroneck, Suffern, Sloatsburg, Spring Valley, Ramapo, and West Haverstraw as exploring the city charter option (Frank C. Moore Papers, Box 19, Folder 1).

24. A contemporary analogy would be the formation of business improvement districts (BIDs), private or not-for-profit organizations that allow residents and property owners within a defined geographical area of a city to offer supplemental services or improvements, typically funded by tax levy on businesses in the district (but also eligible for other potential revenue and grant streams).

25. Mandelker et al. (2014) found that two-thirds of all special districts are in rural areas, serving as a popular alternative to incorporation.

26. Similarly, Howe's (2006) review of village development in the Hudson River Valley distinguishes the creation of "commercial or manufacturing villages," dominant between 1790 and 1825 and corresponding to the opening of commercial transportation corridors from "suburban villages"—villages created to accommodate residential growth along the periphery of urban cities. He likens villages created in the Hudson River Valley in the post-1940s to special district villages—"those created for special purposes, either to make use of zoning and planning powers or religious purposes" (Howe 2006, 103).

27. Teaford (1997) focuses on communities in six counties, including Nassau and Suffolk Counties in New York State. The development of the suburbs there reflected a balance between centralized services and the "village values of a semirural America" (8). Incorporation gave residents "zoning power to protect and preserve the social homogeneity and low density of their villages" within comfortable proximity to the amenities of the large city (10).

28. This new wave of urbanism among millennials, and their preference for the amenities and convenience of urban places, is creating a suburban crisis (Florida 2017). Once "places of prosperity," many suburban communities are confronting the problems of economic decline, declining property values, diminished services, and rising property taxes; older suburbs are hit especially hard" (Florida 2017, 157).

29. The grant of authority is spelled out in village law (Article 15, §7–700) and town law (Article 16, §261), similarly specifying that "For the purpose of promoting the health, safety, morals, or the general welfare of the community, [the board of trustees of a village or town board] is hereby empowered, by local law, to regulate and restrict the height, number of stories and size of buildings and other structures, the percentage of lot that may be occupied, the size of yards, courts and other open spaces, the density of population, and the location and use of buildings, structures and land for trade, industry, residence or other purposes." Town law provides "that such regulations shall apply to and affect only such part of a town as is outside the limits of any incorporated village or city; provided further, that all charges and expenses incurred under this article for zoning and planning shall be a charge upon the taxable property of that part of the town outside of any incorporated village or city" (§261). Both villages and towns may establish planning boards (N.Y. Vill. Law §7–718; Town Law §271) to engage in land use regulations and comprehensive planning (whether or not such planning results in regulations). Both municipal classes may employ a variety of related controls (including special use permitting, site-plan review, subdivision review, cluster development, incentive [or bonus] zoning, the transfer of development rights, and historic preservation laws) as well as the adoption of local laws for the purpose of regulating and controlling land use and development.

30. Whether the new village would have immediate control over the disputed development was questionable. Village law provides that "local laws, ordinances, rules or regulations, which otherwise would apply . . . including but not limited to zoning ordinances, shall remain in effect" for 2 years after incorporation unless replaced through general or special law (N.Y. Vill. Law §2–250 (2015). Additionally, developers had entered into covenants with the town, which some legal experts suggest would remain legally binding even after the village acquired local law authority.

31. The result was similar to a town-village but achieved via different legal processes. There are six coterminous town-villages in existence in New York: Mount Kisco, Harrison, and Scarsdale (all in Westchester County), Green Island (Albany County), East Rochester (Monroe County), and Kiryas Joel (Orange County).

32. The project was delayed by disputes with the town over permits and environmental regulations. In 2015, development got underway, including roadbeds, sewer lines, and the building of a $10 million water-sewer facility. But when the neighboring village of Greenlake withdrew from a shared service arrangement, enrollment in the Tuxedo school district dramatically declined and housing demand waned, stalling the project.

33. Greenville/Edgemont had considered separating itself from the town of Greenburgh in 1965 (Frank C. Moore Papers, Box 17, Folder 2).

34. The Greenburgh town supervisor had invalidated the petitions on the grounds that the proposed boundaries failed to meet the standard of "common certainty"—the petitioners had not satisfactorily defined the boundaries to a degree of common certainty (N.Y. Vill. Law 2–202[c][1]) and were not accompanied by a complete list of regular inhabitants. The court concluded that his findings were "not illegal, based on insufficient evidence, or contrary to the weight of evidence" (Bernstein v. Feiner 2018).

35. Upon incorporation, residents of the new village would no longer pay for anything other than Town A budget items (townwide services). That portion of their tax bill formerly funding Town B budget items (TOV services) would thus become revenue for the new village.

36. As Benjamin (2017) details, allegations of discriminatory intent were judicially rejected in challenges to the incorporation of Pomona, Wesley Hills, Chestnut Ridge, and Montebello (1398).

37. See Congregation of Echo Ridge v. Village of Airmont, Decision and Order, Index No. 034807/2018E; Central UTA of Monsey v. Village of Airmont, New York, 18-cv-11103 (S.D.N.Y., November 28, 2018); Congregation of Ridnik v. Village of Airmont, Case 7:18-cv-11533 (S.D.N.Y., December 18, 2018).

38. The initial attempt was invalidated by the United States Supreme Court on the grounds that it violated the federal constitutional prohibition on the establishment of an official religion. The New York State legislature revised the law multiple times until it passed constitutional muster. See Berger (1995) and Benjamin (2017).

39. The town of Palm Tree was created out of the village of Kiryas Joel and sixty-four acres of adjacent unincorporated land, commencing municipal operation on January 1, 2019. In June 2019, the village of Kiryas Joel enacted Local Law 2, annexing the unincorporated area, thereby making its footprint coterminous with that of the new town. In November 2019, the village voted to approve coterminous town-village status, operating primarily as a village (effective January 1, 2020).

Chapter 2

1. Section 91 provided that, at the meeting called after a vote to dissolve, "it shall be lawful to raise by tax any sum that may be necessary to pay and discharge all the existing debts and liabilities of the said village" (L. 1847, Ch. 426, §91).

2. Governor David Hill expressed a similar sentiment: "If the people make mistakes the people may be trusted to rectify them" (Lincoln 1909c, vol. VIII, 91). Governor Roswell P. Flower echoed that "if the people of a municipality choose to endure misgovernment rather than to correct it, I am not aware that under our theory of government that the State should attempt the correction" (Lincoln 1909d, vol. IX, 30).

3. This is not to argue that villages are communal while towns are centralizing—indeed, towns serve as communal entities as well. Rather, it is only to acknowledge the rather frequent claim in incorporation and dissolution debates that town government does not (and perhaps cannot) always adequately serve the interests of the geographically smaller area of the village or its residents. As I argue elsewhere, the definition of community is based on one's perspective, and municipal boundaries may be drawn (or erased) to reinforce a particular view of what constitutes the community or best serves communal interests.

4. Testimony of Donald Carlson before the New York State Legislative Committee on Towns and Villages Held at Cattaraugus County Center, Little Valley, New York, October 10, 1969, 26. The items included road and equipment maintenance, mileage, and snow removal.

5. Villages are also exempt from many provisions of the Assessment Improvement Law of 1970 (L. 1970, Ch. 956) and are not eligible for state assistance for assessment administration. Villages may terminate their status as an assessing unit through the adoption of a local law.

6. Equalization rates are also used to determine municipal debt and tax limits and to allocate the costs of joint services (such as fire protection). Equalization rates do not address the fairness of assessment practices within a jurisdiction (i.e., the frequency or accuracy of assessments).

7. As Benjamin explains, the adoption of the first general municipal law in 1892 substantially removed the "legal distinctions among types of local governments" (Benjamin 2017b, 25; L. 1892, Ch. 686, §2 and Ch. 685, §1).

8. The committee succeeded the former Temporary Legislative Committee on Town and Village Fiscal and Tax Relationships (created by L. 1954, Ch. 533). As to overlapping services, the Committee found that towns often performed services that were, by statute, restricted to areas of the TOV but were assessed against the town-at-large (thus village residents supported services from which they derived no benefit (Legislative Document No. 47 1956, 15). The Committee further noted that villages were dissatisfied with inequitable state aid, recommending the formula for further study.

9. Among these were to allow dissolution by a simple majority vote (rather than the two-thirds approval at referendum as then required) and to authorize suburban townships to dissolve village functions (Legislative Document No. 86 1968, 25). Others were to grant suburban towns the power to dissolve village functions (Legislative Document No. 24 1967, 17–20), to eliminate the "double taxation" on village residents, to require that the annexation of territory by a village be in the interest of and approved by the town, and that towns exempt villages from the costs of services not provided within village boundaries (Legislative Document No. 24 1967, 20).

10. The recodification of Articles 1, 1-A, 2, and 3 of the Village Law was enacted by the Laws of 1964, Chs. 740, 755, 756, 798, and 856, with Ch. 740 as the primary bill. According to the Committee's report, L. 1964, Ch. 740 "unexpectedly came under attack on the ground that it was in effect a special law [in violation of N.Y. Const. Article IX, Sect. 3(d)(4)] and hence could not have been enacted constitutionally without either home rule requests from all villages of the State to which any part of that article might apply or without the Governor having first declared than an emergency existed which necessitated the passage of that legislation [N.Y. Const., Article IX, §2(b)(2)]" (Legislative Document No. 21 1965, 19). Because such an interpretation would have effectively precluded the recodification of general law of villages, towns, or counties, the Committee prepared a memorandum in defense. A "paramount purpose" of Article IX of the state constitution was to promote "effective local government," an objective that could not be achieved if the constitutional home rule provisions were interpreted to preclude revisions of general laws. "Home Rule and local legislative power were never intended to replace an entire statewide system of Village Law but rather only to provide the means to temper that law to meet local situations" (Legislative Document No. 21 1965, 19). The Committee thus urged gubernatorial approval of the measure.

11. In addressing the delegates to the 1967 Constitutional Convention, however, members of the Association of Towns Resolution Committee sounded a very different note. If residents of a town "feel they can afford the luxury of being a village if they want to pay the price of village government, it is O.K. with [this] Committee and the Association of Towns . . . If they have ceased to be enchanted with their village, they can dissolve it. But this is up to them" (Report to New

York State Legislature and Constitutional Convention Concerning Actions Taken by the Association by the Association of Towns Delegates to its 1967 Annual Meeting Business Session, February 7, 1967 (reprinted in Legislative Document No. 24 1967, 30). The Committee opposed mandated reform and argued for more robust home rule protections.

12. Minutes of the Proceedings of the Joint Legislative Committee on Towns and Villages, held at the Assembly Parlor, the State Capital, November 13, 1969, 85.

13. Ironically, despite its position that reorganization be left to local control, the report of the committee acknowledged consolidation was not likely to be locally approved "*even if there were advantages in such consolidations*" (Legislative Document No. 7 1970, 19, emphasis added). The problem was due to statutory defects but "arose from a combination of local pride, competitiveness, and a failure of local government officials on different levels to have a meeting of the minds on problems or their proposed solutions" (Legislative Document No. 7 1970, 12).

14. Nathan and Benjamin argue that "state-imposed procedural barriers to structural change in local governments are common and usually established in the name of local democracy" (2001, 165). New York's entrusting of dissolution to local action was an exception, although they noted that Article 19 (in effect at the time of the authors' writing), remained "very deferential to local preferences," and as such, "there is little hope for forceful state action to systematically restructure local government" (2001, 177).

15. "The costs of such services shall be a charge upon the taxable property within the dissolved village unless the town board, acting pursuant to law, shall elect to provide such services by establishing a special improvement district, or as a town function" (N.Y. Vill. Law, Article 19, §1914[1]). The law also made provision for the effect on village legislation, requiring that

> unless the plan [accompanying the proposition] shall provide other-wise, all local laws, ordinances, rules or regulations of the village in effect on the date of the dissolution of the village, including but not limited to zoning ordinances shall remain in effect for a period of two years following dissolution, as if the same had been duly adopted by the town board and shall be enforced by the town within the limits of the dissolved village, except that the town board shall have the power at any time to amend or repeal such local laws, ordinances, rules or regulations in the manner as other local laws, ordinances, rules or regulations of the towns. (N.Y. Vill. Law, Article 19, §1910[1])

16. Of these, only Durhamville (incorporated in 1849) seems a candidate for possible dissolution under General Village Law. Its charter was amended by the legislature as late as 1869 (L. 1869, Ch. 546), but the village is not listed in 1897 *Report of Commissioners of Statutory Revision in Relation to Villages*, sug-

gesting it had either abandoned its charter or disincorporated. Local historians could provide no clarity.

17. See Blauvelt v. Village of Nyack (1876). The General Village Law of 1870 did not repeal the General Village Law of 1847, except as it applied to *future incorporations*. Villages incorporated under the 1847 law remained subject to its provisions, including those controlling dissolution. But for villages that incorporated (or reincorporated) under the General Village Law of 1870, there was no mechanism for dissolving. In 1874, the legislature rectified the apparent oversight by amending §32 (the repeal as to future incorporations) to exempt §90 and §91 (the dissolution provisions of the General Village Law of 1847), thus extending the dissolution option to villages incorporated under the 1870 law. In so doing, *Blauvelt* affirmed the power of the legislature to "alter and repeal" general laws for the incorporation of villages, meaning that all village rights and powers acquired through incorporation are "subject to the exercise of that power at any time" (Blauvelt v. Nyack 1876, 155).

18. www.eastlongisland.com/town_of_riverhead/northville/northville_history. com (accessed August 12, 2011). This rural farming community fought successfully fought off industrial development, including the building of multiple nuclear power plants, a fuel desulphurization facility, and a four-lane parkway in the 1970s by having the historic Sound Avenue Road designated a historical corridor in 1975 (Young 2011).

19. Letter from Thomas Carmody, New York state attorney general, to Hon. Mitchell May, secretary of state, April 17, 1914.

20. See http://www.eastwoodneighbor.com/about-eastwood/ (accessed October 8, 2012).

21. Dissolution was considered in the Villages of Elmsford (Westchester County) in 1912, Highland Falls (Orange County) in 1916, Tivoli (Dutchess County) in 1922, East Bloomfield (Ontario County) in 1923, and in the Villages of Sloan (Erie County), Bellport (Suffolk County), Youngstown (Niagara County), and Cold Brook (Herkimer County), all in 1938. See *New Rochelle Pioneer* 1912; *Kingston Daily Freeman* 1915; *Poughkeepsie News* 1922; *Geneva Daily Times* 1938; *Patchogue Advance* 1938; *Patchogue Advance* 1939; *Niagara Gazette* 1938; *Utica Observer Dispatch* 1938; 1938b.

22. A civil suit filed in 1933 for unpaid taxes owed to the former village of Old Forge was reopened in 1936. Again, state legislative action was sought for approval of the town's authority over the settlement of the former village's financial affairs (L. 1939, Ch. 226).

23. The state's reported dissolution of Jamaica Square (Nassau County) in 1931 is an error. Jamaica Square changed its name in 1931 to South Floral Park. There was an effort to dissolve South Floral Park in 1941, but the petition was declared invalid after prolonged legal wrangling (*Brooklyn Daily Eagle* 1940; 1941a; 1941b). South Floral Park remains an incorporated village.

234 | Notes to Chapter 3

24. The point was echoed by Gregory Krakower, director of the Senate Policy Group and special counsel to Senate Majority Leader Malcolm Smith: "One part of the [old] law in particular serves to disempower citizens: elected officials almost always have the power to veto a petition drive—even if a majority of voters wish to consolidate a local government." See http://www.nysenate.gov/blogs/2009/jun/03/power-people-local-government-consolidation-bill-passes-senate.

Chapter 3

1. Consider, for example, the critique offered by the Fiscal Policy Institute as a counterargument to Cuomo's carrots and stick approach to local reorganization:

> Governor Cuomo misleadingly suggests that local governments can solve their fiscal dilemmas by finding substantial efficiencies. Many localities simply do not have the means to make up for the lack of sufficient state aid, and even those that might are constrained by the property tax cap. The governor relies heavily on the notion that consolidating government services could save enormous amounts of money, yet consolidations that make sense have mostly already happened. . . . it is by no means a solution to the local fiscal crisis that is primarily a product of flawed state policies. . . . Increasing the state share of state/local responsibilities is a more sensible way to address the problem, together with targeted relief through an improved property tax circuit breaker to those truly straining under a tax burden (Fiscal Policy Institute 2018, 50).

Evaluating the validity of each of the different claims as to what is the primary (or real) driver of the state's high property tax burden is beyond the scope of this work, although the counterarguments to dissolution as a policy solution are presented throughout.

2. Study efforts advocating local government reorganization include the work of the 1915 Constitutional Convention, the Commission for the Revision of Tax Laws in 1935 (the Mastick Commission), the Temporary State Commission on the Powers of Local Government in 1973, Temporary State Commission on State and Local Finances in 1975 (the Feeney Commission), the Local Government Restructuring Project (spanning 1990–92), the Commission on Consolidation of Local Government (spanning 1990–93), the Commission on Local Government Reform (2002 and 2004), and the Commission on Local Government Efficiency and Competitiveness (2007–8) (the Lundine Commission).

3. As to villages, the Lundine Commission's recommendations were to 1) require townwide approval for a new village and reconsider small villages; 2) ease

procedures for consolidation, citizen petitions, and the creation of coterminous town-villages; 3) reclassify some cities, towns, and villages; and the powers of each class; 4) reduce the number of elected offices (i.e., clerk, receiver of taxes, highway superintendent, etc.); 5) improve local financial data for better citizen review of government efficiency; and 6) make grants and aid available to pursue shared services and consolidations. The commission suggested *a mandatory dissolution referendum* for all villages under 500 in population (29). The report also suggested a review of various cost-driving regulations for local governments (employee and benefit costs, Wicks Law provisions (GML §101 regulating the awarding of contracts for major construction) and purchasing requirements and procurement contracts (Lundine Commission 2008). The Empowerment Act builds on the second recommendation. The creation of a fiscal stress monitoring system (suggestion five) and making grants available to incentive (suggestion six) were added as related policy supports to the Empowerment Act as discussed in detail below.

4. Introduced on May 21, 2009, the Empowerment Act passed the Senate (by a vote of 46–19) and the Assembly (188–26) on June 1 and was signed into law on June 24, 2009. The legislation was supported by a wide variety of state agencies but was adamantly opposed by municipal organizations (including the Association of Towns, NYCOM, the Fireman's Association of the State of New York, the Police Conference of New York, and assorted village representatives writing in their individual capacity) who disputed the central premise of an inefficient local government system (Bill Jacket, L. 2009, Ch. 74).

5. The New York State Constitution, Article IX, §1h(1) gives counties the authority to transfer or abolish units of local government, subject to multiple referenda requirements. The state legislature, however, did not fully implement the counties' constitutional authority when it enacted Municipal Home Rule Law §33-a-(1) in 1970. Instead, they limited counties to abolishing only "offices, departments and agencies" of local governments, not the governments themselves, and limited the county to transferring functions to other units of government. Thus, while transfer of functions could "be done without action by the state or by town boards, it does not appear easy" (Boyd 2008, 16). The Empowerment Act amended Municipal Home Rule Law §33-a-(1) to formally authorize counties to "abolish entire units of local government—including cities, towns, villages and special district—when the level and quality of services are transferred. With these changes to existing law, a county may, in appropriate cases, effect dissolutions, mergers and consolidation of whole units of government, subject to the approval of the voters of the county in a referendum." See Attorney General's Sponsor Memo in Support of Bill, www.reformnygov.com/download_proposal.html.

6. See Attorney General's Sponsor Memo in Support of Bill, www.reformnygov.com/download_proposal.html.

7. Critics of the Empowerment Act point to the village of Brockport (Monroe County), the first community to conduct a dissolution under the new provisions, as illustrative of the law's defects. A petition submitted on March 29, just a week after the Empowerment Act took effect, "forced dissolution" to a vote just sixty-eight days after its validation. The measure was defeated on June 15, 2010, by a vote of 959–652. According to NYCOM and anti-dissolution citizen groups, no pre-vote dissolution study was conducted, and the timeframe was too compressed to allow full consideration of the merits.

8. The official guidelines for calculating the cap can be found at http://www.tax.ny.gov/pdf/publications/orpts/capguidelines.pdf.

9. Override of the property tax cap for school districts must receive at least 60 percent support of voters at referendum. On average from 2012–21, about 24 percent of villages passed local laws overriding the property tax cap. That number was higher from 2012–13 (35 percent), then fell after the tax freeze went into effect in 2015 (falling to 18 percent) and has remained at an average of 23.67 percent from 2016–21. The 2012–21 average was 22.51 percent for towns, 25.97 percent for cities, and 14.9 percent for counties, according to data obtained through the OSC, Open Book New York, Local Government Data.

10. Those indicators included 1) full valuation of taxable real property per capita less than 50 percent of the statewide average; 2) more than 60 percent of the constitutional property tax limit exhausted; 3) population loss greater than 10 percent since 1970; and 4) poverty rate greater than 150 percent of the statewide average (Office of New York State Comptroller 2008, 3).

11. A 2008 Report by the Office of the State Comptroller, for example, highlighted the inequities of retaining general revenue sharing based on municipal classification for village governments, and particularly for those suburban villages that provide the same essential services as cities. By applying aim formulas used for smaller urban cities to statistically similar villages, the OSC found that villages would have received $92.1 more in AIM funding than awarded in the 2007–8 budget (Office of New York State Comptroller 2008, 5). Alternatively, applying the same annual increase in revenue as cities would have boosted funding for urban villages by $10 million (Office of New York State Comptroller 2008, 6). Recalculating AIM based on functional and characteristic similarities would have bumped 279 villages to the same level of revenue sharing as cities and would have given small, urban villages a $90 million increase in funding (1). Although the functions of municipal government have changed, the classifications on which unrestricted state-aid formulas have been based have not, producing a system that is "no longer rational or equitable" (Office of New York State Comptroller 2008, 8).

12. This is true even for villages that "are of similar size and perform similar functions" as cities (Office of the State Comptroller 2008, 5). Recall that in New York, the classification of village or city is not dependent on population, and the range of general services provided by city, town, and village governments has

grown more similar over time. The use of municipal class-based formulas has thus created a persistent inequality in how state assistance is calculated. Additionally, the legislature has frequently overridden the statutory formulas to target aid to the largest cities.

13. The change followed a decision by the United States Supreme Court authorizing states to collect taxes on internet sales. AIM-related funding is withheld and distributed by the OSC upon the DOB certification of AIM eligibility for municipalities. In Erie and Nassau Counties, the intercept of AIM-related payments was complicated by laws requiring disbursement of county sales tax through the county fiscal control boards.

14. The villages of Pelham and North Pelham consolidated in 1975 (Westchester County). East Bloomfield and Holcomb consolidated in 1990 (Ontario County). These are typically included as dissolutions in New York State–reported data but are excluded in the calculations for table 3.2. Consolidation was studied in the following: city and town of Batavia 2009 (Genesee County); village of Albion with towns of Albion/Gaines 2009 (Orleans County); village and town of New Paltz Village 2011 (Ulster County); village and town of Saranac Lake 2007 (Franklin County); village and town of Lewiston 2007 (Niagara County); towns of Shelby and Ridgeway 2005 and 2010 (Orleans County); village of Painted Post and town of Erwin 2011 (Steuben County); village of Dansville and town of North Dansville 2011 (Livingston County); Schuyler and Yates Counties 2014.

15. See http://www.danc.org/files/public/hermon/Final_Dissolution_Study_and_Plan.pdf.

16. See https://www.cgr.org/forestville/docs/ImpactReport.pdf.

17. The property includes multiple parcels, each covered by separate zoning permits and restrictions. A pre-sale request by the college to amend its special-permit status to include residential use beyond approved zoning for dormitories was rejected by the village of South Nyack. Accusations of secrecy surrounding the sale, and news of a joint purchase by an ultraorthodox congregation and real-estate developer, raised alarm over future high-density housing construction (multiple-family residential use). Although the village of South Nyack had no direct say in the sale, some residents were frustrated by what they viewed as a failure to seek other, non–tax-exempt developers for the site. The final sale of the property was judicially approved as meeting the fair market value requirement for a nonprofit transaction and officially closed in the days following the dissolution vote. As of this writing, plans for the site have not yet been finalized.

18. In March 2021, the village of South Nyack filed suit against the Yeshivath Viznitz D'kal Torath Chaim, alleging various code violations and usage unauthorized by permit. Whether the suit will be pursued by the town of Orangetown post-dissolution remains to be seen (Traster 2021). Pursuant to General Municipal Law (GML §790) all debts, liabilities, and obligations of a former village pass to the town upon final dissolution of the village. Debt (including any prior legal

judgements against the village) would remain with the residents of the former village as part of the "legacy district" costs. Pending legal matters continue with the town now substituted in the village's place. The town of Orangetown therefore can decide whether to pursue or drop the suit but must remain as the respondent in pending legal matters against the former village.

Chapter 4

1. According to Cuomo's property tax information page, New York had "the highest local taxes in America as a percentage of personal income—79% above the national average." See https://reforminggovernment.ny.gov/reforminggovernment/propertytaxmap/.

2. Coterminous town-villages are distinct legal entities that may be created in one of several ways: by a home rule request; through the consolidation of a village and town through GML Article 17-A; by a town splitting into two under Town Law, one of which is coterminous with an incorporated village; or by a village incorporating as the whole territory of a town (not otherwise incorporated). Coterminous legal entities have the same geographical footprint (that is, they share the same boundaries). Per the Department of State's legal interpretation:

> Depending on how the coterminous unit is formed, the town and the village function together as a single local government or as two separate local governments. As a single unit of government, the governing body of one unit of the coterminous government serves as the governing body of the other unit. This process results in one of the forms of government being the primary form of government—town or village—effectively eliminating the other as far as administration is concerned. Where the coterminous entity functions as two local governments, separate officers and boards are chosen or selected, and both town and village entities possess governance authority. (New York Department of State 2006)

3. The bucket metaphor is used by the Development Authority of the North Country (DANC) in its contracted dissolution studies.

4. Starting in FY 2018, the funding for some LGE and CREG grants was drawn from the special infrastructure account rather than general funds, making it harder to track in the budget reports. Additionally, the required annual reporting on the efficiency grant programs has not been publicly released since FYE 2017–18. For years of reporting, see New York Department of State 2007; 2009; 2010; 2017; 2018.

5. While there is no singular definition of fiscal stress, there is academic consensus that fiscal solvency includes a local government's ability to 1) maintain service levels, 2) withstand economic disruptions, and 3) "meet the demands of natural growth, decline, and change" (Nollenberger et al. 2003, 2). Fiscally stabile municipalities have more capacity to leverage opportunities and minimize fiscal threats (Hendrick 2011, 10, 23). How localities respond to fiscal stress, however, is not particularly well understood. Indications are that severe stress increases a community's willingness to eliminate services and personnel, or ultimately to reorganize (Maher and Deller 2007, 1567). Still, many communities will use service delivery alternatives and alternative revenue sources to compensate during times of stress, engaging in "municipal pragmatism" (Kim and Warner 2016). The more dramatic step of consolidating or dissolving governing tends to be a last (or later) option policy solution.

6. While the OSC does not make linkages between non-filing and stress designations, the failure to file timely reports does suggest potential transparency, fiscal management, and capacity issues. Non-filing, in other words, may itself reveal problems. A March 2020 report identified ten persistent non-filers (defined as three or more years delinquent). Seven of the non-filers were delinquent in filing annual fiscal reports, two were delinquent in filing constitutional tax limit data, and one was delinquent in its property tax cap filings (Office of New York State Comptroller 2020). Of these seven, three have had dissolution activity: Bloomingburg (Sullivan County) and Cuba (Allegany County) both rejected dissolution at the polls, and one, Windsor (Broome County), had a petition circulated.

7. The enhancements to the fiscal indicators that went into effect in 2018 (with FYE 2017 data) were relatively minor; the environmental indicators were more extensively revised (with scoring and recombination changes to most indicators and two indicators removed entirely, including constitutional tax limits). For full details, see https://www.osc.state.ny.us/files/local-government/fiscal-monitoring/pdf/system-enhancements-local-governments.pdf.

8. Effective for FYE 2011 and beyond, the Governmental Accounting Standards Board (GASB) issued Statement 54, replacing fund balance classifications of reserved and unreserved with new classifications: nonspendable, restricted, and unrestricted (composed of committed, assigned, and unassigned funds). The fund balance represents the cumulative residual resources from prior fiscal years. Villages may legally establish reserves and restrict funds for certain future purposes, such as capital projects. The unrestricted portion of fund balance (i.e., the total of committed, assigned, and unassigned fund balance) may be appropriated to fund programs in the next year's budget and used either for cash flow or to finance future operations.

9. The Office of the State Comptroller has the authority under the New York State Constitution (Article V, §1) and General Municipal Law (Article 3)

to conduct audits to periodically examine the fiscal affairs of local governments. See http://www.osc.state.ny.us/localgov/audits/underaudit.pdf)/ for a review of the audit process and procedure.

10. OSC audits of local governments, including villages, are available at http://wwe1.osc.state.ny.us/auditsearch/auditsearch.cfm. References to individual village audits are noted parenthetically by the OSC audit (report) number.

11. Without an explication of Huefner's methodology or access to the audits from that period of study, I cannot fully replicate his methodology to offer a cross-study comparison of the average number of deficiencies per audit. However, my independent analysis of the audits from 2013 to 2020, which tallies the number of negative findings for each audit from the executive summary of each audit report, produces similar conclusions.

12. The authors caution as well that village leaders may have underreported, as the full impact of the property tax cap still had not been fully realized.

13. "The New York State Constitution places a legal limit on the authority of villages, as well as counties and cities, to impose property taxes. Statutes intended to enforce these constitutional provisions require the comptroller to withhold certain local assistance payments if taxes are levied in excess of a municipality's tax limit." See https://www.osc.state.ny.us/files/local-government/required-reporting/pdf/villages.pdf.

14. For counties, cities, towns, and villages, the constitutional debt limit is a percentage (7 percent) of the five-year average full valuation of taxable property within a municipality, with exclusions for debt issued for "the purpose of water supply and distribution and certain types of short-term borrowing . . . related to sewer projects and certain types of self-liquidating debt" (Office of New York State Comptroller 2019). There also are statutory limitations on general contingency appropriations (monies included in the budget for unforeseen expenditures). For villages, that limit is a maximum of 10 percent of the total of other appropriations excluding debt service and judgments (Office of New York State Comptroller 2016b, Appendix C).

15. As noted in the discussion of the property tax cap, the annual cap applies to the overall *levy*, not the tax rate. Tax rates may sometimes be adjusted downward to stay within the levy limit. Given differences in valuations and assessments, the number of property tax exemptions, and various tax relief programs, changes in the tax levy are a better indicator of the tax burden on residents. Residents, however, are arguably more sensitive to the relative tax rate per $1,000, as it impacts their property tax bills. Thus, the presumption here is that residents pay more attention to the changes in their tax rate per assessed home value or may be sensitive to how much they pay in village taxes relative to town taxes on their property tax bills.

16. The FY 2021 Enacted Budget contained several measures to address liquidity needs of municipalities (FY 2021 Enacted Budget and Financial Plan, 20).

17. About 11 percent of villages have "above average" reliance on the state sales tax (Office of New York State Comptroller 2020b, 4). Eleven counties do not share any state sales tax with their municipalities, two more share only with cities or towns, and one (Suffolk) shares only with villages that have their own police department. There are, then, about ninety villages that do not receive a share of county sales tax (outside AIM-related payments).

18. Pursuant to a legislative grant of emergency authority, Governor Cuomo declared an emergency with Executive Order 202 (March 7, 2020) followed by a series of additional orders suspending and modifying state law in response to the pandemic. Executive Order 202.8, New York State on PAUSE (Policies that Assure Uniform Safety for Everyone), prohibited non-essential workers from the workplace and imposed a shelter-in-place (stay indoors) mandate. The governor made additional modification to state policies in response to region-specific indicators and evolving federal guidelines. Emergency executive powers were rescinded in May 2021.

19. The legislature then had ten days to adopt, by concurrent resolution, its own plan for eliminating the imbalance. If no plan was adopted, the plan submitted by the budget director would take effect automatically. The process exempted certain types of local assistance appropriations from uniform reduction, including public assistance and Supplemental Security Income (SSI) payments. See FY 2021 Enacted Budget Financial Plan, 42.

20. Only seven municipalities (New York City; the counties of Erie, Monroe, Nassau, Suffolk, and Westchester; and the town of Hempstead) were eligible for such funding. Federal assistance was targeted toward education, health care, and unemployment benefits, as well as giving states relief through programs like Enhanced Federal Medicaid Assistance Percentage (eFMAP) and Federal Emergency Management funding.

21. See https://labergegroup.com/spencer/wp-content/uploads/2020/05/Spencer-Public-Information-Meeting-Flyer-050520.pdf.

22. Executive Order 202.26 (March 7, 2020). See https://www.governor.ny.gov/sites/governor.ny.gov/files/atoms/files/EO_202.26_Final_Elections.pdf)/.

23. The vote was (129–72). See https://www.danc.org/media/Municipal%20Studies/Chaumont/Meeting%201%20Presentation.%20Chaumont%20Demographics%20and%20Socioeconomics.pdf.

24. November 18, Proposed Consolidation Interim Report Meeting, November 11, 2020, https://www.youtube.com/watch?v=Odvm2wVXMtI.

25. The proposed and enacted budgets granted counties permanent authority to impose a local sales tax of an additional 1 percent above the state sales tax rate or at their current additional rate (if greater). The amounts withheld from counties in 2020 was $59.1 million (the same as in 2019). In 2020, the fiscal control boards of Erie and Nassau Counties were required to return sales tax distributions to the OSC to meet AIM-related payments to towns and villages in the counties (L. 2020, Ch. 55).

26. Self-governance arguably requires localities to be fiscally self-sufficient, particularly in the current climate of fend-for-yourself federalism in which unreliable state and federal assistance leaves local governments struggling. From the municipal perspective, state-level policies are a significant contributor to local government woes (Aldag, Warner, and Kim 2017; Anjum et al. 2015). State controls, including taxing and expenditure limitations, constrain local autonomy (Brunori 2007; Hou 2015). The "downloading of austerity from one level of government to the next is one way of pushing fiscal stress to the next lower unit in the federal hierarchy—whether from national to state, state to local, or from county to city, town or village. But the buck stops with the lowest level of local government" (Aldag and Warner 2017, 4). Of course, federal and state policies have significant fiscal repercussions for local governments (Wildasan 2010, 59). New York's local leaders report their frustration with state-level policies that they perceive add to their fiscal challenges and often resist the calls for consolidation (Aldag, Warner, and Kim 2017).

27. Municipal bankruptcy is a relatively rare phenomenon that receives a disproportionate amount of attention (Pew Research 2016). Since the passage of the federal Municipal Bankruptcy Act in the 1930s, fewer than 500 municipal bankruptcies have been filed, and zero in New York State where state practice is to impose control board to oversee the finances of distressed municipalities before they reach default.

28. Longevity of an incorporation is not, however, indicative of long-term municipal stability and health. Additionally, it does not appear that his statistical analysis accounts for the fact that thirteen dissolutions since 2010 took place under Article 19 procedures, which had a higher petition threshold and a mandatory pre-vote study process.

Chapter 5

1. In New York, village elections may be administered by the village (as specified in the General Village Law §15-104) or by the county board where approved by local proposition. They are typically biannual and are not all held on the same schedule; village law specifies the third Tuesday in March, but villages may adopt a different date by proposition (approved at least sixty days in advance). Nominations for elected village office may be made by either by political party or by an independent nominating petition (N.Y. Elec. Law §6-206). Thus, even if village elections are nonpartisan (i.e., candidates are not nominated on party lines), local parties or citizen committees may still nominate or endorse candidates based on their stance on dissolution.

2. Sienna College Research Institute Poll, New Yorkers Trust & Rate Job Done by Local Governments as Better Than That Done by State or Federal Governments, February 26. 815 registered voters, +/– 3% margin of error.

3. New York has 572 CDPs. Census Designated Places (CDPs) are closely settled unincorporated places, or geographical areas that are locally recognized by name. They are the statistical equivalent of an incorporated place but lack a governing structure.

4. There is also a distinction in the literature between old regionalism (the promotion of regional interests through the creation or reform of formal governing structures) and new regionalism (which places greater emphasis on intermunicipal cooperation and collaboration between local elected officials, business leaders, community stakeholders, and public-private partnerships).

5. Political fractionalization or fragmentation (whether measured as the number of local governing entities or as the ratio of local government units or elected officials to population or jurisdiction size) has been long recognized as an impediment to effective regional governance (Maxey 1922; Studenski 1930; Merriman, Paratt, and Lepawsky 1933; Wood 1958; Advisory Commission on Intergovernmental Relations 1961; Warren 1978; Rusk 1993; Lewis 1996). Fragmentation creates inefficiencies as smaller municipalities fall below an "optimum service standard," and those costs are passed on to the taxpayers (Bruck and Pinto 2008, 298). Other costs include racial segregation, an increase in patronage and nepotism, corruption, incompetence, and difficulties filling governmental positions in small municipalities (Bruck and Pinto 2008, 298–304). Taxpayers must support redundant physical and political infrastructure. Multiple governing entities arguably diminish citizen identification with the region, encouraging the parochialism of interests. Individual municipalities are ill equipped to deal with larger, regional woes, while local autonomy and self-interest frustrate the cooperation and consensus required to adopt regional approaches and policy solutions. Economic disparities between deteriorating central cities and wealthier suburbs creates inequities in the distribution of services and resources. Population shifts leave cities a declining tax base and a higher demand for services, creating an economic drag on the whole region. Inner-ring suburbs that initially benefited from the exodus eventually experience the same population losses and stagnating economy once associated with the central city. Moreover, interjurisdictional rivalries reduce economic competitiveness and the overall economic health of the region.

6. Norris et al. (2009) found a lack of regional collaboration correlated with fragmentation. "No single jurisdiction was willing to give up anything (especially money and power) to advance the interests of the overall region" (138). Thus, the "real culprit that significantly limits or prevents regional governance is *local governmental autonomy*" (140, emphasis added).

7. The Chautauqua Conference did not endorse a particular vision but was criticized as embracing an "old-style" of regionalism that focused too narrowly on a "preferred model of consolidation" and eschewed the tenets of "new regionalism," which emphasizes a more flexible, incremental approach of intermunicipal cooperation and intergovernmental agreements (Bucki 2008, 147).

8. New regionalism critics argue that it is inadequate to the task without incentives or coercive state action (Basalo 2003, 456). Norris (2001) agrees that new regionalism fails for the same reasons as consolidation: the political and cultural impediments that favor localism are too well entrenched.

9. Municipal reorganization was largely ignored at the Chautauqua conference (Esmonde 2004). In 2000, Erie County executive Joel Giambra questioned the need for villages but "stopped short" of advocating dissolution (Pasciak 2000). After village officials responded with alarm, Giambra proposed a city-county merger that would leave towns and villages intact.

10. There had been only a handful of village dissolution efforts in Erie County. Kenmore rejected a town-village merger in 1971. Alden rejected dissolution in 1986 (by a vote of 762–264). In 1993, a joint village-town committee report studying dissolution of North Collins was tabled. North Collins received shared service grants in 1998 and 2002 and a dissolution study grant in 2008 (Pasciak 2010b). There was a failed petition attempt in Angola in 2004 (deemed deficient because of signatures collected outside the statutory time frame then in effect).

11. In the village of Blasdell, utterance of the word "dissolution" was reportedly verboten; the board refused to engage on the subject but then put forth a resolution for self-study with a $200,000 price tag that was defeated at a referendum (Chandler 2008; Werbitsky 2009). In 2009, East Aurora's mayor preemptively formulated a "one Aurora" plan that was dismissed by the board and contributed to his reelection failure. A subsequent citizen-led petition drive to force a vote was unsuccessful. Orchard Park preemptively invited NYCOM to publicly present on the deficiencies of the new law (Werbitsky 2010; Gordan 2010; 2010b). In the village of Lancaster (which voluntarily downsized its board), the level of hostility raised safety concerns for the pro-dissolution coaliation's petition carriers, and the effort was abandoned (Pasciak 2010).

12. The Study Group defended the board's failure to provide information as cost prohibitive at the current time.

13. The methodology and full results of the poll were not disclosed, but the reported margin of error was +/− 5.7%.

14. Peter Baynes, executive director of NYCOM, made a similar case, arguing that villages account for only 3 percent of property taxes imposed and pointing to other drivers of the property tax burden, including school district taxes (Baynes 2010).

15. In 2005, the village of Sloan was rocked by "unsettling discoveries . . . [that] included shredded documents found in garbage bags behind Village Hall, more documents found floating in a reservoir, erased computer hard drives, questionable bank transfers and checks handed out without Village Board approval" (O'Brien 2008; Zwelling 2005). In yet another scandal, Sloan's highway chief pled guilty to third-degree grand larceny of village property (Gryta 2010; 2010b).

Chapter 6

1. *Stern v. Kramarsky* (1975) addressed municipal spending on a constitutional amendment. Per the opinion of the New York State comptroller, the same principle applies to public expenditures in support of or opposition to any public referenda. As such, towns may "may not use town funds or town employees to prepare a proposed budget or other document for the purpose of showing residents of a proposed village the cost of incorporating or operating a village since a town has no legal standing to oppose the creation of a village and its intrusion into the incorporation process would be a partisan political act rather than an exercise of its proper governmental powers" (Office of the New York State Comptroller, Opinion No. 80-762, 1980).

2. The analysis was limited to the pages' primary content, including posts, photos, links, and attachments that are published by the group administrator(s). Public comments by citizens or residents visiting the pages were not considered as part of the groups' *deliberate* messaging.

Chapter 7

1. Applying their framework of the six non–mutually exclusive variables to the twenty-nine failed votes produces similar findings in the *motivations* underlying dissolute efforts: 87 percent had operational efficiency as a motivating factor, population exodus was a factor in 27 percent, fiscal stress motivated around 20 percent (higher than in the successful cases), and unique factors (like dysfunction or water issues) were prominent in 17 percent. Interestingly, citizen apathy was not a major contributor to any of the cases of failed votes under the Empowerment Act.

2. See Kay and Baker (2015) for an overview of the process tracing methodology.

3. The case studies offer mixed evidence on the role of pro-dissolution policy entrepreneurs but suggest that intra-community figures are most effective against the frequent counternarratives that portray dissolution as fueled by a small, disgruntled minority or by community newcomers or outsiders. Successful dissolution efforts depend on a committed pro-dissolution coalition to carry the effort through the petition and voter education process and any legal challenges that may arise.

4. See, for example, New York State legislative bill numbers offered in legislative session year: S.1824/A01274-B (2011–12); A04707 (2013–15); A04772 (2015–16); and A05636 (2017–18). Of these, only S.1824/A01274-B passed the New York State Senate (34–26) but did not make it out of the Assembly Committee on

Local Government. NYCOM championed revisions that would introduce further procedural and technical limitations into the law (Memorandum in Support of A10432/S.7238). NYCOM supported a sixty-day time limit for the collection of petition signatures, a *required* study process via an appointed committee that includes town representation *prior* to the vote, an extension from 180 days to one year for the formation of the dissolution plan (with the option on the part of the locality to extend that period to two years, and a mandatory referendum on all petition-initiated dissolution plans (Memorandum in Support of A10432/S.7238).

    5. A04707 (2013–14); A04772 (2015–16); A05636 (2017–18).

    6. S0214 (2015–16); S01716 (2017–18); S03067 (2019–20).

    7. S06473/A08411 (2019–20, reintroduced 2021).

    8. See chapter 3, note 3.

    9. Indeed, her entryway into elected politics was sparked by her local activism as a member of a village action committee. Impressed by her work, local Democratic officials appointed her to the Hamburg Town Board in 1994, where she served for more than a decade before becoming Erie County clerk in 2007. In 2011, she was elected to the US House of Representatives (for the 26th Congressional District). After losing her reelection bid, Hochul was chosen by Cuomo to serve as his lieutenant governor. Observers note that no issue is "too local" for Hochul, who has a "granular" understanding of local matters, including zoning and land-use regulation (Mahoney 2021).

    10. Previously, the consolidation of municipal units in Indiana required a special legislative act. Indiana does not have incorporated villages. Townships are geographical and political subdivisions of the county; its municipal units are cities and towns. Towns may reincorporate as cities once their population exceeds 2,000 people. Using the C3 model as their framework for studying the Indiana cases, Taylor, Faulk, and Schaal (2017) concluded support for consolidation was diminished in non-homogenous communities and where there was greater potential for a cost shift from urban to rural residents. They further found higher levels of public support for consolidation where fiscal impacts were modest and the communities more homogeneous. Moreover, they concluded that preexisting functional consolidation (or service sharing) and elite support had little impact on consolidation success.

References

Achter, Paul J. 2004. "TV Technology, and McCarthyism: Crafting the Democratic Renaissance in an Age of Fear." *Quarterly Journal of Speech* 90 (3): 307–26.

Adirondack Daily Enterprise. 1983. "Bloomingdale Group to Study Village Dissolution." March 3, 1983.

Advisory Commission on Intergovernmental Relations (ACIR). 1961. "Governmental Structure, Organization and Planning in Metropolitan Areas." July 1961, A-5. Washington, DC: Advisory Commission on Intergovernmental Relations.

Advisory Committee on Intergovernmental Relations. 1962. "Factors Affecting Voter Reactions to Governmental Reorganization in Metropolitan Areas: Summary of Report M-15." Washington, DC: Advisory Commission on Intergovernmental Relations.

Agranoff, Robert. 2017. *Crossing Boundaries for Intergovernmental Management.* Washington, DC: Georgetown University Press.

Aiello, Tony. 2021. "Highland Falls the Latest New York Village to Attempt to Give Up Independence, Have Local Town Government Run Things." *WLNY News*, July 6, 2021.

Aldag, Austin M., Mildred E. Warner, and Yunji Kim. 2017. "What Causes Local Fiscal Stress? And What Can Be Done About It?" Ithaca: Department of City and Regional Planning, Cornell University.

Aldag, Austin M., and Mildred E. Warner. 2018. "Cooperation, Not Cost Savings: Explaining Duration of Shared Service Agreements." *Local Government Studies* 44 (3): 350–70.

Aldag, Austin M., and Mildred E. Warner. 2018b. "Fix the Cap." *Local State Austerity Policy & Creative Local Response*. Ithaca: Department of City and Regional Planning, Cornell University.

Aldag, Austin M., and Mildred E. Warner. 2019. "How Does Sharing Affect Service Expenditures? An Analysis of 20 Years of Service Costs." Presented at the 2019 Research and Practice in Progress Briefing on Local Government in New York, Rockefeller Institute of Government, Albany, NY, March 14.

Altieri, Gabe. 2017. "Van Etten Dissolution Vote Highlights Fracture Between Village and Town." WSKG News, *National Public Radio*, December 6, 2017.

Amherst Bee. 2010. "Vote 'No' on Dissolution in Williamsville." Editorial. August 11, 2010.

Ammons, Michael N. 2012. *Municipal Benchmarks: Assessing Local Performance and Establishing Community Standards.* New York: M.E. Sharpe.

Amsterdam Daily Democrat and Recorder. 1936. "Empire State Briefs." April 1, 1936.

Anderson, James E. 2011. *Public Policymaking*. 7th ed. Belmont, CA: Wadsworth.

Anderson, Julie. 2013. "OneLyons Takes Legal Action." *Finger Lakes Times*, July 9, 2013.

Anderson, Julie. 2013b. "VanStean Wins Lyons Mayor Seat by 4 Votes." *Finger Lakes Times*, November 19, 2013.

Anderson, Julie. 2013c. "OneLyons Files Specific Objections to Anti-Dissolution Group's Petition." *Finger Lakes Times*, December 13, 2013.

Anderson, Michele Wilde. 2012. "Dissolving Cities." *Yale Law Journal* 121: 1364–1446.

Andriatch, Bruce. 2009. "Deciding if It's Best to No Longer Exist." *Buffalo News*, December 22, 2009.

Andriatch, Bruce. 2010. "Radio Interview by Joyce Kryszak." WBFO, *Buffalo Public Radio*, August 23, 2010.

Anjum, Khadija, Hannah Bahnmiller, Hien Dinh, Alia Fierro, Jieun Kim, Jessica Masters, Disha Mendhekar, Kaitlyn Olbrich, Kyra Spotte-Smith, Keaton Wetzel, Jubek Yongo-Bure, Yunji Kim, and Mildred Warner. 2015. "Facing Fiscal Challenges: Moving Toward a New York State and Local Government Partnership." Ithaca, NY: City and Regional Planning, Cornell University.

Appellants Brief, Bailey et al. v. Village of Lyons. 2013. "Appellants Brief, Bailey, et al. v. Village of Lyons Board of Trustees." State of New York Appellate Division, Supreme Court Fourth Department, Appealed from Supreme Court, Wayne County, Honorable, John Nesbitt, Supreme Court Judge, Index 75906-2013.

Arnosti, Nathan, and Amy Liu. 2019. "The Best Way to Rejuvenate Rural America? Invest in Cities." *New York Times*, April 23, 2019.

Atkins, Richard A. 1968. "Background on Incorporation of Villages as Cities and Jurisdictional Conflicts Among Local Governments." Executive Department Office for Local Government Memorandum, December 17. Franck C. Moore Papers, Box 17, Folder 18.

Atkins, Richard A. 1969. "Village Dissolutions: Reported to the Advisory Board." Executive Department Office for Local Government, Handwritten Notes, January 22. Frank C. Moore Papers, Box 17, Folder 8.

Atkins, Richard A. 1969b. "Background on Incorporation of Villages as Cities and Jurisdictional Conflicts Among Local Governments." Executive Department Office for Local Government, Memorandum, December 17. Frank C. Moore Papers, Box 17, Folder 8.

Avallone, Elaine. 2015. "Herrings Moves Forward with Dissolution Process." *Carthage Republican Tribune*, September 3, 2015.

Bailey et al. v. Village of Lyons, NY Board of Trustees. 2013. "Order to Show Cause Why an Order Should Not Be Given Declaring Village of Lyons in Violation of GML 17-A, Compelling Village to Complete Statutory Duty." June 28, 2013.

Baker, Paula. 1991. *The Moral Frameworks of Public Life: Gender, Politics, and the State in Rural New York, 1870–1930*. New York: Oxford University Press.

Barker, Cyril Josh. 2019. "Seneca Village: Black History in Central Park." *Amsterdam News*, January 31, 2019.

Basalo, Victoria. 2003. "U.S. Regionalism and Rationality." *Urban Studies* 40 (3): 447–62.

Bates, Frank. 1912. "Village Government in New England." *American Political Science Review* 6 (3): 367–85.

Baynes, Peter. 2010. "Guest Editorial." *The Utica Observer Dispatch*, September 21, 2010.

Beck, Amanda W., and Mary S. Stone. 2017. "Why Municipalities Go Out of Business." *Journal of Government Financial Management* 66 (2): 45–49.

Becker, Frank S., and Edwin D. Howe. 1902. *Laws of the State of New York Relating to Villages*. Rochester: Williamson.

Bekiempis, Victoria. 2014. "Is a Catskills Town Divided by Antisemitism or Greedy Developers?" *Newsweek*, October 14, 2014.

Beltramo, Wade. 2008. "Village Dissolution: Understanding the Costs and Benefits." *NYCOM Bulletin*, May–June 2008.

Beltramo, Wade. 2009. "The New N.Y. Government Reorganization and Citizen Empowerment Act: The Latest Effort to Reform New York's Local Governments." *NYCOM Bulletin*, July–August 2009.

Benjamin, Gerald. 1990. "The Evolution of New York State's Local Government System." Paper prepared for Local Government Restructuring Project at the Nelson A. Rockefeller Institute of New York, Albany, NY.

Benjamin, Gerald. 2017. "The Chassidic Presence and Local Government in the Hudson Valley." *Albany Law Review* 80 (4): 1383–1464.

Benjamin, Gerald. 2017b. "Home Rule: Elusive or Illusion." *New York State Bar Association Journal* 89: 25–29.

Berger, Joseph. 1997. "Growing Pains for a Rural Hasidic Enclave." *New York Times*, January 13, 1997.

Berger, Joseph. 1997b. "Dissidents Gain with Kiryas Joel Pact." *New York Times*, March 12, 1997.

Berman, David. 2003. *Local Government and the States: Autonomy, Politics and Policy*. New York: Routledge.

Bernstein v. Feiner. 2018. 95 N.Y.3d 124.

Binghamton Press. 1950. "Lower Taxes Sway Vote: Downsville to Dissolve Village Corporation." March 22, 1950.

Binghamton Press. 1950b. "Downsville to Dispose of Property." August 26, 1950.

Binghamton Press. 1951. "Assembly Votes Dissolution of Downsville: 2 Special Districts Given OK." February 22, 1951.

Binghamton Press. 1951b. "Dewey Gets Downsville Dissolution." February 27, 1951.

Binghamton Press. 1959. "Dissolution Idea." May 6, 1959.

Binghamton Press. 1959b. "Movement to Dissolve Port Dickinson Delayed." August 9, 1959.

Birdseye, Clarence F. 1897. *Supplement to the Second Edition of the Birdseye's Revised Statutes, Codes and General Laws of the State of New York.* New York: Baker and Voorhies.

Bishop, William G., and William H. Attree. 1846. *Report of the Debates and Proceedings of the Convention for the Revision of the Constitution of the State of New York.* Albany, NY: The Office of the Evening Atlas.

Bittinger, Angela. 2015. "It's Time to Dissolve 'a Sinking Ship.'" Editorial. *Dunkirk Daily Observer,* October 31, 2015.

Blauvelt v. Nyack. 1876. 16 N.Y. Sup. Ct. 153.

Blazonis, Sarah. 2013. "Residents Say Goodbye to the Village of Altmar." *Spectrum News,* YNN.Com, June 6, 2013.

Bolger, Timothy. 2016. "Mastic Beach Votes to Dissolve, Making It Third-Shortest-Lived Village in NY." *Long Island Press,* November 17, 2016.

Bosman, Julie. 2018. "School's Closed. Forever." *New York Times,* June 13, 2018.

Boyd, Danile. 2008. "Layering of Local Governments & City-County Mergers a Report to the New York State Commission on Local Government Efficiency and Competitiveness." Albany, NY: Rockefeller Institute of Government.

Boynton, David. 1916. *Actual Government of New York: A Manual of the Local Municipal State and Federal Government for Use in Public and Private Schools of New York State.* New York: Ginn.

Brandon, Craig. 1976. "Rosendale Sacrifices Autonomy for the Good of All." *Utica Observer Dispatch,* April 28, 1976.

Bridges, Eric. 1995. "Implications of a Village Dissolution: Cherry Creek Consolidation Feasibility Analysis." Prepared for Town and Village of Cherry Creek, Chautauqua County, NY. Municipal Partnership Development Project.

Briffault, Richard. 2000. "Localism and Regionalism." *Buffalo Law Review* 48 (1): 1–30.

Bromberg, Daniel E. 2015. "Do Shared Services Achieve Results? The Performance of Interlocal Agreements." In *Municipal Shared Services and Consolidation: A Public Solutions Handbook,* edited by Alexander C. Henderson, 105–22. New York: Routledge.

Bronner, Kevin. 2016. "The New York State Fiscal Stress Monitoring System for Local Governments." Albany Research in Public Administration (ARPA): Report Number 2016-1, August 1.

Brooklyn Daily Eagle. 1895. "Tired of Village Government." October 20, 1895.

Brooklyn Daily Eagle. 1896. "Southampton's Village Charter." January 8, 1896.

Brooklyn Daily Eagle. 1896b. "Sea Cliff's Village Improvement Association." May 19, 1896.

Brooklyn Daily Eagle. 1896c. "Want $50,000 for Good Roads." June 4, 1896.

Brooklyn Daily Eagle. 1896d. "Sea Cliff's Finances." July 10, 1896.

Brooklyn Daily Eagle. 1896e. "Northport Briefs." August 24, 1896.

Brooklyn Daily Eagle. 1896f. "Incorporationists Win." September 30, 1896.

Brooklyn Daily Eagle. 1899. "Babylon's Special Election." April 1, 1899.

Brooklyn Daily Eagle. 1899b. "Northport Incorporation." July 2, 1899.

Brooklyn Daily Eagle. 1940. "South Floral Park Fires Counsel in Dissolution Tiff: Acts Against Leader of Drive to Challenge Status." July 30, 1940.

Brooklyn Daily Eagle. 1941. "Court Postpones Dissolution Rule to Fix Procedure: Justice Cuff Suggests Ruling Delay to Study Village Break-up Process." February 25, 1941.

Brooklyn Daily Eagle. 1941b. "Penny Plans Bill to Dissolve L.I. Village Status." December 5, 1941.

Brookfield Courier. 1919. "An Open Letter for Brookfielders: A Stranger's Impression of Our Village Roads." May 7, 1919.

Brookfield Courier. 1922. "Brookfield Road Bill." April 12, 1922.

Brookfield Courier. 1923. "Notice of Special Village Election." February 21, 1923.

Brown, David L., and Kai. A. Schafft. 2011. *Rural People and Communities in the 21st Century: Resilience and Transformation.* Malden, PA: Polity Press.

Bruck, Andrew, and H. Joseph Pinto. 2008. "Overruled by Home-Rule: The Problems with New Jersey's Latest Effort to Consolidate Municipalities." *Seton Hall Legislative Journal* 32: 287–350.

Brunori, David. 2007. *Local Tax Policy: A Federalist Perspective.* 2nd ed. Washington, DC: The Urban Institute.

Bucki, Craig. R. 2008. "Regionalism Revisited: The Effort to Streamline Governance in Buffalo and Erie County, New York." *Albany Law Review* 71 (1): 111–63.

Buffalo Evening News. 1965. "Hardt Urges More Town Home Rule." October 18, 1965.

Buffalo News. 2010. "Angry Villagers Carrying Torches for and Against Very Local Government." Editorial. March 26, 2010.

Buffalo News. 2010b. "Sloan Residents Discuss Fate of their Village." August 10, 2010.

Burns, Nancy. 1994. *The Formation of American Local Governments: Private Values in Public Institutions.* New York: Oxford University Press.

Burns, Nancy, and Gerald Gam. 1997. "Creatures of the State: State Politics and Local Government, 1871–1921." *Urban Affairs Review* 33 (1): 59–96.

Burrows, Edwin G., and Mike Wallace. 1994. *Gotham: A History of New York City to 1898.* New York: Oxford University Press.

Caber, Terry. 2010. "Communities Vote 'No' on Dissolving." *WIVB News*, September 29.

Carey, Bill. 2014. "Former Altmar Village Clerk Sent to State Prison." CNYcentral.
com, August 4. https://cnyccntral.com/news/local/former-altmar-village-
clerk-pleads-guilty-to-stealing-more-than-117000-from-taxpayers.

Carleo-Evangelist, Jordan. 2014. "A Tax-Cut Ultimatum." *Albany Times Union*,
January 7, 2014.

Carr, Jered. B. 2004. "Perspectives on City-County Consolidations and Its Alternatives." In *City-County Consolidation and Its Alternatives: Reshaping the
Local Government Landscape*, edited by Jered B. Carr and Richard C. Feiock,
3–24. New York: Routledge.

Casey, Pat. 2018. "Court Overturns Ruling for Edgemont Village Incorporation
Referendum." *The Examiner*, October 25, 2018.

Center for Governmental Research. 2008. "Opportunities for Shared Service for
the Village and Town of Allegany." Rochester, NY.

Centrino, Thomas, and Gerald Benjamin. 2014. "Classification of Property for
Taxation in New York State: Issues and Options: Discussion Brief #13."
New Paltz, NY: Center for Research, Regional Education and Outreach.

Cervantes, Nicki. 2010. "Study Urged on Impact of Dissolution." *Buffalo News*,
January 12, 2010.

Cervantes, Nicki. 2010b. "Gaughan Sets His Sights on Dissolving Villages: Emotions
Run High as New Law Making It Easier to Get Petitions Nears." *Buffalo
News*, February 21, 2010.

Chandler, Mathew. 2008. "Gaughan's Opinion of Future of Village Government
Includes His Claim Blasdell Is a Community in Crises." *Hamburg Sun
News*, May 29, 2008.

Chandler, Matt. 2009. "A Sit-down with the King of Downsizing." *Buffalo Law
Journal*, June 25, 2009.

Chapman, Keir. 2019. "Will Dissolving the Village of Chaumont Save Money? They're
Looking into It." *WWNY TV*, October 25. https://www.wwnytv.com/2019/10/25/
will-dissolving-village-chaumont-save-money-theyre-looking-into-it/.

Chapman, Jeff, and Katy Ascanio. 2020. "State Websites Offer Fiscal Data on
Local Governments." *Pew Charitable Trust*, October 20. https://www.pew
trusts.org/en/reasearch-and-analysis/articles/2020/10/20/state-websites-offer-
fiscal-data-on-local-governments.

Cheektowaga Bee. 2010. "It's Time to Get Past the Ugliness." Editorial. August
18, 2010.

Chiappone, Susan. 2014. "Village of Forestville Faces Doubling of Tax Rates in
New Budget." *Buffalo News*, April 29, 2014.

Chiappone, Susan. 2015. "Vote of Dissolution of Village of Forestville Divides
Residents, Officials." *Buffalo News*, October 28, 2015.

Chipp, Timothy. 2008. "Mayors Defend Village Government." *Amherst Bee*, August
20, 2008.

City of Clinton v. Cedar Rapids Railroad. 1868. 24 Iowa 255.

City of Trenton v. New Jersey. 1923. 262 U.S. 182.

Clodgo, Leon H. 2013. "In My Opinion: Divided Loyalties on Keeseville Dissolution." Editorial. *Plattsburgh Press Republican*, June 3, 2013.

Codero, Katelyn. 2020. "Pawling Leaders Agree Shared Services Needed After Consolidation Voted Down." *Poughkeepsie Journal*, December 1, 2020.

Coe, Charles K. 2008. "Preventing Local Government Fiscal Crises: Emerging Best Practices." *Public Administration Review* 68 (4): 759–67.

Cohen, Anthony P. 1985. *The Symbolic Construction of Community*. London: Routledge.

Cone, Jaime. 2018. "VE Fire Department No Longer Responding to Calls." *Ithaca Journal*, June 4, 2018.

Cook, Jaime. 2018. "Harrisville Mayor Says Dissolution Study Was Flawed." *Watertown Daily Times*, May 13, 2018.

Cooley, Thomas, M. 1880. *The General Principles of Constitutional Law in the United States of America*. Boson: Little and Brown.

Cooper, Elizabeth. 2013. "Bridgewater on Brink of Dissolution." *Utica Observer Dispatch*, December 1, 2013.

Cooper, Elizabeth. 2015. "Time Ticking Down on Prospect's Dissolution Decision." *Utica Observer Dispatch,* March 18, 2015.

Cooper, Elizabeth. 2015b. "Prospect's D-Day: Voters Decide Future of Village Tuesday." *Utica Observer Dispatch,* July 20, 2015.

Cooper, Elizabeth. 2015c. "Prospect Votes to Dissolve." *Utica Observer Dispatch,* July 21, 2015.

Corning Evening Leader. 1923. "East Bloomfield." August 16, 1923.

Corning Evening Leader. 1925. "Voting Today at South Corning." March 17, 1925.

Cramer Walsh, Katherine J. 2012. "Putting Inequality in Its Place: Rural Consciousness and the Power of Perspective." *The American Political Science Review* 106 (3): 517–32.

Cramer, Katherine J. 2016. *The Politics of Resentment: Rural Consciousness in Wisconsin and the Rise of Scott Walker*. Chicago: University of Chicago Press.

Cresswell, Sydney, and Anthony Cresswell. 2015. "Communities and Culture." In *Municipal Shared Services and Consolidation: A Public Solutions Handbook*, edited by Alexander C. Henderson, 36–58. New York: Routledge.

Crow, Deserai Anderson, and John Berggren. 2014. In *The Science of Stories: Applications of the Narrative Policy Framework in Public Policy Analysis*, edited by Michael D. Jones, Elizabeth Shanahan, and Mark K. McBeth, 131–56. New York: Palgrave MacMillan.

Cuomo, Andrew. 2010. *The New NY Agenda: A Plan for Action*. Albany, NY: Office of the New York State Governor.

Curry, Tracey. 2010. "Macedon Mayor Hoteling Nixes Planning Board Member." *Wayne Post*, July 14, 2010.

Curry, Tracey. 2010b. "In Macedon, Public Will Falls to Mayor's Will." *Wayne Post*, July 29, 2010.

Curtis, Aaron. 2015. "One Macedon Says Village Dissolution a 'No Brainer.'" *Webster Post*, May 12, 2015.

D'Agostino, John. 2010. "Supporting a Failing Way of Life." Editorial. *Observer Today*, August 20, 2010.

Daily Messenger. 2015. "Our View: Focus on Benefits of Village Dissolution Not Politics." Editorial. March 19, 2015.

Daily Star. 2002. "Village of Andes Kaput." June 4, 2002.

Dedie, Amanda. 2016. "Cherry Creek Puts Dissolution on the Table." *Dunkirk Observer Today*, November 8, 2016.

Dehring, Carolyn A., Craig A. Depken II, and Michael R. Ward. 2008. "A Direct Test of the Homevoter Hypothesis." *Journal of Urban Economics* 64 (2008): 155–70.

DeMola, Pete. 2015. "Keeseville Dissolves After Two Centuries." *Finger Lakes Times,* January 7, 2015.

Devas, Nick, Ian Blore, and Richard Slater. 2004. *Municipalities and Finance: A Sourcebook for Capacity Building.* New York: Routledge.

Dimopoulos, Thomas. 2011. "Late Change to Schuylerville Dissolution Ballot Raises Concerns." *Glens Falls Post-Star,* March 12.

Disturnell, John. 1842. *New York State Guide.* Albany: J. Disturnell.

Disturnell, John. 1843. *New York State Guide.* Albany: J. Disturnell.

Ducker, Walter. 1931. "Advantages and Disadvantages if a Village Incorporates as a City." *Information Concerning the Present Government of the Village of Kenmore Compiled by Village Clerk.* Frank C. Moore Papers, Box 17, Folder 18.

Dullea, Henrik. 1997. *Charter Revision in the Empire State: The Politics of New York's 1967 Constitutional Convention.* Albany: State University of New York Press.

Dunkirk Observer Today. 2016. "Cherry Creek Weighs Future." October 23, 2016.

Dunkirk Observer Today. 2017. "Big Savings in Dissolution." January 31, 2017.

Dunkirk Observer Today. 2018. "Cherry Creek Receives Dissolution Funds." July 7, 2018.

DuVall, Eric. 2010. "Regionalism Has Its Opponents." *Tonawanda News,* June 30, 2010.

Eaton, Amasa Mason. (1902) 2018. *The Origin of Municipal Incorporation in England and in the United States.* Reprint, London: Forgotten Books.

Edmonds, Helen L., and Dwight H. Merriam. 1996. "Land Use and Zoning Law: Recent Developments in the Second Circuit 1996." *QLR* 15 (4): 443–69.

Edwards, Mary M., And Xu Xiao. 2009. "Annexation, Local Government Spending, and the Complicating Role of Density." *Urban Affairs Review* 45 (2): 147–65.

Elazar. Daniel. 1998. *Covenant and Civil Society: Constitutional Matrix of Modern Democracy.* New York: Routledge.

Ellen, Martha. 2010. "Edwards Meeting on Future of Village." *Watertown Daily Times,* September 25, 2010.

Elmira Star Gazette. 2018. "Last-Gasp Citizen Petition Fails, Clearing the Way for Village of Van Etten to Dissolve." August 3, 2018.

Egleston, Nathaniel Hillyer. 1878. *Villages and Village Life with Hints for Their Improvement.* New York: Harper & Brothers.

Esmonde, Donn. 2004. "Roadblocks Revealed by Conversations." *Buffalo News,* June 14, 2004.

Fairlie, John A. 1920. *The American State Series: Local Government in Counties, Towns and Villages.* New York: Century.

Fairport Herald. 1922. "Untitled." April 12, 1922.

Feeney Commission. 1975. *Report of the Temporary State Commission on State and Local Finances.* Vol. 3: *State Mandates.* Albany, NY: Temporary State Commission on State and Local Finances.

Feiock, Richard, C., and Jared Carr. 2000. "Private Incentives and Academic Entrepreneurship: The Promotion of City-County Consolidation." *Public Administration Quarterly* 24 (2): 221–46.

Feiock, Richard C. 2004. "Do Consolidation Entrepreneurs Make a Deal with the Devil?" In *Forms of Local Government: A Handbook on City, County, and Regional Options,* edited by Roger L. Kemp, 39–52. Jefferson, NC: McFarland.

Feiock, Richard C., Jared Carr, and Linda S. Johnson. 2006. "Structuring the Debate on Consolidation: A Response to Leland and Thurmaier." *Public Administration Review* 66 (March): 274–78.

Finch, Jessica. 2008. "Villages Asked to Merge with Towns." *Amherst Bee,* July 16, 2008.

Fiscal Policy Institute. 2018. "New York State Economic and Fiscal Outlook 2018–2019." https://fiscalpolicy.org/wp-content/uploads/2018/02/Government.pdf.

Fischel, William A. 2001. *The Homevoter Hypothesis: How Home Values Influence Local Government Taxation, School Finance, and Land Use Policies.* Cambridge: Harvard University Press.

Fitzpatrick, John T. 1924. *Williamson's Village Laws of the State of New York.* New York: Williamson Law.

Florida, Richard. 2017. *The New Urban Crisis: How Our Cities Are Increasing Inequality, Deepening Segregation, and Failing the Middle Class—and What We Can Do About It.* New York: Basic Books.

Foderaro, Lisa. 2017. "An Upscale Hamlet Weights Whether to Be a Village (Or Not to Be)." *New York Times,* November 5, 2017.

Foderaro, Lisa. 2017b. "Call It Splitsville, N.Y." *New York Times,* November 19, 2017.

Fort Covington Sun. 1974. "Consultants Recommend Fort Covington Dissolve." June 20, 1974.

Frank C. Moore Papers. 1881–1978. M.E. Grenander Department of Special Collections and Archives, University of Albany. Albany, NY.

Freeze, Matt. 2018. "Van Etten: Village Dissolution Process Continues." *Morning Times,* April 24, 2018.

Freeze, Matt. 2018b. "Van Etten: Certified Petition Falls Short by More Than 12 Entries." *Morning Times*, August 7, 2018.

Freeze, Matt. 2018c. "Van Etten: Nearly One-third of Village Petition Void—Three More Signatures Invalid." *Morning Times*, August 9, 2018.

Freeze, Matt. 2018d. "Van Etten: Village Accepts County Funding for Dissolution Process." *Morning Times*, August 21, 2018.

Freeze, Matt. 2018e. "Van Etten: Town, Village Officials Iron Out Dissolution Details—More Joint Meetings Slated." *Morning Times*, September 11, 2018.

Freeze, Matt. 2018f. "Van Etten: Town Tax Rates to Drop in 2019." *Morning Times*, October 26, 2018.

Friedman, Thomas L. 2018. "Where American Politics Can Still Work: From the Bottom Up." *New York Times*, July 3, 2018.

Fries, Amanda. 2013. "Village of Bridgewater Looks to Dissolve Community." *Utica Observer Dispatch*, November 1, 2013.

Gardiner, Bob. 2014. "Salem Voters Back Elimination of Village." *Albany Times Union*, August 6, 2014.

Gardner, James. 2010. "Rioting! In the Suburbs." *Artvoice*, February 25, 2010.

Garragazzo, Wendy. 2011. "Mayor of Leicester Defends Village Status." *Livingston County News*, October 21, 2011.

Gaughan, Kevin P. 2006. "How 439 Politicians Cost Us Effective Government and Why Paying Them $32 Million a Year Costs Us Our Future." *Buffalo News*, December 2, 2006.

Gaughan, Kevin P. 2009. "Struggling to Survive: Bloated Local Government Is Corroding Our Sense of Self." *Buffalo News*, April 26, 2009.

Gaughan, Kevin P. 2009b. "The Local Government Tour." *Artvoice*, July 9, 2009.

Gault, Alex. 2020. "Chaumont Votes to Keep Village Government, Mayor Hopes for New Leadership Moving Forward." NNY 360, November 4. https://www.nny360.com/news/jeffersoncounty/chaumont-votes-to-keep-village-government-mayor-hopes-for-new-leadership-moving-forward/article_2653845c-a1ad-50e8-87f7-4c9d46bb0f09.html.

Geneva Daily Times. 1933. "Village of Old Forge Will Disincorporate." July 12, 1933.

Geneva Daily Times. 1935. "Old Forge Ceases to Be a Village Today." April 1, 1935.

Gephardt v. Wilcox. 1935. 245 A.D. 580.

Germa, Bel, and Mildred E. Warner. 2015. "Inter-Municipal Cooperation and Costs: Expectations and Evidence." *Public Administration* 93 (1): 52–67.

Geruntino, Gino. 2014. "Village of Bridgewater Faces Decision Whether to Dissolve." *WRVO News*, January 31.

Glaeser, Edward. 2011. *Triumph of the City: How Our Greatest Invention Makes Us Richer, Smarter, Greener, Healthier, and Happier.* London: Penguin Books.

Glens Falls Post-Star. 2011. "Vote on Merits, Not Scare Tactics." Editorial. March 15, 2011.

Glens Falls Post-Star. 2015. "Thankfully, Dissolution Talks Will Be Public." Editorial. March 16, 2015.

Goodman, Josh. 2008. "Attempted Merger." *Governing Magazine*, October 31, 2008.

Gordan, Christopher. 2010. "Village Dissolution Could Hit Seniors in Their Pocketbooks." *Orchard Park Bee*, April 1, 2010.

Gordon, Christopher. 2010b. "Town, Village Boards Discuss Efforts of Possible Dissolution." *Orchard Park Bee*, April 8, 2010.

Grad, Frank. 1964. "The New York Home Rule Amendment: A Bill of Rights for Local Government?" *Local Government Law Services Letter* 9: June. Albany, NY: Local Government Law Services.

Grattan, Robert. 1903. *Bender's Village Laws of the State of New York*. Albany, NY: Mathew Bender.

Grattan, Robert. 1914. *Bender's Village Laws of the State of New York*. Albany, NY: Mathew Bender.

Grattan, Robert. 1918. *Bender's Village Laws of the State of New York*. Albany, NY: Mathew Bender.

Groom, Debra J. 2010. "Study States Altmar Residents Would See Lower Taxes if Village Abolished." *Syracuse Post Standard*, May 11, 2010.

Groom, Debra J. 2010b. "Few Questions Arise at Altmar Hearing on Its Dissolution Plan." *Syracuse Post Standard*, July 7, 2010.

Groom, Debra. 2011. "Study States Altmar Residents Would See Lower Taxes if Village Abolished." *Syracuse Post Standard*, May 11, 2011.

Gryta, Matt. 2010. "Highway Chief Pleads Guilty to Embezzlement." *Buffalo News*, March 20, 2010.

Gryta, Matt. 2010b. "Ex-Highway Chief, Warned to Pay $13,000 to Village Soon." *Buffalo News*, July 17, 2010.

Haber, Jeffrey. 2008. "Government Efficiency: The Case for Local Control." Albany, NY: The Association of Towns of the State of New York.

Hakim, Denny. 2012. "Deficits Push N.Y. Cities and Counties to Desperation." *New York Times*, March 10, 2012.

Hamlet of Brewerton Strategic Revitalization Plan. 2008. "Hamlet of Brewerton Strategic Revitalization Plan, September 2008." http://www.anewdayinbrewerton.com/downloads?September_2008_plan.pdf.

Hampton, Deon J. 2016. "Critics of Mastic Beach Want to Unincorporate the Village." *Newsday*, August 28, 2016.

Hampton, Deon J. 2017. "Mastic Beach Locks Up for Last Time as Village Dissolves." *Newsday*, December 30, 2017.

Hampton, Deon J. 2018. "Signs of Revival Emerge in Once-Struggling Mastic Beach, Officials Say." *Newsday*, September 28, 2018.

Hattery, Michael R. 1998. "Wellsville Town-Village Municipal Study Final Report." Cornell University, Local Government Program. Ithaca, NY: Cornell University.

Hattery, Michael R. 2015. "Service Level Consolidation and Sharing Agreements." In *Municipal Shared Services and Consolidation: A Public Solutions Handbook*, edited by Alexander C. Henderson, 59–75. New York: Routledge.

Hauser, Rick. 2018. "Mayor's Column: Where Do My Village Taxes Go?" Village of Perry, News Release, February 22.

Hawkins, Christopher B., and Jared B. Carr. 2015. "The Costs of Services Cooperation: A Review of the Literature." In *Municipal Shared Services and Consolidation: A Public Solutions Handbook*, edited by Alexander C. Henderson, 17–35. New York: Routledge.

Hendrick, Rebecca M. 2011. *Managing the Fiscal Metropolis: The Financial Policies, Practices, and Health of Suburban Municipalities*. Washington, DC: Georgetown University Press.

Henrietta Post. 2014. "For Village of Macedon Boosters, a Tough Sell on Awaits on Dissolution Question." Editorial. November 21, 2014.

Henson, Matt. 2013. "Should the Village of Keeseville Dissolve?" WCAX.com, January 27.

Heveron-Smith, Mary. 1979. "The Time Has Come to Dissolve Savannah." *Finger Lakes Times*, December 29, 1979.

Hice, Jessica. 2017. "Village of Van Etten Hires Firm to Study Dissolution." *Star Gazette*, September 7, 2017.

Hicks, Matt. 2013. "Fire Protection for Town of Van Etten to Be Subject of Public Hearing." *Morning Times*, November 16, 2013.

Hochschild, Arlie Russell. 2016. *Strangers in Their Own Land: Anger and Mourning on the American Right*. New York: The New Press.

Hou, Yilin. 2015. "Local Government Stabilization: An Introduction." In *Local Government Budget Stabilization: Explorations and Evidence*, edited by Yulin Hou, 1–16. Singapore: Springer.

Hough, Franklin B. 1858. *The New-York Civil List, Containing the Names and Origin of the Civil Divisions*. New York: Weed and Parsons.

Hough, Franklin B. 1860. *Civil Lists and Forms of Government of the Colony and State of New York*. New York: Weed and Parsons.

Hough, Franklin B. 1867. *Civil Lists and Forms of Government of the Colony and State of New York*. New York: Weed and Parsons.

Howe, Edward T. 2006. "The Incorporated Villages of the Hudson River Region." *The Hudson River Valley Review* 22 (2): 91–108.

Hudak, Amy. 2016. "Village of Macedon Split Over Dissolution Vote." *WHAM News*, March 16, 2016.

Huefner, Ronald J. 2011. "Internal Control Weaknesses in Local Government: Evidence from Town and Village Audits." *The CPA Journal* (July): 20–27.

Hughes, Herbert H., and Charles Lee. 1999. "The Evolutionary Consolidation Model." In *Forms of Local Government: A Handbook on City, County, and Regional Options*, edited by Roger L. Kemp, 272–79. Jefferson, NC: McFarland.

Hunter v. Pittsburgh. 1907. 207 U.S. 161.

Hyman, J. D. 1965. "Home Rule in New York: 1941–1965: Retrospect and Prospect." *Buffalo Law Review* 15 (2): 335–69.

Ingram, Gregory K., and Yu-hung Hong. 2010. *Municipal Revenues and Land Policies*. Cambridge, MA: Lincoln Institute of Land Policy.

Inman, Robert. P. 2010. *Municipal Revenues and Land Policies*. Edited by Gregory K. Ingram and Yu-hung Hong, 26–44. Cambridge, MA: Lincoln Institute of Land Policy.

Jackson, Kelly. 2009. "Gaughan Plans to Begin Village Dissolution Petitioning in March." *Amherst Bee*, October 21, 2009.

Jakubowski, Casey, and Lisa Kulka. 2016. "Overcoming State Support for School Consolidation: How Schools in the Empire State React." *Journal of Inquiry and Action in Education* 8 (1): 66–80.

Johnson, Linda S. 2004. "Revolutionary Local Constitutional Change." In *City-County Consolidation and Its Alternatives: Reshaping the Local Government Landscape*, edited by Jered B. Carr and Richard C. Feiock, 155–82. New York: Routledge.

Johnson, Linda S., and Richard C. Feiock. 1999. "Revolutionary Change in Local Governance: Revisiting the Rosebaum and Kammerer Theory of Successful City-County Consolidation." *Journal of Political Science* 27 (1): 21–52.

Johnson, Lisa. 2010. "Gaughan with the Villages?" *Lancaster Bee*, March 18, 2010.

Joint Legislative Committee on Towns and Villages. 1969. *Minutes of the Public Meeting of the State of New York Joint Legislative Committee on Towns and Villages*. Henrietta Town Hall, Henrietta, NY, October 9. Frank C. Moore Papers, Box 16, Folder 9.

Joint Legislative Committee on Towns and Villages. 1969b. *Minutes of the Proceedings of the New York State Legislative Committee on Towns and Villages*. Cattaraugus County Center, Little Valley, NY, October 10. Frank C. Moore Papers, Box 16, Folder 9.

Joint Legislative Committee on Towns and Villages. 1969c. *Minutes of Proceedings of a Public Hearing of the Joint Legislative Committee on Towns and Villages*. Historical Museum, Owego, NY, November 12. Frank C. Moore Papers, Box 16, Folder 9.

Joint Legislative Committee on Towns and Villages. 1969d. *Minutes of the Proceedings of the Joint Legislative Committee on Towns and Villages*. Assembly Parlor, State Capital, Albany, NY, November 13. Frank C. Moore Papers, Box 16, Folder 9.

Jones, Michel D., and Mark K. McBeth. 2010. "A Narrative Policy Framework: Clear Enough to Be Wrong?" *Policy Studies Journal* 38 (2): 329–53.

Jones, Michael D. 2014. "Introducing the Narrative Policy Framework." In *The Science of Stories: Applications of the Narrative Policy Framework in Public Policy Analysis*, edited by Michael D. Jones, Elizabeth Shanahan, and Mark K. McBeth, 1–25. New York: Palgrave MacMillan.

Judd, Dennis R., and Annika M. Hinze. 2015. *City Politics: The Political Economy of Urban America*. New York: Routledge.

Kahn, Kathy. 2018. "Two Towns, Different Counties—Same Agenda?" *Rockland County Times*, August 9, 2018.

Katz, Bruce, and Jeremy Nowak. 2017. *The New Localism: How Cities Can Thrive in the Age of Populism*. Washington, DC: Brookings.

Kay, Adrian, and Phillip Baker. 2015. "What Can Causal Process Tracing Offer to Policy Studies? A Review of the Literature." *Policy Studies Journal* 43 (1): 1–21.

Kay, David, and Bryce Corrigan. 2016. "An Empirical Analysis of Intermunicipal Service Sharing and Its Effects on Local Government Spending in New York State." Paper presented at the Rockefeller Institute of Government's 2016 Local Government Research and Practice in Progress Briefing, November 16, Albany, NY.

Kazis, Noah. 2020. "Ending Exclusionary Zoning in New York City's Suburbs." New York University Furman Center, New York, NY. https://furmancenter. org/files/Ending_Exclusionary_Zoning_in_New_York_Citys_Suburbs.pdf.

Kear, Andrew R., and Dominic D. Wells. 2014. "Coalitions Are People: Policy Narratives and the Defeat of Ohio Senate Bill 5." In *The Science of Stories: Applications of the Narrative Policy Framework in Public Policy Analysis*, edited by Michael D. Jones, Elizabeth Shanahan, and Mark K. McBeth, 157–84. New York: Palgrave MacMillan.

Keller, Suzanne. 2003. *Community: Pursuing the Dream, Living the Reality*. Princeton: Princeton University Press.

Kim, Yuni, and Mildred E. Warner. 2016. "Pragmatic Municipalism: Local Government Service Delivery After the Great Recession." *Public Administration* 94 (3): 789–805.

Kingston Daily Freeman. 1915. "What Highland Falls Wants." December 27, 1915.

Kingston Daily Freeman. 1920. "Untitled." January 1, 1920.

Kingston Daily Freeman. 1959. "Board Not Calling for Rosendale Poll." April 3, 1959.

Kingston Daily Freeman. 1959b. "Rosendale Going to Polls on July 14 on Dissolution Vote." June 19, 1959.

Kingston Daily Freeman. 1959c. "Rosendale Voters Deny Harassing Village Board." June 22, 1959.

Kingston Daily Freeman. 1959d. "Dissolution Vote on Tuesday." July 11, 1959.

Kingston Daily Freeman. 1959e. "Rosendale Leaders Are for Dissolution." July 13, 1959.

Kingston Daily Freeman. 1959f. "Rosendale Turns Back Dissolution Move." *Kingston Daily Freeman*, July 15, 1959.

Kittle, Shaun. 2012. "Keeseville Dissolution Study Wrapping Up." *The Burgh*, October 11, 2012.

Klinenberg, Eric. 2018. *Palaces for the People: How Social Infrastructure Can Help Fight Inequality, Polarization, and the Decline of Civic Life*. New York: Crown Publishing Group.

Knotts, Katherine. 2010. "Farnham Mayor on Dissolution: 'It Is Absolutely Wrong.'" *Hamburg Sun News,* September 2, 2010.

Kratz, Alex. 2022. "South Nyack's Drama." *Nyack News and Views*, March 14, 2022.

Krebs, Bill. 2009. "Downsizing Fad the Wrong Medicine for the Ailment." Editorial. *Buffalo News,* December 16, 2009.

Krueger, Matt. 2010. "Gaughan's Door-to-Door Campaign Begins in Sloan." *Cheektowaga Bee,* April 1, 2010.

Krueger, Matt. 2010b. "Dissolution Main Topic at Sloan Meeting." *Cheektowaga Bee,* April 15, 2010.

Krueger, Matt. 2010c. "Sloan Dissolution Vote to Be Held August 17." *Cheektowaga Bee*, June 24, 2010.

Krueger, Matt. 2010d. "Town Supervisor to Join Mayor for Public Meeting on Dissolution." *Cheektowaga Bee*, July 15, 2010.

Krueger, Matt. 2010e. "Gaughan Struggling to Find a Venue." *Cheektowaga Bee*, July 22, 2010.

Krueger, Matt. 2010f. "Dissolution Defeated." *Cheektowaga Bee,* August 18, 2010.

Laberge Group. 2020. "Town and Village of Pawling Interim Study of Consolidation." November. Albany, NY: Laberge Group, Inc.

Lansing, Robert, and Gary M. Jones. 1903. *The Government and Civil Institutions of New York State.* New York: Silver and Burdett.

Lantz, Samantha. 2018. "The Latest in the Van Etten Dissolution Battle: Fire Protection." *WETM News,* May 22, 2018.

Lav, Iris J., and Michael Leachman. 2017. "At Risk: Federal Grants to State and Local Governments Programs for Low- and Moderate-Income Families Could Bear the Brunt of Cuts." Washington, DC: Center for Budgets and Priorities, March 13.

Lawyers Committee for Civil Rights Media Release. 2015. "About Long Island Housing Services et al. v. Village of Mastic Beach and Timothy Brojer," Case No. 2:15-cv-00629.

Lazarus, Reuben. 1964. "Constitutional Amendment and Home Rule In New York State." *New York Law Journal.* Franck C. Moore Papers, Box 16, Folder 1.

Laycock, Douglas, and Luke W. Goodrich. 2012. "RLUIPA: Necessary, Modest, and Under-Enforced." *Fordham Urban Law Journal* 39 (4): 1021–72.

Leblanc-Stenberg v. Fletcher. 1991. 763 F. Supp. 1246.

LeBlanc-Stemberg v. Fletcher. 1995. 67 F.3d 412.

LeCouteur, Amanda, Mark Rapley, and Martha Auguoustinos. 2001. "'This Very Difficult Debate About Wik': Stake, Voice and the Management of Category Memberships in Race Politics." *British Journal of Social Psychology* 40 (1): 35–57.

Lefkowitz v. Reisman. 1988. 144 A.D.2d 465, 534 N.Y.S.2d 2.

Lefkowitz v. Reisman. 1989. 73 N.Y.2d 704, 537 N.Y.S.2d 492.

Legislative Document No. 7. 1970. *Report of the Joint Legislative Committee on Towns and Villages.* Albany, NY: Legislative Documents of the Senate and Assembly of the State of New York.

Legislative Document No. 21. 1964. *Second Report of the Joint Legislative Committee on Villages, State of New York.* Albany, NY: Legislative Documents of the Senate and Assembly of the State of New York.

Legislative Document No. 21. 1965. *Third Report of the Joint Legislative Committee on Villages.* Albany, NY: Legislative Documents of the Senate and Assembly of the State of New York.

Legislative Document No. 24. 1967. *Interim Report of the Joint Legislative Committee to Study and Recodify the Town Law.* Albany, NY: Legislative Documents of the Senate and Assembly of the State of New York.

Legislative Document No. 25. 1956. *Report of the New York State Joint Legislative Committee to Study, Codify, Revise and Make Uniform Existing Laws Relating to Town and Village Governments and Other Matters Related Thereto and to Continue the Work of the Temporary State Commission Heretofore Created for Such Purpose.* Albany, NY: Legislative Documents of the Senate and Assembly of the State of New York.

Legislative Document No. 27. 1971. *Final Report of the Joint Legislative Committee on Towns and Villages.* Albany, NY: Legislative Documents of the Senate and Assembly of the State of New York.

Legislative Document No. 41. 1956. *A Report of the New York State Joint Legislative Committee to Study, Codify, Revise and Make Uniform Existing Laws Relating to Town and Village Governments and Other Matters Related Thereto and to Continue the Work of the Temporary State Commission.* Albany, NY: Legislative Documents of the Senate and Assembly of the State of New York.

Legislative Document No. 47. 1956. *Report of the New York State Joint Legislative Committee to Study, Codify, Revise and Make Uniform Existing Laws Relating to Town and Village Governments and Other Matters Related Thereto and to Continue the Work of the Temporary State Commission Heretofore Created for Such Purpose.* Albany, NY: Legislative Documents of the Senate and Assembly of the State of New York.

Legislative Document No. 86. 1968. *Interim Report of the Joint Legislative Committee to Study and Recodify the Town Law.* Albany, NY: Legislative Documents of the Senate and Assembly of the State of New York.

Leland, Suzanne M., and Gary A. Johnson. 2000. "Metropolitan Consolidation Success: Returning to the Roots of Local Government Reform." *Public Administration Quarterly* 24 (2): 202–21.

Leland, Suzanne M., and Gary A. Johnson. 2004. "Consolidation as a Local Government Reform: Why City-County Consolidation Is an Enduring Issue." In *Forms of Local Government: A Handbook on City, County, and Regional Options,* edited by Roger L. Kemp, 25–38. Jefferson, NC: McFarland.

Leland, Suzzane M., and Kurt Thurmaier. 2004. *Case Studies of City–County Consolidation: Reshaping the Local Government Landscape.* Armonk, NY: M.E. Sharpe.

Leland, Suzzane M., and Kurt Thurmaier. 2005. "When Efficiency Is Unbelievable: Normative Lessons from 30 Years of City–County Consolidations." *Public Administration Review* 66 (4): 475–89.

Leland, Suzanne M., and Kurt Thurmaier. 2014. "Political and Functional Local Government Consolidation: The Challenges for Core Public Administration Values and Regional Reform." *American Review of Public Administration* 44 (4): 29–46.

Levine, Joyce. 2001. "The Role of Economic Theory in Regional Advocacy." *Journal of Planning Literature* 16: 186–93.

Lewis, Paul G. 1996. *Shaping Suburbia: How Political Institutions Organize Urban Development.* Pittsburgh: University of Pittsburgh Press.

Lieberman, Steve. 2022. "South Nyack: What Lingering DPW Sale Could Mean for Village Debt, Taxpayers' Burden." *LoHud News*, March 14, 2022.

Lincoln, Charles Z. 1909. *State of New York: Messages from the Governors: Comprising Executive Communications to the Legislature and Other Papers Relating to Legislation from the Organization of the First Colonial Assembly in 1683 to and Including the Year 1906, Volume VI (1869–1876).* Albany, NY: J.B. Lyon.

Lincoln, Charles Z. 1909b. *State of New York: Messages from the Governors: Comprising Executive Communications to the Legislature and Other Papers Relating to Legislation from the Organization of the First Colonial Assembly in 1683 to and Including the Year 1906, Volume VII (1869–1876).* Albany, NY: J.B. Lyon.

Lincoln, Charles Z. 1909c. *State of New York: Messages from the Governors: Comprising Executive Communications to the Legislature and Other Papers Relating to Legislation from the Organization of the First Colonial Assembly in 1683 to and Including the Year 1906, Volume VIII (1869–1876).* Albany, NY: J.B. Lyon.

Lincoln, Charles Z. 1909d. *State of New York: Messages from the Governors: Comprising Executive Communications to the Legislature and Other Papers Relating to Legislation from the Organization of the First Colonial Assembly in 1683 to and Including the Year, Volume IX (1869–1876).* Albany, NY: J.B. Lyon.

Lingeman, Richard. 1980. *Small Town America: A Narrative History 1620-Present.* Boston: Houghton Mifflin.

Livingston County News. 2011. "To Dissolve or Not to Dissolve?" November 23, 2011.

Lobdell, Keith. 2012. "Keeseville Dissolution Draft Study Picks Third Option." *Denpubs.com*, July 14, 2012.

Lobdell, Keith. 2013. "Keeseville Steps Closer to Dissolution." *Valley News*, August 3, 2013.

Lobdell, Keith. 2013b. "Dissolution Vote in Keeseville October 22." *The Burgh*, October 21, 2013.

Lobdell, Kieth. 2013c. "Keeseville Village Government to Dissolve." *Denpubs.com*, October 22, 2013.

Lockridge, Kenneth A. 1970. *A New England Town: The First Hundred Years*. New York: Norton.

Lowville Journal Republican. 1932. "Village of Old Forge Is Under Examination: State Finds Discrepancies in Village Management." July 28, 1932.

Lucchino, Frank. J. 1994. "Reclaiming Hope: Voluntary Disincorporation in Allegheny County." County of Allegheny, PA: Allegheny County Controller's Office.

Lundine Commission. 2008. "21st Century Local Government: Report of the New York State Commission on Local Government Efficiency & Competitiveness" (Lundine Commission Report). Albany, NY: Office of Local Government Efficiency.

Lutz, Donald. 1988. *The Origins of American Constitutionalism*. Baton Rouge: Louisiana State University Press.

Lyall, Sarah. 1989. "First Year for an L.I. Village Is Anything But Blissful." *New York Times*, April 22, 1989.

Lyall, Sarah. 1990. "Pine Valley, L.I. Fades into Pine Valley R.I.P." *New York Times*, March 24, 1990.

Lyson, Thomas A. 2002. "What Does a School Mean to a Community: Assessing the Social and Economic Benefits of Schools to Rural Villages in New York." *Journal of Research in Rural Education* 17 (3): 131–37.

Mandelker, Daniel R., Dawn Clark Netsch, Peter W. Salsich, Judith Welch Wegner, and Janice C. Griffith. 2014. *State and Local Government in a Federal System*. 8th ed. New York: LexisNexis.

Maher Craig S., and Steven C. Deller. 2007. "Municipal Responses to Fiscal Stress." *International Journal of Public Administration* 30: 1549–72.

Mahoney, Bill. 2021. "'Energizer Bunny:' How Local Politics Made New York's Next Governor." *Politico*, August 23, 2021.

Mahoney, James. 2012. "The Logic of Process Tracing Tests in the Social Sciences." *Sociological Methods and Research* 41 (4): 570–97.

Mangin, John. 2014. "The New Exclusionary Zoning." *Stanford Law and Policy Review* 25 (1): 91–120.

Mann, Brian. 2015. "Dissolution Vote Divides Village of Port Henry." *North Country Public Radio*, October 26, 2015.

Mann, Brian. 2016. "On Narrow Vote Port Henry Dissolves Village Government." *North Country Public Radio*, August 17, 2016.

Marcus v. Baron. 1981. 84 App. Div. 2d 118, 445 N.Y.S.2d 587.

Marcus v. Baron. 1982. 57 N.Y.2d 862.

Marshlow, Robert W. 1964. "Home Rule in New York State: A Brief Summary." Albany, NY: Office of Local Government Executive Department of New York State. Frank C. Moore Papers, Box 16, Folder 1.

Mastick Commission. 1935. "Sixth Report of the New York State Commission for the Revision of the Tax Laws." Albany, NY: New State Commission for the Revision of the Tax Laws.

Marx, Sally. 2017. "Petition Prompts Van Etten Dissolution Discussion." *Ithaca Journal*, August 21, 2017.

Marx, Sally. 2020. "Spencer Village Dissolution Vote Approaching." *Ithaca Journal*, September 3, 2020.

Marx, Sally. 2020b. "Spencer-Van Etten Town Talk: Spencer Dissolution Could Increase Village Tax Rate, Firm Says." *Ithaca Journal*, September 7, 2020.

Marx, Sally. 2020c. "Spencer-Van Etten Town Talk: Spencer Dissolution Rejected By Village Residents." *Ithaca Journal*, September 21, 2020.

Mattera, Nick. 2010. "Despite Benefits, Lewiston Officials Say Residents Are Against the Idea of Consolidation." *Niagara Gazette*, June 28, 2010.

Mattison, Andy. 2010. "Altmar Village Vote Set for November." YNN.com, August 17.

Mattison, Andy. 2010b. "Altmar Votes Yes on Dissolution." YNN.com, November 10.

Maxey, Chester C. 1922. "The Political Integration of Metropolitan Communities." *National Municipal Review* 11 (8): 229–54.

McCabe, Brian J. 2016. *No Place Like Home: Wealth, Community, and the Politics of Homeownership*. New York: Oxford University Press.

McCarty, Lucian. 2011. "Village Dissolution Committee Meets; Discussions That Will Wrap Up in 2013 Get Started." *The Saratogian*, February 22, 2011.

McDonald, Bruce. 2017. "Measuring the Fiscal Health of Municipalities: Working Paper WP17BM1." Cambridge, MA: Lincoln Institute of Land Policy.

McGovern, J. Raymond. 1953. "Creation, Control and Supervision of Cities and Villages by the State." *Brooklyn Law Review* 20 (2): 158–71.

McKinney, William M. 1918. *The Consolidated Laws of New York, Annotated: Book 64, Village Law*. Northport, NY: Edward Thompson.

McKinstry, Lohr. 1992. "Ticonderoga Voters Choose Dissolution." *Plattsburgh Press Republican*, March 18, 1992.

McKinstry, Lohr. 2013. "Hotly Debated Keeseville Dissolution Goes to Vote Tuesday." *Plattsburgh Press Republican*, January 19, 2013.

McKinstry, Lohr. 2014. "Keeseville, Towns Working Out Dissolutions Issues." *Plattsburgh Press Republican*, September 24, 2014.

McKinstry, Lohr. 2015. "Port Henry Dissolution Petition Filed." *Plattsburgh Press Republican*, June 25, 2015.

McKinstry, Lohr. 2015b. "Port Henry Dissolution Vote Looms." *Plattsburgh Press Republican*, October 22, 2015.

Mearhoff, Sarah. 2017. "Village of Van Etten Dissolution Referendum Postponed." *Ithaca Journal*, November 9, 2017.

Medina Journal Register. 1985. "One Village's Answer to the Money Crunch: Disband." December 18, 1985.

Memorandum Decision, Bailey et al. v. Village of Lyons. 2013. "Memorandum Decision, Bailey, et al. v. Village of Lyons Board of Trustees." Supreme Court of the State of New York (County of Wayne), August 27.

Memorandum Decision, Bailey and DeWolfe v. Village of Lyons. 2014. "Memorandum Decision, Bailey & Wolfe v. Village of Lyons." Supreme Court of the State of New York, County of Wayne, N.Y. Slip Op. 30405, February 19.

Memorandum Order, Bailey et al. v. Village of Lyons. 2014. "Memorandum Order, Bailey, et al. v. Village of Lyons Board of Trustees." Supreme Court of the State of New York, Appellate Division, Fourth Judicial Department, N.Y. Slip Op. 03422, May 9.

Mende, Susan. 2015. "Village of Hermon May Dissolve into Town if Voters Approve." *Watertown Daily Times*, September 6, 2015.

Mende, Susan. 2015b. "Hermon Votes to Dissolve Village." *Watertown Daily Times*, October 26, 2015.

Menifield, Charles E. 2017. *The Basics of Public Budgeting and Financial Management: A Handbook for Academics and Practitioners*. Lanham, MD: Hamilton Books.

Merriman, Charles, Spencer D. Parratt, and Albert Lepawsky. 1933. *The Government of the Metropolitan Region of Chicago*. Chicago: University of Chicago Press.

Messinger, Boyd R. 1989. "Local Government Restructuring: A Test of the Rosenbaum-Kammerer Theory." PhD diss., University of Pittsburgh.

Miles, Joyce. 2009. "Government: Is Status Quo Too Costly?" *Lockport Union & Sun Journal Online*, April 12, 2009.

Miller, Jim. 2013. "Round 2: Second Lyons Village Vote Set for Tuesday." *Finger Lakes Times*, March 16, 2013.

Mockler, Kate. 2010. "Village Board Meeting Features Heated Discussion on Dissolution." *Amherst Bee*, February 24, 2010.

Mockler, Kate. 2010b. "Village Dissolution Petitions Expected to Be Filed Today." *Amherst Bee*, June 2, 2010, at 1.

Monticello Republican Watchman. 1947. "Dam Makes Boom Town." December 12, 1947.

Moore, Frank C. 1938. "Letter to Bertha M. Moore." September 10. Frank C. Moore Papers, Box 9, Folder 5.

Moore, Frank C. 1964. "Notes for Home Rule Discussion." March 19. Franck C. Moore Papers, Box 16, Folder 1.

Moore, Frank C. 1967. "Remarks by Franck C. Moore at Meeting of the Fifty Group, the Crossroads, Latham, NY." May 1. Frank C. Moore Papers, Box 17, Folder 2.

Morse, Ricard S., and Carl W. Stenberg. 2018. "Pulling the Lever: The States' Role in Catalyzing Local Change." In *Intergovernmental Relations in Transition: Reflections and Directions*, edited by Carl W. Stenberg and David K. Hamilton, 207–26. New York: Routledge.

Morey, William C. 1902. *The Government of New York: Its History and Administration.* New York: Macmillan.

Moulder, Evelina, and Robert J. O'Neil. 2009. "Citizen Engagement and Local Government Management." *National Civic Review* (Summer): 21–30.

Moule, Jeremy. 2015. "Macedon's Dissolution Decision." *Rochester City Newspaper,* June 3, 2015.

Mount Vernon Chronicle. 1898. "Will Remain as a Village." May 27, 1898.

Myer, Daniel. 2010. "Focusing in on the Future of the Village of Farnham." Editorial. *Hamburg Sun News,* June 24, 2010.

Myer, Daniel. 2010b. "Farnham Residents Should Vote 'Yes' on Village Dissolution." Editorial. *Sun Times,* September 23, 2010.

Myers, David N., and Naomi M. Stolzenberg. 2008. "What Does Kiryas Joel Tell Us About Liberalism in America?" *The Chronicle: Hebrew Union College-Jewish Institute of Religion* 71: 49–53.

Myers, David N., and Naomi M. Stolzenberg. 2012. "Kiryas Joel: Theocracy in America?" *Huffington Post,* December 4, 2012.

Nabatchi, Tina, and Lisa Blogrem Amsler. 2014. "Direct Public Engagement in Local Government." *American Review of Public Administration* 44 (4): 63–88.

Nathan, Richard P., and Gerald Benjamin. 2001. *Regionalism and Realism: A Study of Government in the New York Metropolitan Area.* Washington, DC: Brookings.

New Rochelle Pioneer. 1898. "Mount Kisco Has an Election." May 20, 1898.

New Rochelle Pioneer. 1899. "Pleasantville Still a Village." September 9, 1899.

New Rochelle Pioneer. 1912. "Elmsford Won't Change." July 27, 1912.

New York Association of Towns. 2009. *Memorandum in Opposition.* Association of Towns of the State of New York, May 27, 2009.

New York Conference of Mayors. 1964. "Legislative Program." New York State Conference of Mayors: Albany, NY. Frank C. Moore Papers, Box 16, Folder 19.

New York Conference of Mayors. 1965. "Legal Bulletin: February–August." Franck C. Moore Papers, Box 17, Folder 2.

New York Conference of Mayors. 2010. "Guide to Local Government Dissolution and Consolidation Under General Municipal Law Article 17-A." Albany, NY: New York State Conference of Mayors and Municipal Officials, Municipal Management Series, March.

New York Daily Graphic. 1878. "Scenes from the Hudson: The Village of Nyack—An Interesting and Historical Locality." February 7, 1878, at 653.

New York Department of State. 1983. "Local Government Technical Series: Village Dissolution." Albany, NY: New York Department of State, Local Government Services Division.

New York Department of State. 2006. "Legal Memorandum LG06: What Is a Coterminous Town-Village." Albany, NY: Department of State, Office of General Counsel.

New York Department of State. 2007. "Local Government Shared Services Progress Report: 2005–2007." Albany, NY: New York Department of State.

New York Department of State. 2009. "Local Government Shared Services Annual Report: 2008–2009." Albany, NY: New York Department of State.

New York Department of State. 2010. "Local Government Shared Services Annual Report: 2009–2010." Albany, NY: New York Department of State.

New York Department of State. 2011. *Local Government Handbook.* 6th ed. Albany, NY: New York Department of State.

New York Department of State. 2017. "SFY 2016–2017 Annual Report: Administration of Local Government Efficiency Program." November 7. Albany, NY: New York Department of State.

New York Department of State. 2018. "SFY 2017–2018 Annual Report: Administration of Local Government Efficiency Program." October 2. Albany, NY: New York Department of State.

New York Department of State. 2018b. "Local Government Handbook." Albany, NY: New York Department of State, Division of Local Government Services, November 18.

New York Field Codes. 1865. 5 New York Field Codes 97.

New York Gubernatorial Candidates Debate. 2010. Hofstra University, New York, NY, October 18.

New York State Archives. 1866–1988. Collection N-AR 13243, Village Incorporation Files and Maps, 1886–1988. New York State Archives, Albany, NY.

New York State Executive Budget Briefing Book. 2022. "New York State Executive Budget Briefing Book: FY 2023." Albany, NY: New York State Office of the Governor. https://www.budget.ny.gov/pubs/archive/fy23/index.html.

New York State Department of Taxation and Finance. 2012. "Office of Real Property Tax Services Summary of 2012 Real Property Tax Legislation." Albany, NY: State Of New York Department of Taxation and Finance.

New York State Legislative Commission On State-Local Relations. 1983. "New York's Local Government Structure: The Division of Responsibilities: An Interim Report of the New York State Legislative Commission on State-Local Relations." January 1. Albany, NY: New York State Legislature.

New York State Guide. 1843. *New York State Guide Containing an Alphabetical List of Counties, Towns, Cities, Villages, Post-Offices, Etc.* Albany, NY: J. Disturnell.

New York Sun. 1897. "Mamaroneck Is Seething: Ordinary Mild-Mannered Residents Calling Names." April 26, 1897.

New York Sun. 1899. "Pleasantville Votes to Go On." September 8, 1899.

New York Times. 1877. "A Village Disincorporated." August 11, 1877.

New York Times. 1877b. "The Lessons of Nyack." August 13, 1877.

New York Times. 1894. "The Gould Memorial Windows: Almost Ready to Be Placed in the Little Village Church at Roxbury." March 11, 1894.

New York Times. 1897. "Revisions of Village Laws." May 14, 1897.

New York Times. 1903. "Miss Gould Aids Roxbury." February 27, 1903.

New York Times. 1903b. "Miss Gould Aids Roxbury." November 19, 1903.

New York Times. 1911. "Would Dissolve Village: Only Way His Enemies See They Can Visit Police Justice Stag." June 26, 1911.

New York Times. 1926. "Villages Ask for New Law." September 26, 1926.

New York Times. 1927. "New Village Law Is in Force Today." July 1, 1927.

New York Times. 1937. "18 Villages of State to Seek Home Rule in New Constitution." October 8, 1937.

New York Times. 1939. "Lack of Interest Fatal to Village." November 23, 1939.

New York Times. 1968. "U.S. Court Widens Vote in Villages." November 2, 1968.

New York Times. 1969. "Levitt Urges State Law to Alter Vote Laws." July 6, 1969.

New York Times. 1990. "Pine Valley Voters to Consider Dissolution." March 11, 1990.

Newsday. 2016. "Brookhaven Can Help After Mastic Beach Village's Failure." Editorial. November 27, 2016.

Niagara Gazette. 1938. "Village of Youngstown Accepts Agreement to Use City's Water: Report, Petition, Seeking Dissolution of Village Being Circulated." November 10, 1938.

Niagara Gazette. 1953. "Cost of Adequate Police, Fire Protection in Lewiston, Niagara Called Excessive in Reeds' Report Urging Consolidation." December 3, 1953.

Niagara Gazette. 1958. "Barker Takes Water Issue to Committee." September 6, 1958.

Nollenberger, Karl, Sanford M. Graves, and Maureen G. Valente. 2003. *Evaluating Financial Condition: A Handbook for Local Government.* Washington, DC: ICMA.

Norris, Donald. 2001. "Prospects for Regional Governance Under the New Regionalism: Economic Imperatives Versus Political Impediments." *Journal of Urban Affairs* 23 (5): 557–71.

Norris, Donald, Carl Stenberg, and Tonya Zimmerman. 2009. "Governmental Fragmentation and Metropolitan Governance: Does Less Mean More? The Case of the Baltimore Region." In *Governing Metropolitan Regions in the 21st Century,* edited by Don Phares, 11–38. New York: Routledge.

North Country This Week. 2018. "Opinion: Dissolve Village to Give Town Chance to Thrive Says Resident." Editorial. June 8, 2018.

North Tonawanda Evening News. 1972. "Mourners Few as Village Dies at Age of 95." September 22, 1972.

Novak, William J. 1996. *The People's Welfare: Law and Regulation in Nineteenth Century America.* Chapel Hill: University of North Carolina Press.

O'Brien, Barbara. 2008. "Discoveries Reveal All Is Not Well." *Buffalo News,* June 12, 2008.

O'Brien, Barbara. 2008b. "Gaughan Wants Merger of All 16 Villages: Says They Should Be Absorbed by Towns." *Buffalo News,* July 10, 2008.

O'Brien, Barbara. 2015. "Responsiveness, Efficiency of Villages Deemed Worth the Cost." *Buffalo News,* January 15, 2015.

Ogdensburg Journal. 2018. "Residents Urge Dissolution of Village." Editorial. January 17, 2018.

Office of the New York State Comptroller. 1980. "Opinions of the State Comptroller. Opinion No. 80-762." December 11. Albany, NY: Office of the New York State Comptroller.

Office of the New York State Comptroller. 2004. "2004 Annual Report on Local Governments." Albany, NY: Office of the New York State Comptroller.

Office of the New York State Comptroller. 2006. "Outdated Municipal Structures: Cities, Towns and Villages—18th Century Designations for 21st Century Communities." Albany, NY: Office of the New York State Comptroller.

Office of the New York State Comptroller. 2008. "Research Brief: 21st Century State Aid Formulas: Revenue Sharing." Albany, NY: Office of the New York State Comptroller.

Office of the New York State Comptroller. 2011. "Village of Lyons Financial Condition of the Water and Sewer Funds." Albany, NY: Office of the New York State Comptroller.

Office of the New York State Comptroller. 2013. "Research Brief: Fiscal Stress Drivers and Coping Strategies." Albany, NY: Office of the New York State Comptroller.

Office of the New York State Comptroller. 2013b. "2013 Fiscal Stress Summary for Results for Villages." Albany, NY: Office of the New York State Comptroller.

Office of the New York State Comptroller. 2015. "Local Government Issues in Focus: Revenue Sharing in New York State." Albany, NY: New York State Division of Local Government Services and Economic Development, February, vol. 1 (2): 1–17.

Office of the New York State Comptroller. 2016. "Fiscal Stress Monitoring System Results for Municipalities: Three-Year Review." Albany, NY: Office of the New York State Comptroller.

Office of the New York State Comptroller. 2016b. "Local Government Management Guide: Understanding the Budget Process." Albany, NY: Office of the New York State Comptroller.

Office of the New York State Comptroller. 2017. "Annual Report on Local Government: For Fiscal Year Ending in 2016." Albany, NY: Office of the New York State Comptroller.

Office of the New York State Comptroller. 2017b. "Fiscal Stress Monitoring System: Municipalities in Stress Fiscal Year Ending 2016." Albany, NY: Office of the New York State Comptroller.

Office of the New York State Comptroller. 2017c. "Fiscal Stress Monitoring System Results for Municipalities: Four Year Review, 2013–2016." Albany, NY: Office of the New York State Comptroller.

Office of the New York State Comptroller. 2017d. "Fiscal Stress Drivers and Coping Strategies." Albany, NY: Office of the New York State Comptroller.

Office of the New York State Comptroller. 2017e. "Fiscal Stress Monitoring System Manual." Albany, NY: Office of the New York State Comptroller.

Office of the New York State Comptroller. 2017f. "Fire Protection in New York State: How Is It Provided in Your Community?" Albany, NY: Office of the New York State Comptroller.

Office of the New York State Comptroller. 2019. "Constitutional Debt Limit." Albany, NY: Office of the New York State Comptroller.

Office of the New York State Comptroller. 2019b. "Property Taxes in New York State." Albany, NY: Office of the New York State Comptroller.

Office of the New York State Comptroller. 2020. "A Grade of Incomplete: Persistent Non-Filers of Legally Required Local Government Reports." Albany, NY: Office of the New York State Comptroller.

Office of the New York State Comptroller. 2020b. "Fiscal Stress Monitoring System: Municipalities Fiscal Year 2019 Results; Fiscal Year 2020 Risks." Albany, NY: Office of New York State Comptroller.

Office of the New York State Comptroller. 2020c. "Understanding the Constitutional Tax Limit: Villages." Albany, NY: Office of the New York State Comptroller.

Office of the New York State Comptroller. 2021. "Review of the Enacted Budget State Fiscal Year 2021–2022." Albany, NY: Office of the New York State Comptroller, April.

Office of the New York State Comptroller. 2022. "Aid and Incentives for Municipalities: New York State's Local Revenue Sharing Program." Albany, NY: Office of the New York State Comptroller, February.

OneLyons Press Release. 2014. www.onelyons.com/wordpress/wp-content/uploads/2014/02/ONELYONS-Press-release-Feb-21-2014.pdf, February 21.

OneLyons Press Release. 2014b. www.onelyons.com/wordpress/wp-content/uploads/2014/05/4th-Dept-Appeals-Decision-Bailey-v-Lyons-PRESS-Release1.pdf, May 13.

Order to Show Cause, Bailey et al. v. Village of Lyons. 2013. "Why an Order Should Not Be Given Declaring Village of Lyons in Violation of GML 17-A, Compelling Village to Complete Statutory Duty." Bailey et al. v. Village of Lyons, NY Board of Trustees, June 28.

Order to Show Cause, Bailey and DeWolfe v. Village of Lyons. 2014. "Order to Show Cause, Bailey & Wolfe v. Village of Lyons." Supreme Court of the State of New York, County of Wayne, January 4.

Oswego Farmer. 1922. "In Central New York." September 22, 1922.

Oswego Palladium. 1972. "Municipalities Consider Public Service Mergers." July–August 1972.

Parker, Amasa J., and Albert Danaher. 1906. The Village Law of the State of New York with All Amendments to Date Including Those Made by the Legislature of 1906. Albany, NY: Banks.

Parshall, Lisa K. 2011. "Another Run at Regionalism: Village Dissolution in Erie County, New York." Paper presented at the 2011 New York State Political Science Association Conference, April 8–9, Lewiston, NY.

Parshall, Lisa K. 2012. "Historic Village Government Dissolution in New York State." Paper presented at the Researching New York 2012 Conference, University at Albany (SUNY), November 15–16.

Parshall, Lisa K. 2011b. "The Evolution of Village Government Dissolution Law in New York State." Paper presented at the 2011 Northeastern Political Science Association Meeting, Philadelphia, PA, November 17–19.

Parshall, Lisa K. 2018. "Applying the Narrative Policy Framework to New York State's Village Dissolution Debate." Paper presented at the 2018 New York State Political Science Association, Wagner College, Staten Island, NY, April 13–14.

Parshall, Lisa K. 2019. *The Use of Narrative Policy Framing in the Village Dissolution Debate: Pro- and Anti-Dissolution Messaging in the Brockport and Lyons Dissolution Efforts.* Paper presented at the 2019 New York State Political Science Association Conference, New York, NY, April 11–12, 2019.

Parshall, Lisa K. 2019b. "Dissolving Village Government in New York State: A Symbol of a Community in Decline or Government Modernization?" *Policy Brief: Rockefeller Institute of Government,* June 24.

Parshall, Lisa K. 2020. "Is It Time for New York State to Revise Its Village Incorporation Laws: A Background Report on Village Incorporation in New York State." *Policy Brief: Rockefeller Institute of Government,* January 28.

Parshall, Lisa K. 2022. "A Comparative Look at the Village Dissolution Movement in Ohio and New York: Assessing State-Level Policy Impacts." *Policy Brief: Rockefeller Institute of Government,* January 31.

Pasciak, Mary. 2000. "Giambra Pushes for Villages to Merge with Towns." *Buffalo News,* December 4, 2000.

Pasciak, Mary. 2010. "Activist Begins Petition Drives in 3 Localities." *Buffalo News,* March 25, 2010.

Pasciak, Mary. 2010b. "3 Seek 2 North Collins Board Seats." *Buffalo News,* March 15, 2010.

Patchogue Advance. 1938. "People Uninterested, Village of Landing Is Disincorporated." November 24, 1938.

Patchogue Advance. 1939. "Move to End Village of Bellport in Proposed in Taxpayer's Association." August 12, 1939.

Paz, Isabella Grullon. 2017. "VE Boards Discuss Dissolution of Village." *Ithaca Journal,* July 24, 2017.

People v. Snedeker. 1899. 160 N.Y. 350.

Peshkin, Alan. 1978. *Growing Up American: Schooling and the Survival of Community.* Chicago: University of Chicago Press.

Pew Research. 2016. "State Strategies to Detect Local Fiscal Distress: How States Assess and Monitor the Financial Health of Local Governments." https://www.pewtrusts.org/en/research-and-analysis/reports/2016/09/state-strategies-to-detect-local-fiscal-distress.

Pierce, Nathan J. 2014. "Research Design and the Narrative Policy Framework." In *The Science of Stories: Applications of the Narrative Policy Framework in Public Policy Analysis*, edited by Michael D. Jones, Elizabeth Shanahan, and Mark K. McBeth, 27–44. New York: Palgrave MacMillan.

Pierce v. Village of Ossining. 1968. 292 F. Supp. 113.

Plattsburgh Press Republican. 2015. "Moving Forward for the Citizens." October 30, 2015.

Platsky, Jeff. 2018. "Town Alarmed by Village of Van Etten Finances as Consolidation Approaches." *Binghamton Press and Sun Bulletin*, May 14, 2018.

Platsky, Jeff. 2018b. "Van Etten's Dissolution May Start a Trend in Chemung County, Legislator Predicts." *Binghamton Press & Sun Bulletin*, June 18, 2018.

Polimédio, Chayenne, Elena Souris, and Hollie Russon-Gilman. 2018. "Where Residents, Politics, and Government Meet Philadelphia's Experiments with Civic Engagement." *New America*, November 14, 2018.

Porter, Eduardo. 2018. "The Hard Truths of Trying to 'Save the Rural Economy.'" *New York Times*, December 17, 2018.

Post News Journal. 2015. "Residents Should Approve Forestville Dissolution." Editorial. October 26, 2015.

Post News Journal. 2017. "Cherry Creek Approves Dissolution." February 2, 2017.

Potter, J. 1996. *Representing Reality: Discourse, Rhetoric and Social Construction.* London: Sage.

Powell, Michael R. 2009. "A Struggling Area with Low Prices and a Beach." *New York Times*, April 3, 2009.

Poughkeepsie Eagle News. 1922. "Marlborough Village Votes No Incorporation." March 24, 1922.

Poughkeepsie Daily Eagle. 1924. "Disincorporation Is Turned Down: A Two-thirds Majority Is Lacking by Six Votes." December 8, 1924.

Poughkeepsie Daily Eagle. 1925. "Phinney, Valley Trustees Board President Quits." September 15, 1925.

Poughkeepsie Daily Eagle. 1925b. "Village Board Gets Petition." October 12, 1925.

Poughkeepsie Daily Eagle. 1926. "Valley to Vote Again on Disincorporation." February 19, 1926.

Poughkeepsie Daily Eagle. 1926b. "Pleasant Valley Abandons Charter." March 17, 1926.

Poughkeepsie News. 1922. "Tivoli Tax Association Is Proposed: Main Object of the New Organization Would Be to Push Disincorporation of Village." August 11, 1922.

Problems Related to Home Rule and Local Government. 1938. New York State Constitutional Committee. Albany, NY: J.B. Lyon.

Putnam County Courier. 1897. "Incorporation Talk: The Extinction of Another False Fire, Carmel Compared." October 1, 1897.

Putrino, Carmin R. 1964. "Home Rule: A Fresh Start." *Buffalo Law Review* 14 (3): 484–98.

Randall, Mike. 2016. "Reorganization Study Could Lead to Highland Falls' Dissolution or

Merger with Town of Highlands." *Times Herald*, February 19, 2016.

Recent Developments in Home Rule. 1964. "Recent Developments in Home Rule." December. Frank C. Moore Papers, Box 16, Folder 3.

Reply to Motion, Bailey and DeWolfe v. Village of Lyons. 2013. In the Matter of Jack Bailey et al., Andrew DeWolf (pro se) Petitioner-Appellant, vs. Village of Lyons Board of Trustees, Respondent-Respondent. Appellate Division Docket # CA 13-01917, November.

Reply to Motion, Bailey and DeWolfe v. Village of Lyons. 2014. "Reply to Motion, In the Matter of Jack Bailey et al., Andrew DeWolf (pro se) Petitioner-Appellant, vs. Village of Lyons Board of Trustees, Respondent-Respondent."

Report of the Interim Urban Problems Committee. 1959. "Report of the Interim Urban Problems Committee: Submitted to the Governor and Legislature." Madison, Wisconsin, January.

Resila, Alex. 2014. "Former Altmar Village Clerk-Treasurer Accused of Pocketing Taxpayer Money." CNYcentral.com, March 19.

Resnek, Jacob. 2008. "Plan Afoot to End Tupper Village." *Plattsburgh Press Republican,* August 15, 2008.

Rice, Kathryn, Leora S. Waldner, and Russell M. Smith. 2014. "Why New Cities Form: An Examination into Municipal Incorporation in the United States." *Journal of Planning Literature* 29 (2): 140–54.

Richards, Joanna. 2012. "Village of Chaumont Ponders Pros, Cons Of Dissolution." *North Country Public Radio*, May 29, 2012.

Richland, W. Bernard. 1954. "Constitutional City Home Rule in New York." *Columbia Law Review* 54 (3): 311–37.

Rivera, Robert, and Youanshuo Xu. 2014. "New York Property Tax Cap: Impact Analysis." *State Austerity Policy and Creative Local Response*, December 2014.

Roberts, Sam. 2011. "A Village with the Numbers, Not the Image, of the Poorest Place." *New York Times*, April 20, 2011.

Robinson, Larry. 2016. "Village of Morristown Considers New Dissolution Study." *Watertown Daily Times*, August 12, 2016.

Robinson, Larry. 2018. "Morristown Village Board Accepts Report on Dissolution." *Watertown Daily Times*, January 24, 2018.

Robinson, Larry. 2018b. "Morristown Village Residents Vote to Dissolve by Lopsided Margin." *Watertown Daily Times*, July 27, 2018.

Rochester Bureau of Municipal Research. 1958. "Legal and Fiscal Considerations Involved in the Question Whether East Rochester Should Become a City." Summary Report to the Village of East Rochester Prepared at the Request of, and with the Guidance from the Citizens Committee Appointed by the Village Board to Study This Problem, October 27. Frank C. Moore Papers, Box 17, Folder 2.

Roland, Tim. 2018. "Following Dissolution, Village Largely Unlamented." *Sun Community News*, August 27, 2018.

Roman, Dayelin. 2010. "Lake George Keeps Dissolution from Ballot." *Glens Falls Post-Star,* November 16, 2010.

Rose, Julia. 2014. "Village of Bridgewater Could Be Dissolved After Tuesday's Vote." *CNY News*, March 18, 2014.

Rosenbaum, Walter A., and Thomas A. Henderson. 1972. "Explaining Comprehensive Governmental Consolidation: Toward a Preliminary Theory." *Southern Political Science Association* 34 (2): 428–57.

Rosenbaum, Walter A., and Thomas A. Henderson. 1973. "Explaining the Attitude of Community Influentials Toward Government Consolidation: A Reappraisal of Four Hypotheses." *Urban Affairs Quarterly* 9 (2): 251–75.

Rosenbaum, Walter A., and Gladys M. Kammerer. 1974. *Against Long Odds: The Theory and Practice of Successful Governmental Consolidation*. Beverly Hills, CA: Sage.

Rusk, David. 1993. *Cities without Suburbs*. Washington, DC: Woodrow Wilson Center Press.

Samaha, Albert. 2014. "All the Young Jews: In the Village of Kiryas Joel, NY, the Median Age Is 13." *The Voice*, November 12, 2014.

Sampson, David. 2010. Deputy Attorney General for Regional Affairs, *Speech to the Fredonia Center for Regional Advancement*, Fredonia, NY, August 21.

Savitch, H. V., and Sarin Adhikari. 2017. "Fragmented Regionalism: Why Metropolitan America Continues to Splinter." *Urban Affairs Review* 53 (2): 381–402.

Scanlon, Christina. 2015. "Salem Dissolution Proceeds." *Glens Falls Post-Star,* January 9, 2015.

Scanlon, Christina. 2015b. "Salem Supervisor Questions Special Meeting on Dissolution." *Glens Falls Post-Star*, March 14, 2015.

Scanlon, Christina. 2015c. "Salem Mayor Wavers on Village Dissolution Support." *Glens Falls Post-Star*, March 18, 2015.

Scanlon, Christina. 2015d. "Email Exchange Reveals Truth Behind Special Meeting." *Glens Falls Post-Star,* March 22, 2015.

Scanlon, Christina. 2015e. "Trustee Resigns from Board as Village Dissolution Nears." *Syracuse Post Standard,* May 29, 2015.

Scavo, Carmine, and Emily Washington. 2012. "Government Streamlining Commissions: A Methodology for Measuring Effectiveness." Working Paper 12-28, Mercatus Center, George Mason University, October.

Scott v. Village of Saratoga Springs. 1909. 115 N.Y. Supp. 796.

Schleicher, David. 2017. "Stuck! The Law and Economics of Residential Stability." *Yale Law Journal* 127 (1): 78–154.

Schragger, Richard. 2003. "Consuming Government." *Michigan Law Review* 101 (6): 1824–57.

Schupe, Barbara, Janet Stein, and Jyoti Pandit. 1987. *New York State Population Statistics: A Compilation of Federal Census Data.* New York: Neal-Schuman.

Semuels, Alana. 2021. "As Wildfires Burn, Are U.S. Cities Spending Too Much on Their Fire Departments?" *Time*, September 14, 2021.

Shanahan, Elizabeth, Michael D. Jones, Mark K. McBeth, and Ross R. Lane. 2013. "An Angel on the Wind: How Heroic Policy Narratives Shape Policy Realities." *Policy Studies Journal* 41 (3): 453–83.

Shanahan, Elizabeth A., Michael D. Jones, Mark K. McBeth, and Claudio Radaelli. 2018. "The Narrative Policy Framework." In *Theories of the Policy Process*, edited by Christopher W. Weible and Paul A. Sabatier, 173–213. New York: Westview.

Shanske, Daniel. 2017. "The (Now Urgent) Case for State-Level Monitoring of Local Government Finances: Protecting Localities from Trump's Potemkin Village of Nothing." *New York University Journal of Legislative and Public Policy* 20: 773–825.

Sherman, Doug. 2010. "The Question of Villages." Editorial. *Buffalo News*, August 22, 2010.

Shepsle, Kenneth A. 2003. "Losers in Politics (and How They Sometimes Become Winners): William Riker's Heresthetic." *Perspectives on Politics* 1 (2): 307–15.

Sherwood, Julie, and Tammy Whitacre. 2014. "Macedon v. Macedon: Long Time Discord Continues Between Town and Village." *Daily Messenger*, May 20, 2014.

Smith, Page. 1966. *As a City Upon a Hill: The Town in American History.* New York: Alfred A. Knopf.

Smith, John M. 2000. "Zoned for Residential Uses—Like Prayer: Home Worship and Municipal Opposition in LeBlanc-Sternberg v. Fletcher." *Brigham Young University Law Review* 2000: 1153–84.

Smith, Tara. 2017. "A Community Caved In." *Long Island Advance*, March 16, 2017.

Smith, Tara. 2017b. "What Comes Next? Mastic Beach Votes to Dissolve Village." *Long Island Advance*, November 17, 2017.

Smith, Russell. M. 2018. *Municipal Incorporation Activity in the United States: Patterns, People, and Procedures.* Cham, Switzerland: Springer.

Sommer, Mark. 2017. "Bid Farewell to Cherry Creek, a Farming Village That Will Exist No More." *Buffalo News*, February 4, 2017.

Specht, Charlie. 2010. "Williamsville Gets Back to Business." *Buffalo News*, August 24, 2010.

Specter, Joseph. 2010. "Tax-Battered New Yorkers Look to Government Consolidation." *Poughkeepsie Journal Online*, July 25, 2010.

Spielman, Sarah Trappler. 2018. "A Town Divided." *Tablet*, November 16, 2018.

Special Report of the Commissions of Statutory Revision. 1867. *Special Report of the Commission of Statutory Revision in Relation to Villages.* Albany, NY: New York State Legislature. Frank C. Moore Papers, Box 21, Folder 30.

Spina, Mathew. 2010. "Williamsville Citizens Gathering Information: Pledges Neutrality on Dissolution Issue." *Buffalo News*, March 1, 2010.

St. Regis Falls Adirondack News. 1887. "Notice to the Inhabitants of the Village of St. Regis Falls, NY." June 25, 1887.

St. Regis Falls Adirondack News. 1909. "Local News." September 25, 1909.

St. Regis Falls Adirondack News. 1913. "Local and Personal." February 22, 1913.

St. Regis Falls Adirondack News. 1913b. "Local and Personal." April 12, 1913.

Staff, A. 2020. "What S. Nyack Community Is Saying About Dissolution." *Nyack News and Views*, December 16, 2020.

Stern v. Kramarsky. 1975. 375 N.Y.S.2d 235.

Stemberg v. Fletcher. 1995. 67 F.3d 412 (2d Cir.).

Stone, Deborah. 2012. *Policy Paradox: The Art of Political Decision Making.* 3rd ed. New York: W.W. Norton.

Stolzenberg, Naomi M., and David N. Myers. 2021. *American Shtetl: The Making of Kiryas Joel, a Hasidic Village in Upstate New York.* Princeton: Princeton University Press.

Studenski, Paul. 1930. *The Government of Metropolitan Areas in the United States.* New York: Arno Press.

Suffolk County News. 1895. "Good for Them—Why Not for Us!" October 25, 1895.

Suffolk County News. 1930. "Conditions Have Changed." May 16, 1930.

Suffolk County News. 1939. "Only 17 of 38 Property Owners Vote and the Village of the Landing Is Dissolved." December 1, 1939.

Sun Community News. 2015. "Congrats, You're Dissolving. Now Step on the Gas." Editorial. November 4, 2015.

Swanson, Bert E. 2004. "Alternative Explanations for the Adoption of City-County Consolidations in Jacksonville/Duval County Florida." In *Case Studies of City County Consolidation: Reshaping the Local Government Landscape,* edited by Suzanne M. Leland and Kurt M. Thurmaier, 28–54. Armonk, NY: M.E. Sharpe.

Syed, Anwar Hussain. 1966. *The Political Theory of American Government.* New York: Random House.

Taczkowski, Richard. 2007. "Goal of Government Efficiency Can't Be a One-Man Show." Editorial. *Buffalo News*, December 20, 2007.

Taddeo, Sarah. 2015. "Lyons Laments Loss of Local Police Force." *Rochester Democrat and Chronicle*, February 13, 2015.

Taddeo, Sarah. 2015b. "Macedon to Schedule a Third Vote on Dissolution." *Rochester Democrat and Chronicle*, March 11, 2015.

Tall, Deborah. 2016. *From Where We Stand: Recovering a Sense of Place.* Syracuse, NY: Syracuse University Press.

Tan, Sandra. 2010. "Neighboring Homes, Different Taxes." *Buffalo News*, August 13, 2010.

Taylor, Charles D., Dagney Faulk, and Pamela Schaal. 2017. "Remaking Local Government Success and Failure Under Indiana's Government Modernization Act." *Journal of Public and Nonprofit Affairs* 3 (2): 155–75.

Teaford, Jon. 1979. *City and Suburb: The Political Fragmentation of Metropolitan America, 1850–1970*. Baltimore: Johns Hopkins University Press.

Teaford, Jon. 1997. *Post-Suburbia: Government and Politics the Edge Cities*. Baltimore: Johns Hopkins University Press.

Temporary State Commission on the Constitutional State Convention. 1967. "Report 13: Local Government." Albany, NY: The Temporary State Commission on the Constitutional State Convention.

Thomas, Cara. 2017. "Village of Barneveld Moves Toward Dissolution." *Central News New York*, May 25, 2017.

Times of Wayne County. 2015. "Two Macedon Trustees Call for Village Dissolution." November 16, 2015.

Toscano, Bill. 2014. "Salem Moving Toward Dissolution Vote." *Glens Falls Post-Star*, March 30, 2014.

Toscano, Bill. 2014b. "Salem Dissolution Petition Submitted." *Glens Falls Post-Star*, April 3, 2014.

Toscano, Bill. 2014c. "Report Outlines Saving to Salem if Village Dissolves." *Glens Falls Post-Star*, July 28, 2014.

Tocqueville, Alexis, de. 1835. *Democracy in America*. New York: G. Dearborn.

Trachtenberg, Alan. 2007. *The Incorporation of America: Culture and Society in the Gilded Age*. New York: Hill and Wang.

Traster, Tina. 2020. "The 11th Hour—South Nyackers Have a Tough Decision to Make." *Rockland County Business Journal*, December 14, 2020.

Traster, Tina. 2021. "South Nyack Dissolution Plan Approved; Lawsuit Against Yeshiva Could Be Inherited by Town of Orangetown." *Rockland County Business Journal*, August 2, 2021.

Tucker, Caroline. 2012. "Voters Approve to Dissolve Village of Lyons." *Rochester First*, March 18, 2012.

Tulis, Spencer. 2014. "Lyons Dissolution Police Stress Department's Impact." *Finger Lakes Times*, October 9, 2014.

U.S. v. Railroad. 1882. 105 U.S. 263.

U.S. v. Village of Airmont. 1996. 925 F. Supp. 160.

Utica Daily Press. 1932. "Many Old Forge Taxpayers Sign." October 10, 1932.

Utica Daily Press. 1932b. "Petition Asks Special Vote at Old Forge." November 17, 1932.

Utica Daily Press. 1934. "Zoller Rejects Old Forge Vote: Grouping of Questions Nullifies Election to Dissolve Village." August 20, 1934.

Utica Daily Press. 1940. "Town Board Ordered to Issue District Bonds." N.D.

Utica Observer Dispatch. 1932. "Action Started Against Village Taxpayers in Arrears: Old Forge Acts to Force Back Tax Payments." June 5, 1932.

Utica Observer Dispatch. 1932b. "Report Cites Economy Need at Old Forge." July 19, 1932.

Utica Observer Dispatch. 1934. "Move to Abandon Adirondack Village Charter Blocked: Old Forge Vote on Dissolution Declared Void." August 19, 1934.

Utica Observer Dispatch. 1935. "Old Forge Factions Divided on Benefits Expected from Dissolution of Village." November 10, 1935.

Utica Observer Dispatch. 1938. "Dissolution as Village Afoot at Cold Brook." January 4, 1938.

Utica Observer Dispatch. 1938b. "Village Dissolution Proceedings Placed in the Hands of Uticans." June 1, 1938.

Utica Observer Dispatch. 2015. "Village of Prospect Receives Grant to Help with Its Dissolution." September 3, 2015.

Vanstean, Terry. 2014. "Why the Village of Lyons Should Not Be Dissolved." *Finger Lakes Times,* March 16, 2014.

Veselkova, Marcela. 2017. "Narrative Policy Framework: Narratives as Heuristics in the Policy Process." *Human Affairs* 27 (2): 178–91.

Veilkind, Jimmy. 2011. "Small Government Big Costs: How Green Island Stacks Against Its Neighbors." *Albany Times Union,* August 1, 2011.

Vielkind, Jimmy. 2011b. "Cuomo's Law Highlights a Thicket of Local Government Entities, Eliminates Almost None of Them." *Capital News,* August 25, 2011.

Village Committee of the New York State Constitutional Convention. 1938. New York State Constitutional Convention, Committee on Village Government, July 12. Frank C. Moore Papers, Box 9, Folder 4.

Village of Cherry Valley. 2008. "Meeting Minutes: November 17, 2008." Village of Cherry Valley, NY.

Village of Liberty Joint Study Committee Report. 2008. "Findings, Recommendations & Proposed Consolidation Plan." Village of Liberty, NY.

Village of Odessa Scoping Report. 2010. "The Dissolution of the Village of Odessa: A Portrait of a Community without a Village Government." The Working Group Dissolution Scoping Report.

Village of Pawling. 2020. "Consolidation Proposal: What It Means to You and the Village of Pawling." http://www.villageofpawling.org/wp-content/uploads/2020/10/Consolidation-Brochure.pdf.

Virkler, Steve. 2017. "Harrisville Dissolution Study Nearing Completion, with Implementation Plan Expected Soon." *Watertown Daily Times,* November 13, 2017.

Virkler, Steve. 2018. "Harrisville Trustees Agree to Hold Vote on Dissolution." *Watertown Daily Times,* February 13, 2018.

Virkler, Steve. 2018b. "Harrisville Looking to Conduct Feasibility Study on Dissolution." *Watertown Daily Times,* July 28, 2018.

Vogel, Charity. 2005. "Listen Carefully; This Area Has Two Choices: A New Approach to Regionalism or Even Deeper Chaos." *Buffalo News,* March 6, 2005.

Wachhaus, Aaron. 2014. "The Ties That Bind: Community, Topos, and Municipal Dissolution." *Administration and Society* 46 (9): 1109–29.

Wallace, Benjamin Bruce. 1911. "Origin and Development of Village Government in New York." PhD diss., University of Wisconsin.

Wallis, Allan. 1994. "Inventing Regionalism: The First Two Waves." *National Civic Review* 83 (2): 447–68.

Warner, Mildred. 2015. "Municipal Size, Resources, and Efficiency: Theoretical Basis for Shared Services and Consolidation." In *Municipal Shared Services: A Public Solutions Handbook,* edited by Alexander Henderson, 3–16. New York: Routledge.

Warren, Charles. 1978. "Regional Reform: Prospects and Alternatives." *Southern Review of Public Administration* 2 (1): 14–29.

WCBS. 2016. "Accounting Error Threatens Future of Mastic Beach Village Government." *WCBS News,* May 6, 2016.

Werbitsky, Eileen. 2009. "Blasdell Rejects Study on Dissolving." *Buffalo News,* June 11, 2009.

Werbitsky, Eileen. 2010. "Village, Town Anticipating Dissolution." *Buffalo News,* April 1, 2010.

Weiner, Joseph L. 1937. "Municipal Home Rule in New York." *Columbia Law Review* 37 (4): 557–81.

Werner, Edgar A. 1888. *Civil List and Constitutional History of the Colony and State of New York.* Albany, NY: Weed and Parsons.

Whittle, Patrick. 2011. "Mastic Beach Mayor, Residents at Odds." *Newsday,* September 7, 2011.

Wick, Karl, and Susan B. Wick. 2003. *Esopus.* Mount Pleasant, NC: Arcadia.

Wildasan, David E. 2010. "Intergovernmental Transfers to Local Governments." In *Municipal Revenues and Land Policies,* edited by Gregory K. Ingram and Yu-hung Hong, 49–76. Cambridge, MA: Lincoln Institute of Land Policy.

Williams, Fred O. 2008. "Gaughan's Call Gets a Strong 'No': Officials from 12 Villages Reject Proposal to Dissolve to Reduce Government Bloat." *Buffalo News,* August 14, 2008.

Williams, Stephen. 2014. "Population Drop Worsens Problems in Adirondacks." *Daily Gazette,* June 8, 2014.

Willard, Lucas. 2014. "Salem Residents Vote to Dissolve Village." WAMC, Northeastern Public Radio, August 6, 2014.

Wilson, James Q. 1973. *Political Organizations.* New York: Basic Books.

WKTV. 2017. "Dissolving the Village of Barneveld." *WKTV News,* April 14, 2017.

Wong, Cara J. 2010. *Boundaries of Obligation in American Politics: Geographic, National, and Racial Communities.* New York: Cambridge.

Wood, Robert C. 1958. "Metropolitan Government." *American Political Science Review* 52 (1): 108–22.

Wright, Jeff. 1981. "Vote on Village Dissolution Likely." *Plattsburgh Press Republican*, July 22, 1981.

Wurthnow, Robert. 2013. *Small-Town America: Finding Community, Shaping the Future.* Princeton: Princeton University Press.

Wurthnow, Robert. 2018. *The Left Behind: Decline and Rage in Rural America.* Princeton: Princeton University Press.

WWNYTV News. 2018. "Vote Set for June on Dissolving Village of Morristown." April 5, 2018.

Young, Beth. 2011. " 'Save Our Sound Avenue' Event Sounds Warning on Development." *North Shore Sun*, May 18, 2011.

Zhang, Pengju. 2019. "The Non-Randomness of Municipal Government Reorganization: Evidence from Village Dissolution in New York." *American Review of Public Administration* 49 (8): 914–30.

Zhang, Penju. 2022. "The Fiscal and Economic Impacts of Municipal Dissolution: Evidence from New York." *International Tax and Public Finance.* Forthcoming.

Zhang, Pengju, and Marc Holzer. 2020. "Do Small Local Governments Fare Well? A Survey of Villages in New York." *American Review of Public Administration* 50 (1): 77–91.

Zwelling, Michael. 2005. "Sloan Keeps Report on Probe Secret." *Buffalo News*, June 15, 2005.

Index

www.ingramcontent.com/pod-product-compliance
Lightning Source LLC
Chambersburg PA
CBHW030643270326
41929CB00007B/179